THE GENUINE OLD FASHIONED DOWN-HOME HOME GROWN OFFICIAL TEXAS COOK-BOOK

Text: Caleb Pirtle III

Published by Leisure Time Publishing, Inc., a division of Heritage Worldwide, Inc., Dallas, Texas.

Publisher:	Rodney L. Dockery
General Manager & Editorial Director:	Caleb Pirtle III
Regional Publishing Director:	Suzanne Breitbach
Project Editor:	Betty Miser
Recipe Editor:	Diane Luther
Production Coordinator:	Erin Gregg
Production Manager:	Vickie Craig

Photography: Tourism Division, Texas Department of Commerce, Austin, Texas

Photographers: Richard Reynolds, Michael Murphy and O. C. Garza.

Additional Photography: Waxahachie Chamber of Commerce and the Texas Panhandle Heritage Foundation.

Manufactured in the United States of America.

First Printing

Printed by:
Heritage Worldwide, Inc./Leisure Time Publishing, Inc.
9029 Directors Row
Dallas, Texas 75247
Telephone: (214) 630-4300

Contents

Foreword

Texas has its own distinctive heritage.

And flavor.

It is a proud land formed with the diversity of many cultures from many nations, and you can find the influences of those ethnic groups in its foods and throughout its communities and cities, both large and small.

That focus is reflected in *The Genuine, Old-Fashioned, Down-Home, Home-Grown, Official Texas Cookbook.*

The recipes all have a definite Texas flavor.

They were prepared for us by those Texas food manufactures who are an integral, vibrant part of the Texas Department of Agriculture's popular "Taste of Texas" program.

The recipes thus mirror the best cooking that Texas has to offer. They were developed by Texans for Texans, using Texas-made food products.

We certainly respect the time and effort that each company took in the creation of these favorite recipes, and we chose to include them in the book in much the same form as when received by Leisure Time.

However, in order to create a broader awareness of the many great products made in the state and to benefit you in your efforts to proudly support them, we have taken the liberty of customizing ingredients in the recipes with genuine Texas-made products.

You can, of course, use a wide-variety of similiar ingredients in most of the recipes, but we strongly recommend Texas products in order to give your cooking that distinctive and unforgettable Taste of Texas.

We certainly appreciate the Texas Department of Agriculture for its support of a cookbook that showcases Texas-made products, as well as for reviewing the recipes.

Through the years, the Texas Department of Agriculture has done a great job developing and promoting its "Taste of Texas" campaign. And we—like you—are proud to have the opportunity to support the program.

Editorially, *The Genuine, Old-Fashioned, Down-Home, Home-Grown, Official Texas Cookbook* is a visual and verbal portrait of scenic, historic and recreational Texas.

Therefore, it's not just a cookbook.

It is a travel book as well.

And we appreciate the assistance of Phil Davis, assistant director, and Michael Murphy, media manager, of the Tourism Division of the Texas Department of Commerce. They made sure we had the right information and the right photography to reflect the flavor and the difference that is Texas.

THE
LAND OF
PLENTY

"I must say as to that I have seen of Texas it is the garden spot of the world, the best land and the best prospects for health I ever saw is here....That, I have no doubt, is the richest country in the world, good land and plenty of timber, the best springs, good mill streams, good rains, clear water, and every appearance of health and game a-plenty."

——*Letter from David Crockett*
to his children, written in
San Augustine, January 9, 1836

*T*exas, from the roots of its very beginning, was a land of plenty, full of promise and full of promises kept, but only for those tough enough and determined enough to stake a claim in its sometimes rich, sometimes stubborn soil.

It was a country beyond the last frontier, blessed with beauty, cursed with isolation, as gentle as the April blossom of a cactus plant, as forbidding as its thorns. Great pines reached for the clouds. Mountain peaks defied them. Restless sand dunes drifted down to the sea. Deserts prayed to the sun. Wayward rivers had no particular place to go and were never in much of a hurry to get there. Royal palm trees looked like strangers lost in a strange land. The prairies seemed to roll on endlessly and aimlessly with nothing taller than buffalo grass to interrupt the view of a faraway crease where earth and sky finally came together, painted with the pink, gold and purple bruises of sunset. And timbered valleys of cedar and juniper hid amongst those burly hills that formed the rugged, rock-crested backbone of a beckoning countryside as tenacious as it was tempting.

In time, it became a whole other country, one that bound together the hopes and dreams, the customs and tongues of many lands, of many people.

Long ago, I sat with the last of the old-time, Texas maverick historians, R. Henderson Shuffler, and listened to him say, "Some of the wildest myths I've ever heard concern the people of Texas. Texans are always pictured as wild, woolly, and full of fleas...the big rich, the cowboy, the unlettered, the unlearned with a fist like a ham and a heart of gold.

"Most think of early Texans as a bunch of hell-roaring bumpkins in buckskin who came brawling across the frontier, shoved the Indians and Mexicans out, and settled down to shooting each other at high noon in front of the village saloon."

He paused for a moment, and an impish twinkle danced in the corner of his eyes. Shuffler continued, "Well, the truth happens to be just as colorful, just as fascinating, and tremendously more self-respecting than the myth.

"The one great thread running through the real group picture is its diversity. This wasn't just a land of tall, gallant Anglos or fast-riding Mexican cowboys from south of the border.

"There were a good many Negroes, Chinese, French, Czechs, Indians, Germans, and even one old Jewish conquistador, who whipped this country known as Texas. In fact, we've found more than two dozen ethnic groups that came and greatly influenced the development of the state.

"They all played a part in making Texas what it is today, good or bad. They were just a bunch of foreigners. But they joined arm-in-arm, stood shoulder-to-shoulder, and referred to themselves, with pride and defiance, as 'Texians.'"

The Spanish sent missionaries to bring the good news of a Spanish God to the Indians. A few renegades accepted what they heard and became Christians. The nomadic Plains Indians, however, did not take the Bible nor the scriptures that the European holy men offered. They took something more useful to them: Spanish guns and Spanish horses.

The Irish Catholics came, but they were only seeking refuge from the persecutions of Protestant England. The French Catholics swarmed across Texas in 1803, shortly after Napoleon sold the Louisiana Territory to the United States. Spanish

Venison A La Bourguignonne

1 lb Broken Arrow Ranch Venison Chunks, cut into bite-sized pieces

½ cup Guadalupe Valley Texas Red Wine

1 Menchaca™ Brand Bay Leaf

1 onion, stuck with 2 cloves

1 clove garlic

½ cup green onions, chopped

1 tsp Hilltop Herb Farm Thyme

1 tsp Brooke's Seasoning Salt

½ tsp ground pepper

1 tsp Hill Country Farms Country Style Mustard

1 cup beef broth

1 slice thick-sliced bacon

1 cup small whole onions

4 oz mushrooms, sliced ¼" thick

2 tbsp cornstarch

¼ cup water

1 (12 oz) pkg noodles, cooked

Hilltop Herb Farm Parsley to garnish

- Put venison, red wine, bay leaf, onion and garlic in ziplock bag. Marinate in refrigerator for several hours.
- Remove venison from marinade and reserve the marinade.
- Spray a skillet with non-stick oil, and brown venison in skillet over medium heat.
- Add green onions, herbs, spices, mustard, broth and enough marinade to just cover meat.
- Bring to a boil, cover, and simmer gently until meat is tender (about 1½ hours).
- 30 minutes before serving, add the whole onions and mushrooms to the venison and let cook.
- Taste and correct the seasonings.
- While cooking venison, fry the bacon, drain and chop into small pieces.
- Mix the cornstarch with water. Slowly pour into the venison pot, stirring continuously until thickened.
- Serve over noodles, and garnish with the bacon and parsley.
- Freezes well.
- Serves 5.

nerves suddenly wavered. To them, the French were invaders, not neighbors, and the Spanish, like the Indians, felt more comfortable holding on to bullets than Bibles.

The Germans found a new home amidst the foothills. And the frontier became scattered with settlers from Scotland, England, Switzerland, Belgium, Holland, France, Ireland, and even Spain. In 1836, news reached Poland that the Texians were loading up their guns for a war with Mexico. The Polish could not stand the thought of missing another fight. After all, they had been revolting against Austrian rule for years. So they loaded their guns, too, grabbed a boat, and headed for Texas, in search of a general named Sam Houston who just might be needing a few good men.

The Norwegians journeyed to the banks of the Bosque River, looking for a place where they could find greater religious and political freedoms. In 1852, the Czechs were sailing into Galveston, upset because their attempts to form a Slavic state back in the homeland had failed miserably. They were still enslaved by Austrian rule, and the new immigrants had fled rather than serve in the Austrian army, an insult worse than the threat, the promise, of death. Frightened Jewish refugees were simply in search of a hiding place, far from the war-torn ghettos of Russian Poland, the Ukrainian steppes, and Eastern Prussia. Italians trekked to the Brazos River valley, broken by poverty and their fierce opposition to compulsory military service. In Texas, they would fight. In Texas they had something—land of their own—worth fighting.

The coming of the railroad beckoned the Chinese. They nailed tracks to the good earth, stretching first to Dallas, then on westward to the borders of El Paso. And after the turn of the century, when General Black Jack Pershing invaded Mexico, pursuing the elusive bandits of Pancho Villa, he depended on the Chinese to provide his men with such vital necessities as candy, cigarettes, and food, even while he rode deep into a foreign and hostile territory.

The heritage, the traditions of the past run rich and deep within the bloodlines of Texas. Throughout the state, even today, can be found traces of Europe, a touch of Asia, all tied together with the rawhide legacy of a homespun frontier. As

Hasenbraten

1 Texas Rabbit Processing Rabbit, cut into pieces
2-4 slices bacon
salt and pepper
3 tbsp Gandy's Butter
1 onion, chopped
1 cup Gandy's Sour Cream
¹/₂ lemon, sliced
1 tbsp White Wings Flour
Fiesta Season It All, to taste
¹/₂ lemon, juiced

- Rub the rabbit with the bacon, then wrap each rabbit piece with some bacon.
- Season the rabbit well with salt and pepper.
- Melt the butter in a roasting pan, and place rabbit in it.
- Add onion, cover, and roast in a 400 degree oven for 30 minutes, basting frequently.
- After 20 minutes, pour on sour cream and continue cooking.
- When done, transfer meat to a warm platter. Garnish with lemon slices.
- To the drippings in the roasting pan, add flour, seasoning and lemon juice. Blend and heat thoroughly. Serve in gravy boat to accompany rabbit.
- Serves 4.

German Sauerkraut

3 tbsp Borden's Butter
2 lbs cabbage, washed and shredded
1 onion, chopped
1 Texas Orchards Apple
salt and pepper to taste
water to cook
1 potato, raw
¹/₂ cup Fall Creek Vineyards Emerald Riesling

- Melt butter in large pot and stir in cabbage thoroughly.
- Add onion, apple and salt and pepper to taste.
- Fill pot with water. Cook until tender, about 10 minutes.
- Grate in potato.
- Stir in wine, heat thoroughly and serve.
- Serves 4.

Variations:
- Instead of wine, season with a dash of paprika, 1 tbsp of sugar and ¹/₂ cup cream.
- Substitute Texas Brut Champagne for white wine. This goes very well with venison or pheasant.

Shuffler always pointed out, "There are still locales where the old cultures are preserved with amazing purity."

Panna Maria, for example, is the oldest Polish settlement in North America, with the oldest Polish church, the remnants of those early-day "freedom fighters." At Danevang, citizens still speak Danish. In Ennis, names in the phone book look as though they have been smuggled right out of a Czechoslovakian village. New Braunfels and Fredericksburg, nestled in the Texas hills, are trimmed with the gingerbread architecture of Germany. And only their Schutzenfests are louder than their Sangerfests. Nothing is better than their wurst.

The Dutch traveled into Nederland. The Norwegians found homes in Bosque and Kaufman Counties. One settler gazed across Four Mile Prairie in 1869 and wrote: "In its natural aspects, this country resembles Denmark and is very pretty. Brownsboro, on the other hand, is more like Norway, as the land is very hilly and even has high ridges and large pine woods."

The Wends, virtually ignored by time and circumstance, banded together near Giddings. The ancient church at Serbin retains its Wendish tradition: the men occupy the balcony, and the women and children all sit on downstairs pews.

Henri Castro brought his French settlers to the banks of the Crystal Medina River, and he named the community he built, appropriately enough, Castroville. The houses are typical of an Alsatian village, and some people still speak the Alsatian language. Another French colony—for the socialistic, well educated and highly skilled—was called La Reunion. The colony failed. The city next door didn't. It became Dallas.

*T*exas became the legacy of the common man who showed uncommon devotion and dedication to the land around him.

Settlers, then cowboys, and finally farmers staked their claims to the beckoning Texas soil. They carved trails through forests, across the plains, and beyond the caprock, venturing into land where no one but the Indian had dared ride before. They became the God-fearing, sometimes God forsaken, stepchildren of an unfriendly and wind-swept prairie.

The Dutch are one of many ethnic cultures showcased at San Antonio's Folk Life Festival.

Eastern civilization turned its head toward the far side of the Mississippi River, and men and women began their lonely trek westward. They had no other place to go.

They were, as legendary J. Frank Dobie always said, men and women who were carved out of the old rock. As one old cowboy said, the early Texans—those who built the foundation upon which the state grew—were nothing more than creatures of circumstances, the circumstances of an unfenced world.

And around their homes, their graves, grew communities, then villages, and finally cities. Wagon ruts, then highways, followed the tracks of their fading footprints. Their names were not particularly important, either then or now. But their handiwork, their sweat, their determination formed the economic backbone of Texas.

They collected cattle off the prairie and drove them to northern markets in Kansas. In time, barbed wire fences were strung across the prairies, and ranches grew up around the old cattle trails.

They settled the land and tilled the soil, and their farms were the beginning of a wide-sweeping and far-reaching agricultural industry.

Their ancestors had spoken many languages.

Their skins were many colors.

But they were all Texans.

Teddy Roosevelt spoke for many when he recalled his own years on ranch and farmlands.

"We worked under the scorching sun, when the wide plains simmered and wavered in the heat...We knew toil and hardship and hunger and thirst...but we felt the beat of hardy life in our veins, and ours was the glory of work and the joy of living."

Those who chose to settle the frontier worked hard, then as now.

They irrigated the land with their blood and their sweat.

Even when adversity confronted them, they were too determined to run, too stubborn to quit.

The land beckoned only the strong.

It had no use for the weak nor the timid.

And the strong survived.

The land was their hope.

Chilies Stuffed With Texas Chevre
Goat Cheese And Sun-Dried Tomatoes

8 fresh New Mexico or Anaheim chilies, roasted and left whole
½ lb Larsen Farms Texas Chevre Goat Cheese
2 oz cream cheese, softened
8 red bell peppers, roasted
¼ cup olive oil
½ tsp salt
1 tbsp Imperial Sugar, or to taste
1 tbsp balsamic vinegar
½ cup sun-dried tomatoes packed in olive oil, drained and chopped fine

- Peel the chilies carefully (wear rubber gloves), leaving them whole, slit them lengthwise, and discard the seeds.
- In a food processor, puree the goat cheese with cream cheese, transfer the mixture to a bowl, and chill it until firm.
- In the cleaned food processor, puree the bell peppers, with the oil, salt, sugar and vinegar for 3-4 minutes, or until mixture is smooth. Transfer the sauce to a bowl and chill, covered, for 1 hour.
- Arrange the chilies on a work surface and lay them open flat.
- Fill each chili with about 2 tbsp of the cheese mixture. With a knife make a ⅜" canal in the cheese mixture.
- Fill canals with 2 tsp of tomatoes, and press the chili and the cheese mixture around the tomatoes to enclose them.
- Transfer the stuffed chilies as they are made to a plate, cover and chill them for 2 hours.
- Divide the sauce evenly on 8 serving plates.
- Cut each chili with a serrated knife into 5-6 slices, and lay on top of sauce on each plate.
- Serves 8.

The land held their promise, their homes, their farms, their future.

The land became Texas.

*T*rough the years, the diversity of those cultures has been carefully blended into the culinary heritage of Texas. When the French stepped ashore, bringing with them the first flag to fly over Texas, they discovered that the abundance of shellfish along the Gulf coast could easily become the base for oyster stews and shrimp gumbos. After awhile, they began adding sassafras powder to the gumbo to thicken it, creating gumbo filet. The Indians had long been drying the herbal sassafras leaves and pounding them into a powder on a stone mortar. The French felt right at home on the coastline. After all, those marshlands were ideal for growing rice, which soon became a staple of their cuisine in the New World.

The French influence can also be tasted in Jambalaya, an aromatic concoction of delicate seasonings and herbs that included shrimp and oysters, perhaps chicken, and sometimes even bacon or ham. And those early French settlers were forever serious about their coffee. It needed to be black. It needed to be strong. It was never considered to be a luxury, only a necessity. And, when blessed with a slug of brandy, the coffee was said to keep away chills or fever, maybe even adding a few years to their lives. To Texas, the French left a legacy of gumbo, dirty rice, and beignets.

The French later got together with the Spanish, and the magical blend of their cooking became known and respected as Creole.

Spanish missionaries trudged into East Texas to spread the gospel of Christianity to the Indians. The Indians showed them how to raise corn, beans, and melons, sometimes feeding the priests, according to old diaries, tamales and mush. The early colonists from Spain depended on the woodlands around them for survival, combining their old world recipes with turkey, buffalo, deer, antelope, plums, persimmons, berries, and wild grapes. But always they regarded corn as the foundation for most of their meals, even though a British diplomat, who joined

Semillon Herb Pie©

*2¹/₂ lbs Pilgrim's Pride
Boneless Chicken Breasts,
cut into strips
salt
freshly ground pepper
2 tbsp Fredericksburg Herb
Farm Fresh Lemon Thyme
4 slices white bread,
crusts removed
4 tbsp Oberhellmann Vineyards
Bell Mountain Semillon Wine
2 tbsp water
2 tbsp Fredricksburg Herb
Farm Chopped Fresh
Lemon Verbena
grated zest of 1 lemon
2 eggs
salt and pepper, to taste
pastry for 2 large pie crusts
1 egg yolk*

- Preheat oven to 300 degrees.
- Season the strips of chicken with salt and pepper and roll them in the lemon thyme.
- Soak the bread in a mixture of Semillon wine and water, squeeze well, and add the bread to the meat mixture, along with the lemon verbena, the lemon zest, eggs and salt and pepper to taste.
- Roll out ²/₃ of the pastry about ¹/₈″ thick; line the bottom and sides of a 9¹/₂″ springform mold. Top with the chicken strips.
- Roll out the remaining pastry in a circle large enough to cover the pie. Place the pastry over the pie and trim and crimp the edges, sealing the top to the side crust.
- Roll out any pastry scraps and cut out leaf shapes for decoration.
- Brush the crust with the beaten egg yolk and decorate with pastry leaves. They will stick to the egg glaze.
- Brush the leaves lightly with the yolk.
- Bake for 1³/₄-2 hours.
- If the pastry browns before the pie is done, cover with foil for the remaining cooking time.
- Remove the pie from oven and cool on a rack.
- Serve at room temperature.
- Serves 6-8.

©1990 Varney's Chemist Laden
 Fredericksburg Herb Farm
 Fredericksburg, Texas

11

a Spanish family for dinner, reported: "Eating cornbread is like eating cooked sawdust." In time, corn was gradually replaced by rice.

The Spanish developed a process for squeezing certain stalks of corn and making a sweet syrup. And many of the pioneers cherished the lowly persimmon. The women favored a persimmon pudding, and the men would fight over a good, warm persimmon beer.

Mexico turned Texas cooking hot, being responsible for adding chilis, coriander, comino seeds, oregano, and garlic to just about every corn and bean dish that reached a Texas table. Mexico's political control of the region only lasted from 1821 to 1836, but its brand still heats up Texas foods. In fact, tortillas, chalupas, frijoles, and chili con carne are synonymous with Texas cooking. Many of those who settled the Texas frontier firmly believed that chili, when it was hot and strong, and it was always hot and strong, could protect them against colds and malaria, as well as clarify their blood. Others simply swore that a good bowl of chili was an effective aphrodesiac.

After Texas became a Republic, it made a strong, bold and concerted effort to attract immigrants from Europe. After all, Texas had land, lots of land. And those Scandinavians, Czechoslovakians, Germans, Italians, and Polish who journeyed to Texas shores brought new seeds for the farmlands and new ideas for the kitchen.

The Czechs prepared Kolaces. The Italian pioneer women taught their daughters the fine art of preparing pasta. For the Germans, the wurst was best. The Polish pickeled their pepper beans and made herb pies. The Orientals made a delicacy out of bean sprouts. And the French hauled vension from the field and turned it into a concoction called La Bourguignonne.

During its years as a member of the Confederacy, Texas adapted to old-fashioned, Deep-South and Western cooking. The blacks, working out in the fields, introduced hoppin' john and hoe cakes and chitterlings.

And the cowboy relied on his sourdough starter. He would take one cake of yeast and dissolve it in two pints of warm water, then add two tablespoons of sugar, four cups of flour, and one raw potato, cut in fourths.

Kolaces

1½ cups warm milk
2 cakes soft yeast
¾ cup Imperial
Granulated Sugar
4 egg yolks
4 cups Light Crust
All Purpose Flour
¼ cup each shortening
and butter, melted
Hill Country Farms Peach,
Apricot, Strawberry or
Raspberry Preserves

Topping:

½ cup Light Crust
All Purpose Flour
1 cup Imperial
Granulated Sugar
⅛ tsp "Adams Best" Vanilla
softened butter to
moisten dough
melted butter to
brush after baking

- Heat the milk and add yeast, sugar and egg yolks. Let the mixture foam.

- Gradually add flour, working the dough until it doesn't stick to your hands when touched. The dough should be very soft.

- Let the dough rise until double. Pinch it down and let it rise until double again.

- Then, with a tsp or tbsp, depending on the size of the kolace desired, cut balls from the dough and spread them on baking sheets.

- Brush the balls with melted shortening and butter and let them rise until double. When they have risen, poke indentations in the center to hold the fruit preserves.

- Fill and sprinkle with a topping of flour, sugar and enough butter to make it moist, adding vanilla.

- Let the filled kolace rise, then bake at 350 to 375 degrees until lightly browned.

- Brush warm kolaces with melted butter.

- Makes 3 dozen.

On many occasions, the taste of Texas is hot.

Hopping John

1 onion, chopped
1 bell pepper, chopped
1 lb J-B Sausage, sliced
2 cups dried blackeyed peas,
cooked (measure before cooking)
1½ cups cooked Comet
Long Grain Rice

- Saute onion, pepper and sausage in large skillet.
- Combine all ingredients. Serve hot.
- Serves 6-8.

Red Eye Gumbo

2 qts Brazos Beef Red Eye
1 large green bell pepper
1 medium onion
6 stalks celery
½ tsp Fiesta Garlic Powder
½ tsp gumbo file
2 cups okra
2 lbs shrimp
1 lb crabmeat
3 cups cooked Comet
Long Grain Rice

- Pour red eye into large saucepan or stew pot.
- Chop onions, bell peppers and celery.
- Add vegetables and spices to pot and cook for 10-15 minutes.
- Chop okra, shrimp and crab to desired size and add to mixture.
- Simmer for 15-20 minutes.
- Serve over rice or add rice to gumbo prior to serving.
- Serves 6-8.

As one cowboy cook, Richard Bolt, wrote: "Mix all ingredients in a crock and let rise until very light and slightly aged. The time required for this depends on the temperature. If the weather is very hot, the starter will be ready for use in 10 to 12 hours. If the weather is cold, it will require more time for the starter to become ready for use. When the starter is light and bubbling, it is ready for use. Do not let the sponge get too sour because this will cause the water to rise to the top, and when this happens the bread will not rise properly. Keeping the starter warm enough to work good in the wintertime is important, so I have wrapped the crock in a blanket and put a burning lantern in my teepee with my sourdough and myself. Sourdough starter is as tempermental as a woman, so treat it like your wife—with tender, loving care."

Southern cooking, in those days, had a much different slant in its recipes. In **The First Texas Cookbook**, published in 1883 by the First Presbyterian Church of Houston, Texas, the Honorable J. C. Hutcheson told how to cook cornfield peas:

"Go to the pea-patch early in the morning and gather the peas, take them home in a split basket. Take them in the left hand and gouge them out with your right thumb until it gets sore, then reverse hands. Look the pea well in the eye to see its color, but cook them anyway, as no color exempts the pea from domestic service, still the gray eye and white lips and cheeks are to be preferred. Throw the shelled peas mercilessly into hot water and boil them until they 'cave in.' When you see they are well subdued, take them out and fry them about ten minutes in gravy—plenty of gravy, good fat meat gravy, and try to induce the gravy to marry and become social with the peas. When you see that the union is complete, so that no man can put them asunder, and would not wish to if he could, put them in a dish and eat them all."

Texans with down-home Southern backgrounds preferred hog jowls and turnip greens; grits; crackling cornbread; okra, either boiled or fried; and hush puppies, cornmeal muffins that were created, so the rumor persists, to throw to the dogs around a campfire at night in order to keep them quiet.

Texas cooking is a proud reflection of its past. The recipes may change with the passing of years, but they will always have

Parmesan Stuffed Pasta

½ qt chicken broth
1 tbsp tomato paste
2 tbsp olive oil
2 tbsp butter
1 small onion, chopped
2 oz unsmoked bacon
3 cloves Fiesta Fresh Garlic
1½ lb boneless stewing beef
1 stalk of celery
1 sliced carrot
a pinch of cinnamon
3 cloves
1 cup Messina Hof Cabernet Sauvignon
6 tbsp bread crumbs
9 tbsp grated fresh Parmesan cheese
2 Twin Rivers Eggs, well beaten
a grating of nutmeg
4-6 large pasta shells, uncooked
additional Parmesan cheese to top

- Heat the broth with the tomato paste; set aside.
- In a heavy, round 3 qt enameled or earthenware covered stewing pot, heat the olive oil and butter.
- Add onion, garlic, bacon and beef, brown the meat on all sides over low heat for 10 minutes.
- Pour in hot broth, which should just cover meat, and add celery, carrot, cinnamon, cloves, and wine. Let simmer until liquid is reduced to a thick gravy (or 9 hours).
- Put broth mixture through a sieve and set meat aside (meat may be eaten as a second course).
- Mix the bread crumbs and Parmesan into the broth along with eggs and nutmeg. It should form a thick, stiff paste. If the paste is too soft, add more bread crumbs and Parmesan.
- Use as a filling in hand rolled pastas.
- Stuff pasta shells.
- Bake according to directions for pasta shells, topping with additional Parmesan cheese, if desired.
- Serves 3-4.

the distinctive flavor of the many ethnic groups who carved the state out of a rugged frontier and gave it the pride, the vibrance that mirrors the independent Texas spirit.

Those who would be Texians came from many nations.

Their culture was varied. So was their food.

Yet, in time, they became as one.

They were part of the old rock, solid and proud, upon which the foundation of Texas could be built. Their labors, their determination, their vision, the fight in their eyes caused Sam Houston to say, when he was governor of the state: "Texas could exist without the United States, but could the United States, except at very great hazard, exist without Texas?"

EAST TEXAS

"What we got, if it was important at all, we got from the ground. The lumber men came and took our pines that was growin' down in the thicket. The oil men sucked black gold from out of the innards of the earth. And me? All I ever got from the ground was fish bait, but I guess that's all I ever really needed when you get to thinkin' about it."

———East Texas farmer
from Dime Box

*E*ast Texas wears bib overalls and a smile. It's a grits and red-eye gravy sort of place, whose past is as white as the cotton that lay in the fields, as black as the oil that left the good earth stained the color of money. It's a land hidden in the shadow of the pines, where the hopes and dreams of man have forever been tied to the gifts of the soil.

The countryside rolls gently across great forests, and its backroads wind from farmstead to farmstead, past little crossroad communities that bear such names as Malta, Moscow, Old Egypt, Bethlehem, Macedonia, and Klondike. Hound dogs battle the thickets, in search of the elusive coon. Big bass explode from the topwater of lakes Sam Rayburn, Toledo Bend, Lake O' The Pines, and Tawakoni.

Deep East Texas, it's been said, is a softer, more gentle land, and gentlemen were required to live upon it. It possesses four national forests which shade almost a million acres of pine, magnolia, cypress, wild plum, oak, bay, and sweetgum. And in springtime, the darkness of the woodland is ablaze with the crimson of azaleas, the fragile blossoms of the dogwood, blowing gently like a blizzard of white in the restless winds. What this nation needs, some have said, is a national flower to call its own. The piny woods folks who settled in Tyler say they have the flower.

The rose.

But then, the folks who settled in Tyler are somewhat prejudiced. They refer to their city as the "Rose Capital of the World," and they have the credentials to prove it. More than two hundred nurseries produce half of the nation's commercially grown roses within a fifty-mile radius of Tyler. The city itself boasts the largest maintained rose garden in the United States, if not the world. And it sells and ships out fifteen million rose bushes a year.

*E*ast Texas is interlaced with the lore of a time when the land was untamed and unspoiled, and those who trekked the secret pathways of its forests fought and died for a land that became their homeland.

The pride of Nacogdoches, one of Texas's most historic cities, is the Old Stone Fort, constructed as a trading post about 1779 by Captain Gil Y'Barbo. Later it was to be used as a prison, a fortress, a newspaper office for the first two publications printed in Texas, and, finally, a courthouse where men fought with words instead of fists. They preferred fists.

The first shots of the Texas Revolution were fired on Nacogdoches in 1832. When the East Texas loaded their guns and marched off to war, they dumped their shelled corn between the walls of the old fort so there would be food awaiting them when they finally returned from battle. And it was within those solemn red adobe walls that James Bowie, with his knife, and David Crockett, with his long rifle, were administered the oath of allegiance by Mexican authorities only days before they were to meet and die in a little chapel known as Alamo. The Old Stone Fort now stands as a museum on the wooded campus of Stephen F. Austin State University.

War tore apart a gentle land.

The Alabama and Coushatta tribes fled into the sanctity of the Big Thicket to keep from fighting one. They had never been fighters. They didn't wear feathers, didn't even own a war

Appetizers

Fresh Herb Nibble-Ettes

*3 tbsp **each** Patty's Herbs
Fresh Basil, Italian Parsley,
Chives, and Marjoram,
finely chopped
2 tbsp **each** Patty's Herbs
Fresh Italian or Greek Oregano
and Thyme, finely chopped
1 (1.6 oz) pkg buttermilk
dressing mix
1/2 tsp Fiesta Garlic Powder
1 tsp Hungarian paprika
1 cup light vegetable oil
1 (24-34 oz) pkg goldfish or
oyster crackers*

- Mix herbs, dressing mix, garlic powder, paprika and oil, and pour over crackers in large bowl.
- Store in air-tight container.
- Nibble-Ettes may be stored in freezer for a long period of time.
- Great for appetizers, with soup, salads and crumbs for casseroles.
- Makes 3-4 cups.

Variation:
- Fresh Dill Nibble-Ettes can be made by substituting 1/2 cup chopped fresh dill for the other fresh herbs.

The legacy of the Indian stretches from the piney woods to the far western corner of the plains.

Party Dip

½ cup Borden's Plain Yogurt
½ cup Borden's Cottage Cheese
1 (15 oz) can Popeye Chopped
Spinach, drained
1 green onion, sliced
1 tsp Old San Antonio Style
Dark Chili Powder
¼ tsp dillweed
1 tsp lemon juice
fresh vegetables, crackers or
bread sticks

- Combine yogurt and cottage cheese, and stir until smooth.
- Stir in spinach, onion, chili powder, dillweed and lemon juice.
- Cover and chill until ready to serve with fresh vegetables, crackers or bread sticks.
- Makes 1½ cups.

Lurline's Picante Bean Dip

2 (15 oz) cans East Texas Fair
Picante Pintos, pureed in food
processor or blender
1 (6 oz) carton guacamole dip
8 oz Cheddar cheese, grated
1 medium tomato, diced
3 green onions with
tops, chopped
Texas Fresh Tortilla Chips
Tru-Tex Picante Sauce

- Spread pureed beans on plate.
- Spread guacamole dip on top in a circle.
- Sprinkle with cheese, tomato and green onions.
- Put crispy tortilla chips around the edge.
- Serve picante sauce on the side.
- Serves 10-12.

bonnet when Seminoles began hunting them down like wild, frightened animals. Beneath the East Texas pines they found their "Alibamy," meaning a place of rest. The year was 1816.

Now the Alabama and Coushatta Indian Reservation, between Livingston and Woodville, is a 4,444-acre recreational area. The Indian Chief Railroad line meanders and dips through the rugged underbrush, opening up a rare, untouched world of wild orchids, tupelo gum, honey locusts, shagbark, and the American hornbeam. In a living Indian village, tribesmen work at crafts and arts handed down by generations. The Na-Ski-La dancers perform the Hopi hoop dance, the shield dance, snake dance, friendship dance, and the basket dance of prayer. And young bright-eyed maidens still wander into the thickets to gather reeds from the river, pine needles and cones from the forest, so their mothers and grandmothers can weave baskets, as did their ancestors, dying them with rich colors made from natural herbs and berries.

The Caddoan Mounds State Historic Site near Alto cry out from a forgotten era, preserving three great ceremonial mounds that were built five centuries before Columbus landed in the Americas. Years of patient excavation have uncovered 100,000 artifacts, yet the origin of the ancient tribe remains an unknown. They came into the forests and had vanished by the time the first Anglo explorers trekked across soil that would be East Texas. Within the park is the replica of a bee-hive shaped house, used by the tribe and crudely constructed with materials and tools that would have been available to the mound builders. The Indians could have finished the house in eight hours. It took the archaeologists two and a half months.

*E*ast Texas is deeply Southern, in spirit and in truth, framed by the white-columned charm of Jefferson; the veiled ante-bellum beauty of San Augustine, reverently calling itself with good reason the "Cradle of Texas;" the Victorian legacy of Navasota, its 19th-century buildings fashioned primarily from limestone or brick simply because disgruntled Confederate soldiers left the town in charred ruins back during the late 1860s. And Navasota swore that it would never burn again.

Jefferson was known by many names: the River City, the

Vegetable Dip

1 large carrot
½ cup chopped TIE Brand
Bell Pepper
½ small onion, chopped
½ TIE Brand Cucumber, peeled
and seeded
3 sprigs cilantro, chopped
1 (8 oz) ctn lite cream cheese
¼ tsp Adams Minced Garlic
1 tsp lime juice
½ tsp Texas Gunpowder®
Ground Jalapeño Powder
chips or crackers

- Shred carrot in food processor.
- Add bell pepper, onion, cucumbers, cilantro and cream cheese. Mix.
- Add garlic, lime juice and Texas Gunpowder®.
- Mix, chill and serve with chips or crackers.
- Makes about 2 cups.

Jalapeño Cream Cheese Dip

1 (5.5 oz) jar Fischers & Wieser
Hot Red Jalapeño Jelly
1 (8 oz) brick cream cheese
Texafrance Bagel Chips

- Pour jalapeño jelly over brick of cream cheese.
- Serve with bagel chips.
- Makes 16-24 servings.

Party Pretzels

1 stick margarine
1 pkg Manana Mexican Dip Mix
1 lb pretzels

- Melt margarine. Stir in dip mix.
- Lay pretzels in large pan. Pour margarine mixture over pretzels and stir well to coat all of them.
- Bake at 250 degrees for 25 minutes or until mixture has dried on pretzels.
- Serve in a large bowl by themselves or with prepared Manana Mexican Dip.
- Serves 10-12.

Baghdad on the Bayou, the bread basket of the Western Confederacy. Steamboats churned steadily up the Big Cypress, and, in time, Jefferson became the second largest port in Texas. It was even considered by many to be the most cultured city south of St. Louis, the home of saloons, race tracks, cock fights, and gambling halls where the stakes were always high. Jay Gould, the notorious railroad tycoon, looked down upon Jefferson and proudly predicted, "Jefferson is destined to become the iron city of the South, the grandest industrial city in Texas."

It was Jay Gould who swaggered into town with the notion of bringing the Iron Horse itself to the Baghdad of the South, laying the track right down the middle of Main Street, and he wanted Jefferson to pay for it all.

Jefferson did not look upon Gould with any particular awe or reverence. Jefferson did not need the railroad, its power brokers contended, not as long as the city's commerce was anchored devoutly to the decks of those steamboats that kept coming to its banks from New Orleans.

Jay Gould had always been a hard loser. He angrily told city officials: "Bats will roost in your belfries. Trees will grow through the roofs of your buildings, and grass will grow in your streets." As the Wizard of Wall Street checked out of the grand Excelsior Hotel, he scratched at the bottom of the register's page: "The End of Jefferson."

His curse would forever haunt Jefferson. The natural dam down on the river suddenly broke, and the steamboats could no longer wedge themselves between those narrow, muddy channels that sliced through Big Cypress. The water drained away. So did Jefferson's population, dwindling to 3,000.

Jefferson today looks much as it did in the 1870s, carefully preserved and authentically restored. Almost fifty historical medallions hang on its homes, churches, and 19th-century structures, more than any other city in Texas. The doors to the Excelsior House, a hotel built in the 1850s by a riverboat captain, have never been closed. And in its rooms have slept two Presidents, General U. S. Grant and Rutherford B. Hayes; the man Hayes defeated for the Presidency, James G. Blaine; America's songbird, Jenny Lind; John Jacob Astor, Oscar Wilde,

Famous Cheese Dip

1 (10 oz) can Ro*Tel Tomatoes
and Green Chilies
1 lb pasteurized American
cheese, melted
El Galindo Tortilla Chips

- To tomatoes and green chilies, add pasteurized cheese which has been melted in a double boiler or microwave (for additional thickness, add more cheese).
- Mix together.
- Serve warm as dip with tortilla chips.
- Makes 2½-3 cups.

Spinach-Stuffed Mushrooms

3 doz large Monterey First
Harvest Fresh Mushrooms
(about 1½ lbs)
¼ cup Borden's Butter
or Margarine
1 small onion, finely chopped
1 (15 oz) can Popeye Chopped
Spinach, drained
½ cup dry bread crumbs
1 clove garlic, minced
½ tsp nutmeg
¼ tsp pepper
⅛ tsp dry mustard
½ Borden's Sour Cream
grated Parmesan cheese

- Preheat oven to 350 degrees.
- Wipe mushrooms. Remove and chop stems. Set caps on baking sheet. Set aside.
- Melt butter in medium skillet over medium-high heat.
- Add onion and mushroom stems, and saute 5 minutes until tender.
- Squeeze spinach dry. Add spinach, bread crumbs, garlic, nutmeg, pepper and mustard to onion mixture. Mix well.
- Stir sour cream into spinach mixture.
- Fill mushroom caps with spinach mixture. Sprinkle cheese over mushrooms.
- Bake 15 minutes.
- Serve warm.
- Makes 36 appetizers.

W. H. Vanderbilt, and, of course, the dreaded Jay Gould. His hand-scrawled curse predicting "The End of Jefferson" can still be seen in an old register in the Excelsior House lobby.

Across the street sits the gleaming "Atalanta," Gould's own private railroad car. The ladies of the Jessie Allen Wise Garden Club found it abandoned in a briar-thicket pasture in Jacob's Community, purchased it for a mere $1,200, and charge thousands of visitors a dollar each to tour the magnificent and priceless relic. Gould may have sentenced the city to die. But his regal and fancy car is now making money for the little antebellum town on Big Cypress Bayou. Jefferson, it seems, is having the last laugh on the old railroad tycoon, even if it's only a chuckle, a hundred years too late.

*J*efferson had depended on a river, and the river became dry and caked with mud. Just beyond, Caddo Lake was born during the New Madrid Earthquake of 1812 affecting two million square miles. An old Indian, his skin like a piece of sun-wrinkled leather, claimed to have been a witness the night the quake tore open the earth. He said: "Once there was a prairie where we hunted buffalo. But that was before the earth had chills and fever and shock. In the night the village sank. Then the water rolled over our home grounds and we fled to the hills."

A band of fishermen and farmers journeyed to the banks of the lake and nailed together a little settlement naming it, without much fanfare, Potter's Point.

On one fateful morning, two fishermen, Tom Allen and Will Teel, rowed away from the point, casually patrolling the trotline that stretched out across a lily pad bayou. For bait they were using the soft white flesh of mussels that lived in the warm, shallow water of Lake Caddo. The pair would gingerly slice away the outer edge of the mussel's shell, insert a knife point, and quickly pry the shell apart. It was an old practice. They had been doing it for years.

But that day in 1909 would be different. It was late in the evening when they found it—a pearl no larger than a pencil eraser lying in the tender, waxy flesh. The two men curiously

San Antonio Style Chicken Wings

12 chicken wings
1 cup Pace® Picante Sauce
⅓ cup catsup
¼ cup Killer "B" Honey
¼ tsp ground cumin
⅔ cup Dairy Brand Sour Cream

- Cut wings in half at joints; discard wing tips.
- Combine ⅓ cup of the picante sauce, catsup, honey and cumin; pour over chicken.
- Place in refrigerator; marinate at least 1 hour, turning once.
- Drain chicken, reserving marinade.
- Place on rack of foil-lined broiler pan.
- Bake at 375 degrees for 30 minutes.
- Brush chicken with reserved marinade: turn and bake, brushing generously with marinade every 10 minutes, until tender, about 30 minutes.
- Place 6″ from heat in preheated broiler; broil 2-3 minutes or until sauce looks dry. Turn, broil 2-3 minutes or until sauce looks dry.
- Spoon sour cream into small clear glass bowl; top with remaining ⅔ cup picante sauce. Serve with chicken.
- Makes 24 appetizers.

Layered Taco Dip

2 (9 oz) cans Amigos Bean Dip
1 cup shredded Monterey Jack cheese
6 avocados, pared and mashed
1 tbsp lemon juice
⅔ cup Ricos Picante Sauce, or to taste
1 (3 oz) pkg cream cheese, softened
2 tbsp Briannas Creamy Italian Dressing
1 pkg Wick Fowler's Taco Seasoning Mix
1 cup shredded Cheddar cheese
1 bunch green onions, chopped
1 cup lettuce, finely shredded
1 medium tomato, finely chopped
½ cup sliced black olives
Guiltless Gourmet Baked Tortilla Chips

- In a 9″x13″ glass dish, spread beans. Sprinkle with Monterey Jack cheese.
- In a bowl, mix avocados, lemon juice and picante sauce; spread over beans. Blend cream cheese, creamy Italian dressing and taco seasoning mix together until smooth and spread over avocado mixture.
- Top mixture with Cheddar cheese, green onions, lettuce, and tomato. Garnish with black olives.
- Serve with tortilla chips.
- Serves 15-20.

Rice 'N' Cheese Spread

1 cup cooked Texmati Rice
½ lb Cheddar cheese, grated
1 tbsp minced onion
3 tbsp minced green pepper
3 stuffed olives, chopped
3 tbsp Hell on the
Red Pickle Relish
1 tbsp chopped pimento
1 hard cooked Pilgrim's Pride
Egg, chopped
½ cup finely crushed
saltine crackers
¼ cup mayonnaise
¼ tsp salt
assorted crackers

- Combine first 7 ingredients. Add egg, cracker crumbs, mayonnaise and salt, mixing well.
- Pack in small crock or shape into a log.
- Serve with assorted crackers.
- Makes 2 cups.

Mystery and beauty surrounds the channels of Caddo Lake.

Spinach Balls

1 (14 oz) can Popeye Curly Leaf
Spinach, drained and chopped
1 cup herb-seasoned stuffing mix
½ cup grated Parmesan cheese
3 Twin River Eggs
6 tbsp Vandervoort's Butter,
softened

- Preheat oven to 375 degrees.
- Lightly grease baking sheet;
  set aside.
- Squeeze spinach dry. Combine
  spinach, stuffing mix and cheese.
- Stir in eggs and butter. Mix well.
- Shape into 1″ balls. Place on
  prepared baking sheet.
- Bake 15-20 minutes until
  lightly browned.
- Serve hot.
- Makes 35 balls.

Great Balls of Fire
Texas-Size Cheese Balls

2 tsp Aunt Betty's Fire Mix
2 tsp water
1 (8 oz) pkg cream cheese,
softened
1 (8 oz) pkg processed Cheddar
cheese, shredded
1 cup crumbled blue cheese
¾ cup chopped Regal
Texas Pecans

- Mix Fire Mix with water.
- Cook in microwave on HIGH
  1 minute to thicken.
- Mix cream cheese, Cheddar
  cheese and blue cheese with
  the Fire Mix liquid. Save a dab
  to pour on top for topping.
- Add pecans. Mix and form into
  2 cheese balls.
- Sprinkle a dab more of the dry
  mix on cheese balls.
- Pour a dab of liquid on top.
- Decorate with pecans.
- Chill well until tasting time.
- Makes 2 large cheese balls.

mailed the small pearl to Dr. Owens, a buyer of precious stones in Newport, Arkansas. Owens frantically wired back: "I'm on my way to Caddo Lake to set up a purchasing agency to handle as many pearls as can be found."

The secret that lay beneath the tepid waters of Caddo was a secret no longer. Wagons and hacks came rambling down the dusty roads to Britt's Gap, Alligator Bayou, Perch Gap, Little Green Break, and Towhead. Overnight the banks were lined with digging, clawing fortune hunters who all crawled on hands and knees into the mossy water with a "mother-of-pearl" gleam in their eyes, feeling around the lake floor for mussels with their bare feet. Fishermen were no longer fishermen, and farmers forgot about their crops. On the shoreline their women waited with vats of boiling water, old hoe files, and butcher knives to eagerly pry open the shells. They dug white pearls from "washboard" mussels, pink pearls from "white eye" mussels, and wine pearls from "buttermilk" mussels.

News of the pearl boom at Potter's Point riccocheted across the country. Buyers promptly rode into East Texas, setting up shop beneath the shade of a pine and clutching satchels filled with mony. Those high-dollar speculators began bidding as quickly as the pearls were pulled from the water, offering "silver, gold, or greenbacks," with prices ranging from $100 to $600.

The great million-dollar pearl boom, always hectic and sometimes frantic, lasted three years before coming to an abrupt end. The gates and locks at the old dam were removed, and the dam in Mooringsport, Louisiana, was raised. One morning, water came rushing into the bayou below Potter's Point, and the mussel beds were hidden again far below the murky surface of a lake too deep for the hunters to touch bottom anymore. Pearl camps were sadly abandoned. Fishermen returned to their trotlines. Farmers went back to their crops.

*E*ast Texas soil was never selfish with its gifts. Deep in the Big Thicket, back in 1865, a farmer used mules to power his drill bit, and he dug the state's first oil well simply because he saw his hogs covered with oil from the seepage. The ground was black with what he called Texas tea. Indians had found the

Sesame Pepper Cheese Log

1 (3 oz) pkg cream cheese
1/4 cup Llano Blush Wine
3 tbsp The Pepper Palate
Sweet Pepper Relish
1/4 tsp salt
3/4 lb Monterey Jack cheese,
grated
1/3 cup Menchaca Brand™
Sesame Seeds

- Beat cream cheese until soft.
- Blend in wine, pepper relish, salt and cheese.
- Shape into a log 2" diameter and about 10" long.
- Toast sesame seeds in 400 degree oven until golden, about 5 minutes.
- Roll cheese log in sesame seeds.
- Chill until firm, about 2 hours.
- Makes 1 lb log.

Texas Chili Dip

2 lbs ground beef
1 pkg West Brand Chili Mix
1 (8 oz) can tomato sauce
with bits
1 (10 oz) can Ro*Tel Tomatoes
with Green Chilies
1 lb Longhorn cheese, cut into
small pieces
El Galindo Tortilla Chips

- Prepare meat and chili mix according to directions.
- Heat tomato sauce, tomatoes and cheese in double boiler until cheese melts.
- Blend cheese and meat mixtures.
- Serve very hot with tortilla chips.
- Serves 12.

black gold oozing from the earth years earlier and had bathed in it for medicinal purposes. Early settlers had greased their wagon axles with it.

Most of those first early-day wells were dug by hand when production was measured in pints rather than barrels. It is said that E. H. Farrow rode two horses to death, racing to Nacogdoches to wire the news that the first well had come in.

Oil brought hope, then wealth, to the poverty-stricken, drought-forsaken farmlands of the 1930s. Dad Joiner had raised a ramshackle wooden derrick above Daisy Bradford's farm, and he promised that he would tap into "a treasure trove that all the kings of the earth might covet."

Who was to doubt him? After all, Dad Joiner, almost seventy years old and crippled, had ridden into Rusk County with forty-five dollars in his pocket, quoting the Bible like a preacher possessed, and quietly buying up oil leases from hungry farmers who thought a dollar an acre was big money. It did not matter to them that geologists had already explored the land and proclaimed it barren.

Dad Joiner was a poet, a prophet, a promoter, and, most likely a fraud. He made his money selling cheap oil leases to rich widows whose names he found listed as "next of kin" in the obituary columns of Dallas newspapers. He once confided to a friend, "Every woman has a certain place on her neck, and when I touch it they automatically start writing me checks."

Dad Joiner's partner in the East Texas oil venture was Doc Lloyd, all 320 pounds of him. He had been a druggist, veterinarian, and a government chemist who prospected for gold in Idaho, the Yukon, and Mexico. He had ridden with Pancho Villa, been married six times, and conducted the Dr. Alonzo Durham Great Medicine Show, drifting from town to town, peddling patent medicines he had concocted from oil.

Doc Lloyd passed himself off in East Texas as a world renowned geologist, and he swore that there was oil luking beneath Daisy Bradford's farm. Dad Joiner vowed, "We're going to get us the well of the world."

At 1,098 feet, the drill bit jammed. Joiner squared his shoulders, took a deep breath, and drilled again, even though a geologist ridiculed him, saying, "I'll drink every barrel of oil

Cocktail Meatballs

Meat Balls:
2 lbs hamburger meat
1 cup chopped onions
1 cup finely chopped
bell peppers
1 cup finely chopped celery
1 cup bread crumbs
2 Fenton's Eggs
2 tsps salt
1 tsp pepper
Sauce:
1 (15 oz) can tomato sauce
1 (12 oz) can Lone Star Beer
1/2 cup Claude's Brisket Sauce
1 1/2 cup Claude's Steak Sauce

- Mix all ingredients for meatballs together in large mixing bowl. Then shape into quarter-size meatballs.
- Place on cookie sheet and brown in oven at 325 degrees for 20 minutes.
- Meanwhile, mix ingredients for sauce and simmer covered for 20 minutes.
- After meatballs are browned, add to sauce and simmer for 1 hour.
- Great for parties as an appetizer, or as a main dish served over rice.
- Makes 24 meatballs.

Cajun Turkey Bites

3/4 lb Plantation Smoked
Turkey Breast
1/3 cup mayonnaise
1 tbsp Adams Minced Onion
1 1/4 tsp Adams Oregano
3/4 tsp Adams Ground Cumin
1/2 tsp Adams Garlic Powder
1/4 tsp Rosehill Culinary Herbs
Thyme
Shotgun Willie's Hot Pepper
Sauce, to taste
1 1/4 cup finely chopped
Clear River Pecans

- Cut turkey into 3/4" cubes; set aside.
- Combine remaining ingredients except nuts in medium bowl, mix well.
- Add turkey, tossing to coat evenly with mayonnaise mixture; roll each cube in chopped nuts. Chill loosely covered on waxed paper-covered cookie sheet until ready to serve, no lnger than 6 hours.
- Serve on cocktail picks.
- Makes about 36 appetizers.

you get out of that hole." At 2,518 feet, the drill pipe deep inside his second ill-fated well twisted off.

Joiner prepared to tackle the good, but stubborn, earth again. "You can't drill there," Daisy Bradford told him.

"Why not?"

"That's where I'm planning to put in my garden."

Joiner's crew pushed the equipment on down hill until one of the skids broke on a rock. Undaunted, Doc Joiner smiled a sad smile and said softly, "We'll drill right here." There was no place else to go. He had finally run out of money, time, and patience. Women weren't writing him checks anymore.

Early on the morning of October 5, 1930, more than five thousand had gathered in a clearing beside Daisy Bradford Number 3 to see whether the hole would be wet or dry, a money maker or a heart breaker. The ordeal, win or lose, was just about over. When the fire died in the boilers, men ripped the tires from their trucks and threw them in the flames. And the work continued, unceasing, amidst the smoke and the stench of burning rubber. Without any warning, about nine o'clock that night, there was a rumble deep in the ground, and the earth began to tremble. The crowd went wild, and so did the well.

The gusher came in, and the face of East Texas would forever be stained the color of oil. It transformed Kilgore and Longview, Overton and Gladewater into boom towns beyond the wildest imagination, draping the sky and roughnecks alike with black prosperity as thick as molasses.

The legacy of the oil boom is showcased in the three million dollar East Texas Oil Museum at Kilgore College. It is an authentic tribute to the men, like my father, who provided the muscle and grit to hammer out a field that ultimately produced 4.5 billion barrels of oil, a field that still has not emptied Doc Joiner's "treasure trove for kings."

Within one 24-hour period, Kilgore would grow from 800 to 8,000. For awhile, seven wells came in every two weeks, then it was seven a day, and finally a hundred a day. Ultimately there would be 25,987 producing wells covering 140,000 acres in five counties. But it was Kilgore that held tightly and jealously to the world's richest acre.

Sausage Roll Ups

3 cups Pioneer Biscuit and
Baking Mix
1 cup grated Swiss cheese
½ tsp red pepper
¼ tsp salt, optional
¾ cup Gandy's Milk
¼ cup vegetable oil
¼ cup Texas Hill Country
German Mustard
1 lb bulk pork sausage; cooked,
drained and crumbled

- Preheat oven to 400 degrees. Grease a baking sheet liberally.
- Combine biscuit mix, cheese, pepper and salt, if desired; stir in milk and oil.
- Divide dough into 3 equal portions. Turn dough portions onto surface sprinkled with additional mix. Knead gently 4-5 times. Roll each portion into a 7"x12" rectangle.
- Spread 1 tbsp plus 1 tsp mustard over each rectangle. Sprinkle ⅓ sausage over dough.
- Roll up tightly in a jellyroll fashion, beginning with long side; pinch seam and ends to seal. Wrap in wax paper and chill until firm. Repeat with remaining ingredients.
- Cut rolls into ½" slices; place on prepared baking sheets.
- Bake 15 minutes or until golden brown.
- Makes 60 appetizers.

Spicy Shrimp Dip

1 btl Al's Barbeque Sauce
3 tsp horseradish
boiled shrimp

- Mix barbeque sauce and horseradish together.
- Serve as a dip for cold boiled shrimp.
- Makes 1½ cups.

$\mathcal{N}$arrow highways of history thread their way across the hills of a wooded land whose timbered acreage virtually equals the combined forest areas of New England. Marshall was a rich and powerful city when Texas seceded from the Union in 1861, and it served as the Capital of Missouri and headquarters for the Trans-Mississippi Postal Department during the War Between the States. The Ginocchio National Historic District surrounds the 1896 Victorian Ginocchio Hotel, and relics of Marshall's heritage are stored away in the old, restored Harrison County Courthouse. Crockett, the fifth oldest town in Texas, was the site of the Mission San Francisco de los Tejas, the first Spanish mission in Texas. A replica of the 1690 log chapel stands in an 118-acre state historic park, alongside the old Rice Stagecoach Inn. And not far away are the springs where David Crockett and his men camped on their journey to the Alamo. They almost did not make it. Angry farmers who had settled the piny woods almost hanged them, mistaking Crockett for a horse thief who had plagued the countryside.

Nederland's Windmill Museum pays tribute to the Dutch who came to plow the land. Its La Maison Des Acadiens is a museum that carefully preserve's the French influence that wove itself into the culture of the area. Lufkin is wedged between Angelina and Davy Crockett National Forests, and it should have been merely a forgotten crossroads on the edge of the thicket. The railroad was supposed to have gone through Homer, six miles away, but, alas, the construction crew got into an old-fashioned, bare-knuckled, drunken brawl and wound up in jail. By the time they got out, some wise, far-sighted town officials had marked the route of the steel rails through Lufkin. So it was Lufkin that prospered. And it was Homer that became a forgotten crossroads on the edge of the thicket.

Brenham, known as the "Bluebonnet Capital of the World," holds fast to the antique architectural legacy of its German ancestry. And nearby, at Washington-On-The-Brazos, a band of Texans gathered in 1836 on the banks of the Brazos River to carve out their Declaration of Independence from Mexico. The Star of the Republic of Texas Museum displays artifacts from those turbulent days of freedom won and freedoms lost. The

Beverages

Honey Minted Iced Tea

2 qts water, divided
⅓ cup loose tea or 15 tea bags
2 cups Texsun Orange Juice
1 Rio Queen Orange, cut in half and thinly sliced
8-10 sprigs Patty's Herbs Fresh Mint
1 cup Lone Star Honey

- Bring 1 qt water to a full rolling boil in a saucepan. Remove from heat.
- While water is still bubbling, add the tea all at once. Steep for 5 minutes.
- Stir and strain into container holding 1 qt cold water. Cool at room temperature.
- Add remaining ingredients.
- Pour into ice-filled glasses.
- Makes 10-12 servings.

restored Winedale Inn, a stagecoach stop for wayward travelers during the war years rises regally off the prairie at Round Top, a land scarred often and reverently by the footprints of Sam Houston. His home was at Brenham. The old Baptist Church where he worshipped, when he worshipped, still stands.

The room where Houston died, however, the earth that holds his grave, is at Huntsville. Much of his controversial life and work is reflected in the cluster of buildings within the city's Sam Houston Memorial Park: the famed "Steamboat House," where Houston spoke his final word, "Texas," and the general's law office, carriage house, and one of his stately homes. The shortest highway in Texas leads to his grave, to his tombstone that bears Andrew Jackson's pointed eulogy: "The world will take care of Houston's fame." It has.

For twenty-five scenic miles, between Rusk and Palestine, stretches the longest, narrowest, most unusual state park in Texas. It is a railroad track that, at one time, served an honest-to-goodness working railroad, back when trains rumbled regularly into the old iron smelter at Rusk. Now its steel rails glisten beneath the Texas State Railroad, as passenger cars are pulled along by four vintage steam engines. They chug daily along between the Victorian stations at Palestine and Rusk, passing across winding creeks and on through cool forests that have known but show no traces of ever being trammeled by the footsteps of man.

*W*ay down deep in the pine and magnolia shadows of East Texas, in a land called "the biological crossroads of North America," the last remaining botanical wilderness in Texas had to be saved from the deadly hum of a chainsaw.

The Big Thicket, where men have wandered lost only a few yards from the highway, has long been a sanctuary of folklore and mystery, flavored somewhat by the winking of ghost lights and the far-away cry of the legendary ivorybill woodpecker, so large that backwoodsmen named them "mygods" or "godamightys." It was a dark, forbidden country, roamed by the bobcat, puma, Mexican tiger, and black bear, where the lonely whippoorwill and church-wills-widow would softly sing the sun

Peach Smoothie

*2-3 Brazos Valley Orchard's
Ripe Peaches
1 cup Texsun Orange Juice
2 cups Texas Gold
Vanilla Ice Cream
2-3 oz peach schnapps, optional*

- Peel, pit, and slice fresh ripe peaches. Put into blender and puree.
- Add ice cream and orange juice. Blend thoroughly.
- Pour into glasses.
- For an "enhanced" drink, add 1 oz of peach schnapps to each glass.
- Makes 2-3 servings.

Low Calorie Texas Peach Cooler

*1 cup cold Sealtest Skim Milk
1 medium E & B Peach
Orchard Texas Peach, sliced
with skin on
1/8 tsp vanilla
dash of cinnamon*

- Combine all ingredients in electric blender and blend until smooth.
- Place in freezer 30 minutes.
- Blend again and serve.
- Serves 1.

Shotgun Willie's Bloody Mary

Shotgun Willie's Bloody Mary Mix, Thick'N Mild or Thick'N Spicy
tequila, gin, vodka or rum
ice
Shotgun Willie's 3-Barrel Pepper Sauce
celery
lime slices
Shotgun Willie's Jalapeno Stuffed Olives

- Combine 3-4 parts Bloody Mary mix and 1 part of the choice of spirits.
- Pour the liquid into glasses over ice and stir.
- For those who prefer added spice in their lives, add the pepper sauce to taste.
- Garnish with celery stalks and lime slices. As a finishing touch, sink a jalapeno stuffed olive in the Bloody Mary just before drinking.

Old farm cabins at Heritage Gardens are rustic memories of life deep in the piney woods.

Chocolate Milk Shake

Make with or without electric blender.

1/2 tsp "Adams Best" Vanilla
2 tsp Adams Chocolate Extract
1 cup Hygeia Low Fat Milk
2 cups crushed ice
artificial sweetener to taste
(amount equivalent to
approximately 2 tsp sugar)

With Blender:

• In blender, combine vanilla, chocolate extract, milk, ice and sweetener to reach the 3 cup mark. Blend at low to medium speed for 1-2 minutes, or until ice is pulverized and mixture is thick and frothy.

Without Blender:

• Combine all ingredients except crushed ice in glass. Stir well.

• Serves 3-4.

Soda Fountain Punch

1 qt Lady Borden
Vanilla Ice Cream
7 cups cold Dr Pepper
1/2 tsp Adams Rum Flavor,
optional

• Place ice cream in a 4 qt punch bowl.

• When softened, beat with rotary beater until smooth.

• Gradually add about 2 cups cold Dr Pepper, beating until well mixed.

• Pour in remaining Dr Pepper and mix well with a spoon.

• Makes 20 servings.

down. Its trees are among the world's largest, its plant life among the smallest. Hidden in those vast tunnels of hardwood and pine are at least twenty-one varieties of exotic wild orchids, as well as twenty-five varieties of ferns. It has the world champion eastern red cedar, black hickory, holly, plane tree, red bay, yaupon, sparkleberry, common sweetleaf, and silver bell. A national park study revealed: "The forest contains elements common to the Florida Everglades, the Okefenokee Swamp, the Appalachian region, the piedmont forests, and the large open woodland of the coastal plains. Some large areas resemble tropical jungles in the Mexican states of Tamaulipas and Vera Cruz."

Once it was, as it is named, a big thicket, blanketing 3,350,000 acres with a strange, almost mythical botanical wilderness. Then, as the twentieth century pierced the thicket like a splinter of light, lumbermen came, and they brought with them their chainsaws, and the hardwood timber began to rapidly vanish beneath the teeth of the saw and the blade of an axe. The last vital acres of the grandiose Big Thicket began disappearing at the rate of fifty acres a day.

The Big Thicket Association, headed by Dempsie Henley, the mayor of Liberty, and backed by Senator Ralph Yarborough decided to fight. As Henley sadly said, "It takes only five minutes for a chainsaw to fell a magnolia tree that took a thousand years to grow."

Their long hours of hard, tenacious work finally paid off, and on October 11, 1974, the President signed into law a bill creating an 84,500 acre Big Thicket National Reserve.

Canoes are available to float its gentle streams. Hiking trails cut back through tall, untainted timber, particularly at Big Thicket Gardens in Woodville, an unspoiled setting for such plants as the mandrake, sasafras, strawberry bush, witch hazel, bloodroot, and orchid. Old logging tools and pioneer artifacts are found at Saratoga's Big Thicket Museum, poignant reminders of a backwoods people who always said they "lived yonder a piece," who "pitched" a crop when they planted one, who referred to a quarrel as a "cuss fight," and who thought a religious conversion was simply a "perfessin'."

Near Woodville, Clyde Gray assembled remnants of those

Soups, Stews & Chili

Guacamole Soup

2 ripe medium avocados
1½ cups Rosser Wasser Rock
Brand Spring Water
1 cup Milk-E-Whey Goat's Milk
2 tbsp lemon juice
2½ tsp Brooke's Seasoning Salt
dash of Two Sisters
Pepper Sauce
1 medium tomato, chopped
lemon slices to garnish

- Cut avocados lengthwise into quarters; remove pits and peel.
- Mix avocado, water and goat's milk in blender until smooth.
- Stir in lemon juice, seasoning salt and pepper sauce thoroughly.
- Fold tomato into soup; chill.
- Garnish each serving with a lemon slice.
- Serves 4-6.

hard, unforgiving early days in the thicket at his Heritage Village and Gardens. He found a little 1906 school house at Midway and the weather-torn post office of Pluck in an old hay barn near the ruins of a ghost town. On the wall hung a faded wanted poster, offering "$5,000 for Jesse James and $10,000 in gold coins for Sam & Belle Star." The aged Tolar cabin was carted in from Hillister, a hand-made chair factory brought from Burkeville. Gray dug a wooden cane mill from beneath the waters of Beech Creek, where it had lain untouched for seventy-seven years. He towed in Richmond's first fire truck. From Town Bluff came an antique general store. And, finally, he persuaded an old moonshiner to piece together the copper cooker and coils of a genuine, authentic moonshine still.

Gray's Heritage Village and Gardens has become the final resting place for fragments of once-forgotten ghost towns on once-forsaken roads.

*O*n a cold, harsh winter day in 1901, the earth far below the thicket began to grumble and complain at 1,020 feet, and Texas wildcatters held their breath. Oil exploded in fire and glory, erupting like a volcano gone wild, throwing mud, rock and embers two hundred feet above the fields at Spindletop, a sometimes cynical, sometimes sacred place that had held men's hopes and robbed them of their last few dollars. The drill pipe broke into pieces like brittle strands of macaroni, and the well raged angrily for ten days, blowing out a hundred thousand barrels of oil a day before it was finally brought under control. Derricks sprouted everywhere. Lease hounds went crazy. Refineries sprang up. And land—cheap, worthless farm and timber land—was suddenly selling for $200,000 an acre. The Lucas gusher forever changed the face of Beaumont. In time, it transformed Houston from a struggling town in a mosquito-infested bayou into one of the world's great and beautiful cities.

Beaumont has faithfully recreated the spirit of the boom town at Gladys City, alongside the Lucas Gusher Monument. It contains such clapboard buildings of the era as a post office, power plant, livery stable, blacksmith shop, wooden derricks, and, of course, a saloon. The Spindletop Museum is located on

Summer Fruit and Wine Soup

4 cups hulled Paw-Paw's Fresh
Strawberries or Raspberries,
or both
½ cup Messina Hof
Johannisberg Riesling
1 cup Borden's Plain Yogurt
1-2 cups Artesia Still Natural
Artesian Mineral Water, chilled
(depends on your preference
for thickness)
¼-½ cup sugar (adjust for
sweetness of fruit)

- Whirl berries in blender with Johannisberg Riesling.
- Strain to remove seeds, if you wish.
- Return to blender with yogurt, water and sugar.
- Taste and adjust water and sugar, for consistency and sweetness.
- Chill for at least 1 hour.
- Serve before meal as an appetizer or as a light lunch.
- Serves 4.

Texas Chicken Noodle Soup

2 cups Take Stock
Chicken Stock
1 cup water
1 cup raw chicken pieces
½ cup shredded carrots
½ cup finely sliced celery
and celery tops
½ cup dry fine egg noodles or
alphabet letter noodles
½ tsp salt
½ tsp finely ground black pepper

- Combine chicken stock, water, chicken pieces, carrots and celery in large soup pot until tender.
- Add noodles. Simmer over medium high heat for 15-20 minutes, until noodles are tender.
- Season to taste and serve.
- Serves 4-6.

the campus of Lamar University.

Houston still possesses the energy of those rough and tumble millionaires who worked and fought for their fortunes and left behind a magnificent city. They feverishly pumped petroleum into the city like plasma, gambled on land like it was a poker hand, and won without ever having to show their cards.

One man came heard the tales of Houston's developers, and wrote: "After you have listened to the talk of these pioneer veterans for some time you begin to feel that the creation of the world, the arrangement of the solar system, and all subsequent events, including the discovery of America, were provisions of an all wise Providence, arranged with a direct view of the proper advancement of the commercial interests of Houston."

Such an attitude still persists.

Houston was, after all, the first word spoken by man on the moon that historic summer. Neil Armstrong calmly reported, "Houston, Tranquility Base here. The Eagle has landed." Only twenty-five miles to the south, NASA's Lyndon B. Johnson Space Center provides the key link from liftoff to splashdown. Many of the buildings are open for self-guided tours. On display in the Exhibit Hall is Mercury Faith 7, in which Gordon Cooper orbited the earth in 1963. Alongside is Gemini 5, the cramped craft that carried Cooper and Charles Conrad for an eight-day ride in space. And nearby is the Apollo 9 command module that transported David Scott, Russell Schweickart, and James McDivitt to the first test docking with a lunar module. They are high-tech equipment that became antiques within two exhilerating decades of space exploration. A Gallery of Astronauts honors the courage and dedication of a rare breed of men and women who dared reach for the stars. Visitors can see Mission Control, the nerve center for all U. S. manned flights. And they can amble off for a look at the mission simulation and training facility with its Skylab Orbital Workshop, or take in the flight acceleration facility, the largest man-rated centrifuge operating in the free world.

Houston has, over the years, become a major entertainment center. The Astrodome, labeled by the Reverend Billy Graham as the eighth wonder of the world, was the first all-purpose air conditioned domed stadium on the face of the

Fresh Vegetable Soup

2 cups Take Stock
Vegetable Stock
1 cup fresh vegetables,
diced or julienned
1/2 tsp salt or
Lantana Salt Free Seasoning
2 tbsp dry sherry
1/4 tsp thyme

- Simmer all ingredients for 25 minutes until vegetables are tender.
- Serve warm with good bread.
- Serves 4-6.

Mexican Bean Soup

4 slices Farm Pac Brand Bacon,
diced
3/4 cup onion, chopped
3/4 cup celery, chopped
1 clove garlic, minced
1 (4 oz) can Old El Paso®
Chopped Green Chilies
1 (16 oz) can Old El Paso®
Refried Beans
1/4 tsp black pepper
1/4 tsp Fiesta Chili Powder
several dashes of hot pepper sauce
1 (13 1/2 oz) can chicken broth
Cheddar cheese, shredded
Old El Paso Nachips®
Tortilla Chips, broken

- In a 2 qt saucepan, cook bacon until crisp.
- Add onion, celery and garlic. Cover and cook over low heat, stirring occasionally, for 10 minutes or until vegetables are tender but not brown.
- Add green chilies, beans, pepper, chili powder and hot pepper sauce.
- Stir in chicken broth. Bring to a boil.
- Serve in bowls; sprinkle cheese and tortilla chips over each serving.
- Serves 4-5.

Microwave:
- In a 2 qt microwave-safe casserole, microwave bacon on HIGH for 3-5 minutes or until crisp.
- Add onion, celery and garlic; cover and microwave at 50% power for 5 minutes or until vegetables are tender, stirring occasionally.
- Add green chilies, beans, pepper, chili powder and hot pepper sauce. Stir in chicken broth.
- Microwave on HIGH for 5-6 minutes or until soup boils.
- Proceed as directed above to serve.

The growth of Houston is reflected in the city's Wortham Center.

Tangy Bean Soup

1 lb dried beans (black, pinto or kidney)
8 cups no-salt beef broth plus enough water to cover
1 large onion, chopped
2 cloves garlic, minced
¼ cup chopped green pepper
¼ cup chopped celery
½ cup shredded carrots
2 minced jalapeños, optional
1 tbsp dried parsley
1 tbsp dried cilantro
¼ tsp paprika
¼ tsp black pepper
1-2 Menchaca™ Brand Bay Leaves
1 tbsp low-sodium soy sauce
½ cup Gourmet Garnishes French Riviera Dressing

- Wash beans, soak overnight; drain and rinse. Add to beans all ingredients except soy sauce and dressing.
- Bring to a boil, reduce heat and simmer for 1 hour. Add more water if needed, plus soy sauce and dressing.
- Simmer for another hour or until beans are tender. Discard bay leaves.
- Serves 10.

Broccoli Cheese Soup

2 cups Pioneer Country Gravy, prepared
1 (10 oz) pkg frozen chopped broccoli, thawed
2 cups grated sharp Cheddar cheese
1 tbsp Parmesan cheese
1 tbsp minced onion

- Prepare gravy mix according to package directions.
- Add remaining ingredients. Blend well. Simmer until thoroughly heated.
- Serves 4.

Note:
- If a thinner soup is preferred, add milk or water to desired consistency.

earth. Judge Roy Hofheinz, the late Texas-styled wheeler-dealer, always swore that he was inspired to build the Astrodome by the ancient Romans, who covered their coliseum with awning in bad weather. He once predicted: "The stadium will take its place right alongside the Eiffel Tower and the great wonders of the world in construction." It certainly revolutionized the way mankind would forever watch professional sports. The Astros and the Oilers both played on a rug indoors first.

Through the years, the great domed stadium became a kind of sports theater-in-the-round. It hosted the world's largest indoor crowds for a circus, a rodeo, a prize fight, a basketball game, and a tennis match. Matadors have fought bulls, Portuguese style, inside the Astrodome. Motorcycles and midget automobiles have raced. There have been fat stock shows and demolition derbies. Karl Wallenda even walked a tightrope across its ceiling.

When Ernie Banks, the great Chicago Cubs shortstop played his first game indoors, he looked around at the confines of the dome and asked, "Is it still considered the eighth wonder of the world?"

"It is," he was told. "Why?"

"I thought it might have moved up," Banks said.

Next door, the Astroworld is an amusement park, sprawling for 65 acres across the East Texas farm land. It weaves high energy entertainment throughout ten colorful and distinctive theme areas, offering more than a hundred shows and a wild assortment of white-knuckled, hold-your-breath thrill rides that defy gravity but never the odds.

Houston is almost always on stage at the legendary Alley Theatre and the pompous, prestigious Jesse H. Jones Hall for the Performing Arts. The Alley was historically plain, warm, intimate, and honest, its stage wedged into a hot, crowded little studio. On overflow nights, the audience sat atop a piano, on piano benches, on radiators, and on window sills. But the Ford Foundation said, "The Alley is one of the few significant professional theaters in the country outside of New York." Now the Alley has a luxury, contemporary home, and its architecture, some say, greatly resembles a fortress. One British director simply decided that the theatre "responds to

Lentil Soup

1 (1¼ oz) pkg Wick Fowler's
Bean Seasoning
8 cups Utopia Springs
Spring Water, chilled
1 lb dried lentils
2 stalks celery, chopped
1 medium onion, chopped
2 carrots, sliced in rounds
1 clove fresh garlic, minced
1 (16 oz) can tomatoes, diced
½ cup Ranch House Ham, diced
2 tsp salt

- Place all ingredients in a large sauce pan. Bring to a boil.
- Reduce heat and cover. Simmer 45 minutes to an hour or until beans are tender.
- Stir occasionally and add water if necessary.
- Serves 6-8.

Beefed-Up Blackeyed Pea Soup

2 lbs B3R Beef, ground
¼ cup minced green pepper
1 cup cream of chicken soup,
undiluted
2 (14 oz) cans chicken broth
1 qt water
1 pkg Wick Fowler's
Bean Seasoning
1 (28 oz) can whole tomatoes,
undrained
1 (16 oz) pkg blackeyed peas,
frozen or
1 (15 oz) can East Texas Fair
Fresh Shelled Blackeyed Peas
1 small onion, chopped
1 cup chopped celery
½ tsp salt, or more to taste
cornbread, crackers or
French bread

- Brown beef with green pepper; then drain.
- In a large soup pot, pour in beef mixture and remainder of ingredients. Bring to a boil, cover and simmer for about 1 hour.
- Serve with cornbread, crackers or chunks of French bread.
- Makes 4½ quarts.

Americans" appetities for the castles which they never had in their own heritage." He just may be right. The colonnaded Jones Hall is the $7.4 million gift of Jesse H. Jones's son, John T., who remembered his father once telling him earnestly that Houston should have a grand and glorious home on whose stage symphony, dance, opera, and theater would be proud to perform. What Jones wanted, Jones got, even after death.

Houston's Museum District encompasses wide, tree-lined boulevards, parks, and picturesque fountains, looking much like the scenic backdrop for an old master's painting. The Museum of Fine Arts, the cultural core of Houston since 1924, features more than eleven thousand works, linking together the beauty, the impression of Assyrian, Christian, Egyptian, medieval and Roman art, some pieces dating as far back as 2500 B. C. The Contemporary Arts Museum dares focus on experiments in all kinds of media from the war years of the 1940s to the present. It is bold. It is avant garde. It is a sometimes poignant, sometimes cockeyed slice of Americana's best. Rice University itself is an artistic showplace, with Byzantine and Medieval Italian architecture. And at the University of St. Thomas is the Rothko Chapel, hidden in the inner sanctum of its own mystery. Inside are the last works of New Yorker Mark Rothko. His paintings are dark, misunderstood, and foreboding, with figures, faces, crosses, and doves all slowly fading into focus. Mrs. Dominique de Menil, who commissioned the paintings, said: "This was Mark Rothko's greatest adventure. His colors became darker and darker as if he was bringing to us the tragic mystery of our own perishable condition. He was capturing the unbearable silence of God."

To the east of Houston is that sacred patch of ground beneath the San Jacinto Monument where General Sam Houston, in eighteen bloody minutes, caught Santa Anna asleep, with his pants down and once and forever won independence for Texas. The park has a towering spire, taller than the Washington Monument, to be sure, and a museum that contains mementoes from the men who led Texas during its brawling years. Nearby, moored to its last dock, the battle-scarred Battleship Texas has come home to retirement after service in two world wars.

54

Hot Tamale Soup

1 lb ground chuck
½ cup chopped onion
½ cup chopped bell pepper
1 tsp Adams Chili Powder
1 tsp Adams Ground Cumin
3 (14.5 oz) cans beef broth
1 (10 oz) pkg frozen corn
1 (15 oz) can Old El Paso®
Mexican Beans
12 Pedro's Tamales, shucks
removed and sliced

- Brown ground chuck with onion and bell pepper.
- Add remaining ingredients.
- Simmer 30 minutes, then add tamales.
- Heat thoroughly and serve.
- Serves 6-8.

Sausage Stew

6 Nicholson's Dried Beef Sticks
1-2 bell peppers, diced
½ onion, sliced
2 fresh tomatoes, chopped, or
1 can of stewed tomatoes
1 celery stalk, chopped
6 tsp catsup
1 cup water

- Mix all ingredients in skillet.
- Simmer in skillet 15-20 minutes.

Nestled within the tall shadows of Houston, Bayou Bend and its historical collection is Miss Ima Hogg's legacy to the past. And Sam Houston Historical Park is tucked away at the feet of skyscrapers. Those twenty-one acres originally served as the city's first park. Now they hold a quaint assortment of grand old homes and churches, surrounding a bandstand, that was saved from destruction by the Harris County Heritage and Conservation Society. The park reeks of nostalgia, though its antiquity is reflected sharply in the chrome and glass of the giant buildings that rise above it. The stark contrast between old and new, between log and steel is startling.

Houston is never far from the madding crowd. The thicket has the solitude, a silence broken only by bass jumping amidst the lily pads. A Southern wind lingers in the tall pines. A rose blooms. There is the smell of crude oil in the air. The columns of an ante-bellum mansion glisten in the moonlight. A coon dog strikes a warm trail. And all is well within the gentle land of cornbread, cane syrup, and clabber.

NORTH TEXAS

"I found the usual public square flanked by windowless shops know as 'stores' and an angular courthouse in the middle, around which the waiting teams and saddle horses stood at hitching posts...everything was laid out in a square, that blight on many things American. I felt pleased that the Lord had made the heavens and earth himself, for had the contract been let locally all things might have been in straight lines like a Scot's plaid."

—*An early-day traveler's view of a North Texas town*

$\mathcal{N}$orth Texas wears silk suits when it has to, faded denim when it wants to, and the smile of a gambler who bluffed, when he should have folded, and beat the odds when he didn't have a chance. It's an aristocratic land, full of cotton farms and bald prairies, that possessed no natural assets, other than great chunks of raw land, yet grew to greatness simply because it was hammered together by a legion of men and women who were too stubborn to quit and too proud to ever leave a job undone.

Dallas symbolizes the spirit of all of North Texas. But then, Dallas has always chosen to be a little different. There was no real reason for Dallas to have ever been founded in the first place and even less reason for it to have survived. It sits solidly on a prairie of dry, black dirt that cracks open during droughts and looks more like mud gumbo when the rains come. Its only natural waterway is the Trinity River, which, through the ages, is either barely damp or flooding.

Yet Dallas prospered for almost thirty years before the first railroad came thundering through its city limits. And neither oil nor gas ever bubbled naturally from beneath its streets.

Former Mayor Robert Lee Thornton, however, best summed up the intangible driving force that makes Dallas run. He said, "Dallas is a city which makes a man do more than he would in any other city."

Peter Stewart, for example, formed a foundation that paid $2.5 million for an acre of land in the middle of downtown Dallas just so he could build a park. Thanksgiving Square, a hall for music and the arts, a quiet place for rest, relaxation, and meditation, where rushing waterfalls drown out the harsh, ragged sounds of a city on the move. Stewart told me, "Kings or emperors had temples at the cermonial centers of their ancient cities. In Europe you see cathedral squares. So it's not a new idea." Maybe not. But only in Dallas, where land is vanishing beneath the foundations of tall buildings, where acreage carries premium price tags, would men invest millions so that people they didn't even know could find a place of inspiration in the frantic-paced heart of a city.

Dallas was destined to be great, even when it was nothing more than a village of sticks and stones that John Neely Bryan had stuck together alongside the banks of the unpredictable Trinity back in 1841. His log cabin, the first home built in Dallas, still stands alongside the courthouse. Neely brought commerce to his little town, operating a ferry across the river, running the post office, paving the way for Dallas to become the world's largest market for buffalo skins. In those days, an early visitor wrote that the village "seemed too immature to do any business, but lay sweltering in the sun waiting for the future."

The future was built on oil. Even though Dallas never had any producing wells to call its own, it became a nerve center for America's petroleum industry, with more than 120 oil-oriented firms with a million or more dollars in assets headquartered in the city. For many, oil, the luck of the wildcat well, has been the seed of their fortunes.

In time, Dallas emerged as one of the nation's prized fashion centers, dressing itself with gowns from France and Stetsons from Texas. It all began, perhaps, with Stanley Marcus who, for many years, was the guiding genius behind the legendary Neiman-Marcus, a business founded, he once said, on bad judgment. In 1907, Herbert Marcus, his sister, Carrie

Elizabeth's Ranch Chili

1 lb Broken Arrow Ranch
Venison Chili Grind
½ cup chopped onion
2 tsps cooking oil
4 oz tomato sauce
2 cups water
3 tbsp Fiesta Chili Powder
(vary to taste)
1 tsp Menchaca™ Brand Paprika
½ tsp salt
½ tsp Menchaca™ Brand
Red Pepper
1 clove garlic
1 tsp Fiesta Ground Cumino
1 (14½ oz) can tomatoes, chopped
1 tbsp flour
2 tbsp warm water

- Add the venison and onion to the oil, cooking over medium heat until venison is brown.
- Add the remaining ingredients, cover and simmer about 1 hour or until meat is tender. Stir occasionally while cooking.
- Correct seasonings to taste. Thicken with flour mixed with warm water.
- Serves 5-6.

Dallas is a city with a difference.

59

Neiman, and her husband, A. L. Neiman, found themselves with $25,000 to finance a new business. They had to choose between buying a department store or taking an unknown soft drink franchise in Missouri. They chose the department store. They turned down Coca-Cola.

The Trade Mart is a part of the renowned Dallas Market Center, a giant 125-acre complex that, perhaps, holds the golden key for city's future. To Market Hall, the Apparel Mart, the Home Furnishings Mart, the Decorative Center, and the Trade Mark come 250,000 retail store buyers each year, all looking for furniture, gifts, housewares, appliances, toys, jewelry, electronics, and clothing. As a result, Dallas has solidified its reputation as the commercial crossroads for four of the largest metropolitan areas on the continent: New York, Los Angeles, Chicago, and Mexico City. And the mammoth, seven-story World Trade Center is the Texas connection across the oceans.

Dallas is no longer merely lying in a sweltering sun waiting for the future. The future is here. It is now. Dallas became a success for one simple reason. Noboby ever convinced Dallas that it couldn't.

*D*allas considers itself rich in many ways.

The Mid-Cities have become one of Texas' most prominent destination areas. Arlington's Six Flags Over Texas is a sprawling theme park of live musical shows, big-name country and hard rock entertianment, and rip-snorting thrill rides, based loosely on the state's colorful history. In Grand Prairie, the Palace of West and Ripley's Believe It or Not Museum graphically depict some of the world's most outrageous characters and oddities. Elephants, zebras, camels, white tigers, and giraffes roam the African-styled veldt of The International Wildlife Park. And Trader's Village crowds hundreds of dealers, with junque and antiques, into a shoppers bazaar it calls the World's Largest Flea Market.

The culture of Dallas is more refined. The Virginia Meadows Museum, part of the Owen Fine Arts Center on the Southern Methodist University campus, displays four centuries

German Sausage Stew

1 (12 oz) pkg Hans Mueller Bratwurst, cut in 1/2" slices
1 (12 oz) pkg Hans Mueller Smoked Bratwurst, cut in 1/2" slices
1-2 bell peppers, diced
1/2 onion, sliced
2 fresh tomatoes or
1 can of stewed tomatoes
1 celery stalk, chopped
3 tsp Hans Mueller Dusseldorf Mustard
1 tsp catsup

- Place ingredients in skillet, cover and simmer 15-20 minutes.
- Serves 4-6.

Beef Jerky Stew for Hunting and Backpacking

12 oz Nicholson's Beef Jerky, diced
1-2 bell peppers, diced
1/2 onion, sliced
2 fresh tomatoes or
1 can of stewed tomatoes
1 stalk celery
3 tsp mustard
3 tsp catsup
1 cup water

- Combine all ingredients.
- Simmer 15-20 minutes.
- Serves 3-4.

of Spanish art and a sculpture court, as well as paintings by international masters. On the walls of the Dallas Museum of Art hangs the priceless works of Renoir, Gauguin, Monet, and Matisse. Its sculptures reflect the passion, the noble creativity of Rodin and Henry Moore. The Biblical Arts Center surrounds an immense and dramatic religious painting of the Miracle of Pentecost, interpreted by special lighting and narration. And within the center's three art museums are replicas of Saint Paul's Gate of Damascus and Christ's tomb.

Tucked away in the rocks and timber, the architectural luxury and splendor of Turtle Creek is the daring, remarkable Dallas Theatre Center, described as a "windowless asymetrical enigma, round which you have to walk half a circle before even finding the main entrance. Inside, the twisting staircases and elliptical foyers create the appearance of a ship, and also the sense of movement." The theatre, like the spirit of Dallas, has every right to be different. For it is the only one ever designed by Frank Lloyd Wright.

He was once asked, "Why did you develop such an odd design for the theatre?"

Wright only smiled. "Because I wanted to liberate the stage from the shackles of tradition," he said. "Besides, I always believed that going to the theatre should be a grand adventure."

Downtown, the infamous sixth floor of the Texas Schoolbook Depository Building, where Lee Harvey Oswald allegedly fired the deadly assasin's bullets into President John F. Kennedy, has opened as a museum and monument to the most frightening gunshots of all. In one chilling moment, they changed the course of American history and a nation's destiny. On Dealy Plaza below, a cenotaph and Memorial Park stand stoically beside the ill-faded spot on the motorcade route where a President was slain.

At Old City Park, the Dallas County Heritage Society has pieced together poignant remnants of North Texas's past. There is Millermore, in all of its Greek Revival glory, the muted, antique promise of a frontier where man could better himself. William Brown Miller built it on land he bought for a dollar an acre. The society bought the home for a dollar, and thus saved Millermore from the wrecking ball. Nearby sits the rustic log

Red Eye Chili

1 lb ground pork
3 lbs ground chili meat
1 (32 oz) jar Brazos Beef
Red Eye
2 cups chopped onion
½ cup chopped celery
6 tbsp Adams Chili Powder
1 tbsp Adams Oregano
¾ tbsp salt
¾ tbsp Adams Garlic Powder
¾ tbsp Adams Malabar Coarse
Black Pepper
3 cups water
1 (16 oz) jar Brazos Beef
Caliente, optional
5 tbsp masa flour
2-3 tbsp water

- Cook meat in frying pan until lightly done (light gray in color), pouring liquid off periodically.
- Add meat and red eye to chili pot.
- Saute onions and celery together in the frying pan until translucent.
- Add to chili pot.
- Add chili powder, oregano, salt, garlic powder, black pepper and 3 cups water, and cook slowly, stirring occasionally (add caliente for spicier, hotter chili, if desired).
- Make a paste of masa and 2-3 tbsp water, add to chili pot and cover.
- Cook slowly 1½-2 hours, stirring occasionally to prevent sticking.
- Serves 6.

Vegetarian Chili

1¼ cups combination dried
pinto and kidney beans
1 cup hamburger-flavored TVP
(textured vegetable protein)
2 tbsp vegetable oil
1 pkg West Brand Chili Mix
⅞ cup boiling water
Texmati Brown Rice, cooked
cheese, shaved or grated

- Place kidney and pinto beans (or beans of your choice) in pan and cover with water. Cook 1-1½ hours, being sure water is not completely absorbed, adding more as necessary.
- After beans are cooked, add boiling water to the TVP. Stir, then saute TVP mixture in vegetable oil.
- Add chili mix, then add beans with 2 cups water. Simmer 30 minutes, adding more water as necessary. You may add chopped tomatoes or onions for different tastes.
- Serve on brown rice, then top with cheese shavings.
- Serves 6-8.

cabin of Richard Montgomery Gano, a physician, rancher, minister, soldier, surveyor, and legislator who learned how to survive on a rugged land.

The girl's school, with its McGuffey readers, was nailed to the prairie in the 1850s. The landowner's office has been furnished with business-like simplicity. The section house, heated by a wood-burning stove, lit by a coal oil lamp, was for railroad men, back in a time when they were paid $2.40 a day. It wasn't much. But it was better than earning "six bits" a day down at the cotton mill. The Drummer's Hotel, formerly a stagecoach inn, advertised it had first class accommodations, but no running water or electricity. And the old general store looks much as it did during the days when it served as a lifeline to the dirt farmer and black land settlers of North Texas.

So much of Dallas is still linked to an earlier time. Back in 1936, Texas was planning a celebration to pay homage to its first hundred years, a celebration that needed dimension, distinction, and importance. But above all, it needed the right location. The Centennial probably should have been in Austin. That, after all, is the state capital. Or San Antonio, where the Alamo fell and a legend was born. Or Houston, where independence was really won.

Of all the major cities in Texas, only Dallas had no rightful historic claim to even bid for the great fair. Nevertheless, Dallas dispatched a delegation to Austin, one that had drive, energy, determination, and $3.5 million in its pockets. That was a lot of money in the midst of the Great Depression. Dallas wasn't singing the blues. Dallas wound up with the Centennial.

The legacy of that celebration—Fair Park—is still important to the national image of Big D, focusing on the arts, weaving together the past and future of technology in Texas, and serving as one of the finest cultural and educational facilities found in the country.

The cornerstone of Fair Park is its magnificent Music Hall, built in the 1920s for $2.5 million. To its stage come the symphony, opera, ballet, and the Dallas Summer Musicals. Standing tall and aristocratic at the tip of Fair Park's esplanade, the Texas Hall of State mirrors the events of the state's turbulent past. Artifacts and shadow box dioramas tell the

Turkey Chili

2 lbs Plantation Turkey,
diced or ground
1 (8 oz) can tomato sauce
2 (8 oz) cans water
1 pkg Wick Fowler's 2-Alarm or
Family Style Chili Kit
¼ cup warm water

- Brown turkey in a non-stick or lightly oiled skillet over low heat.
- Transfer turkey to a 3 qt saucepan and add tomato sauce and water.
- Add contents of all packages in chili kit except masa. Cover and simmer chili for 30 minutes.
- Dissolve masa with warm water and stir into chili until smooth. Simmer another 15 minutes.
- Serves 6.

Shrimp and Okra Gumbo

2 cups fresh or frozen okra, diced
2 tbsp oil
1 stick Borden's Margarine
4 tbsp flour
½ bell pepper
1 onion
2 stalks celery
3 cloves garlic
3 qts water
1 tbsp Worcestershire sauce
1 tbsp chopped green onion,
optional
sprinkle of file powder,
optional
2 tbsp Muzzy's Magic Cajun
Seafood Seasoning
2 lbs peeled shrimp
2-3 cups cooked Doguet's
Extra Fancy Fine Rice

- Fry okra in 2 tbsp oil for 10 minutes, stirring constantly, as not to burn. Use aluminum dutch oven, do not use black iron pot. Remove okra and set aside.
- Add margarine and flour and make a roux in same pot. Brown until chocolate brown, stirring constantly.
- Chop vegetables and add them to roux.
- Add okra and cook 5 minutes or until wilted.
- Add water and Worcestershire sauce, seafood seasoning and cook 1½ hours.
- Add shrimp and cook 30 minutes or until tender.
- Serve with rice in a soup plate.
- Serves 8.

legendary stories of Coronado's trek across the Llano Estacado in search of the seven cities of gold, of the massacre at the Alamo, and of revenge and the ultimate victory at the Battle of San Jacinto. The museum also traces the state's economy from the wild, long-legged longhorns to that first great oil gusher at Spindletop.

The Health and Science Museum, however, does not reflect the past. Its focus is firmly on the present, helping promote the scientific miracles of tomorrow with graphic displays that introduce studies of nutrition, dental health, and astronomy.

In the Dallas Garden Center, plants have been artfully placed to create the cool, leisurely effect of a tropical forest, with banana trees and palms shading a winding brick walkway. The Dallas Aquarium displays more than 225 species of fish, reptiles, amphibians, and mammals in tanks that resemble the creatures' natural habitat. It is one of the larger inland aquariums in the United States. And for the past five decades, the Dallas Museum of Natural History has been showcasing the heritage of Texas beyond the skyscrapers. It has fifty exhibits of wildlife, all prowling their natural habitats, and the finest collection of mounted state birds that has ever been assembled.

*N*othing has changed.

Across the grounds of Fair Park, each October, sprawl the State Fair of Texas, an extravaganza of sights and sounds that ranks in attendance with the world's great trade fairs in Paris, Milan, and Toronto. It is sometimes chaotic, always polished, highly-sequined and high tech, and every year, more than three million jam their way through its gates to study man's accomplishments in his own land.

It all began back in 1886, when the acreage was still Captain Gaston's hog wallow, and Colonel Frank Holland was clamoring for a state fair to "advertise the opportunities of this section of the nation." Big D businessmen joined forces and scraped together $177,028 for that very first "Dallas State Fair." They did not believe they could lose on the venture. After all,

Sauces

Texas Style Barbeque Sauce

1 cup catsup
4 tbsp Shadowfox Farms
Herbal Vinegar
4 tbsp Worcestershire Sauce
1 tsp prepared mustard
1 cup water
2 tbsp Menchaca™ Brand
BBQ Seasoning
1 tbsp brown sugar
2 tbsp butter or margarine
½ tsp salt
2 tsp Menchaca™ Brand
Dehydrated Chopped Onion
2 tbsp lemon juice
1 tbsp Pek O' Wood
Liquid Smoke
dash of hot pepper sauce

- Combine all ingredients in a saucepan and simmer over low heat for 15 minutes.
- Use as a basting or dipping sauce with chicken, pork, or beef.
- Place meat in refrigerator overnight for maximum flavor enhancement.
- Makes 2 cups sauce.

they had tradition behind them, and they had a brand spanking new ten thousand dollar racetrack. In 1886, it was common knowledge that a big, big fair had to have horse racing in order to succeed. But when the lights finally dimmed on the festivities, the thoroughbreds had won, and the fair had lost— to the unpopular tune of $128,823.

The struggles had begun amidst frustration, and despair. In 1895, however, John Philip Sousa and his band marched into Dallas, and the fair, at last, showed a profit, even though restaurant row went up in flames. In 1900, the Chicago Fire Company came south and produced a major fireworks display in an old baseball park, but some of the seats collapsed. And damage suits ran quickly up to $150,000. Then came 1903 and the greatest disaster of all. The Texas legislature abolished betting on horse races, and oldtimers predicted that the State Fair had gone to the post for the final time. Without horse racing, they wondered, just what else was there? There was, of course, a mermaid, described as having a "lovable-looking upper torso and the lower body of a speckled trout." Buffalo Bill Cody produced a Wild West Show. And crowds fought to see an 80,000-pound whale preserved in embalming fluid.

Fair President C. A. Keating, by 1904, was frantically searching for a substitute for horse racing. He was, to say the least, a desperate man. He brought in the Morris Electric Volcano, a knife-and-battle ax contest, the Texas Mule School, a fireworks display of the Last Days of Pompeii with a cast of 250, and a newfangled sport called football. Trinity University and Dallas Medical College battled to a scoreless tie, and it was the beginning of a frenzied football era upon Captain Gaston's hog wallow on the outskirts of Dallas.

Through the years, the State Fair of Texas has thrown a spotlight on mankind's greatest innovations. It introduced thousands to the new world of motion pictures, even showed them their first automobiles. It featured a remarkable gadget called television, even though about all anyone could see on the screen at the time was wavy lines and test patterns. Some products changed the world. Some didn't, like the multipurpose machine of 1889 that was designed to churn butter, rock a cradle, and keep flies off the table, all at the same time.

Fresh Tomato Sauce

2 tbsp extra virgin olive oil
1 clove Fiesta Fresh Garlic, minced
4 Big State Fresh Tomatoes, peeled and seeded
fresh basil leaves
salt and pepper

- Heat oil in saucepan until hot and add garlic. Saute briefly until golden brown in color.
- Coarsely chop tomatoes and then add to pan and bring to simmer.
- Remove from heat, add coarsely chopped basil leaves and salt and pepper to taste.
- Makes 1-1½ cups.

Oriental Marinade for Chicken, Ribs or Shrimp

1 cup Hill Country Farms Special Gourmet Sauce
6 tbsp soy sauce
6 tbsp Messina Hof Cabernet Sauvignon Wine or Moyer Texas Brut Champagne
3 tsp Worcestershire sauce

- Combine ingredients in glass, pottery or stainless steel container, blend.
- Place item to be marinated in pan, add marinade mixture, cover and let stand at room temperature 1 hour, if longer time is desired or needed, place in refrigerator; turn several times during this period.
- Marinating times vary according to cut or type of meat; overly long marination may kill the original flavor of the meat.
- Remove from marinade mixture, reserve liquid.
- Place meat on grill, baste with remaining liquid during cooking time. Cook to suit taste or until tender.
- Cooking time will vary with items, type of grill and degree of heat used.

The State Fair's facilities, including the World Exhibits Center, New Dimensions Pavilion, Women's Building, Electric Building, International Bazaar, and Agricultural Building, carry a $100 million price tag. But then, when a fair tries to cater to more than ten million Texans scattered across 254 diversified counties, it has to do things in a big way or wind up forgotten, and nobody forgets the State Fair of Texas. There are jams and jellies, art and needlepoint, all competing for blue ribbons. And thousands of 4-H and FFA members bring their prize animals—cattle and pigs, sheep and chickens—to be judged and sold, some for as much as $30,000.

Standing above it all, never out of sight, is Big Tex, fifty-two feet tall, his shoulders thirty-one feet wide, wearing a seventy-five gallon cowboy hat. And it is only proper that Big Tex has become the patron saint of the State Fair of Texas. After all, he symbolizes the Texas legend.

Big Tex has an oil well pipe for a backbone.

*B*ack in the 1930s, Texas was slowly trying to dig its way out of that economic drainage ditch called the Great Depression. Thousands of unemployed were walking the streets of its cities, looking for a job or a handout. Oil was selling for a dime a barrel, and milk for three cents a quart. Though gripped by a financial calamity, when nobody had a nickel to spare, Texas was determined to have its world's fair.

Fort Worth undaunted when Dallas was chosen to host the Centennial. As newspaper publisher Amon Carter snapped, "We'll show Dallas how the cow eats the cabbage." Fort Worth's slogan for those with the Depression blues was: "Go to Dallas for education, but Fort Worth for entertainment."

Carter immediately hired Billy Rose, the highest paid impressario in show business, the producer of Broadway's "Jumbo," paying him a thousand dollars a day for a hundred days to package Fort Worth's own personal extravaganza, with or without the blessing of the state centennial commission.

As Rose walked off the plane, he told the crowd, "You people stick with me and I'll make a big state out of Texas."

A reporter asked, "Will you miss Broadway?"

Out West BBQ Sauce

Figaro Hickory Liquid Smoke
catsup
water

- Mix one part liquid smoke to three parts catsup.
- Add water for taste or thickness and simmer.
- Brush on your favorite meat before grilling outdoors or in oven.

Meat Marinade

2 tbsp Muzzy's Magic Cajun
Seafood Seasoning
1½ cup salad oil
¼ cup Worcestershire sauce
¾ cup soy sauce
1½ tsp Adams Parsley Flakes
½ cup wine vinegar
3 cloves Fiesta Fresh Garlic,
crushed
⅓ cup lemon juice

- Blend all ingredients in blender for 30 seconds.
- Can be used immediately or stored in refrigerator until needed.
- Makes any cut of meat juicy, tender and tasty. For best results, soak meat 2-8 hours.
- Makes about 5 cups.

Creamy Picante Dressing

⅔ cup mayonnaise
⅓ cup Daisy Brand Sour Cream
½ cup Pace® Picante Sauce

- Combine ingredients; mix well. Serve as a dressing for salads.
- Makes 1½ cups.

Variations:
- Substitute ⅓ cup mayonnaise for sour cream.
- Add ½ tsp ground cumin.

Rose only glared at him. "I am Broadway," he snapped.
"How can you compete with Dallas?"

"Easy," Rose predicted. "We'll give 'em a bold ball of fire. We'll have a 'Lonely Hearts Ball' weekly where all the lonesome women can come and find a partner in a drawing. I'll get Shirley Temple, Mae West, Guy Lombardo, Jack Benny. I'll get a thousand beautiful girls for the Frontier Follies. I'll have a Texas pageant to be called 'The Fall of the Frontier' or 'The Battle of San Jacinto' or some other Texas name. I'll have two thousand Indians and one thousand cowboys, and guess who wins? I'll sign up a chorus line of five hundred pretty girls." He grinned, then added, "I plan to drive Dallas nuts."

Fort Worth danced its way out of the Depression upon the grounds that surrounded Casa Manana, described as "the largest cafe-theater in the universe, the most fabulous outdoor arena of entertainment in existence, the house of tomorrow." On its stage, stripper Sally Ann Rand hid her naked body behind fans and balloons, and Fort Worth publically thanked her for bringing "culture and progress to Tarrant County." Slot machines rattled in the honky-tonk atmosphere of Pioneer Palace, and pigs raced on a forty-foot-long bar where beer was served for ten cents a glass. Two million people came, and their nickles and dimes renewed both the spirit and the pocket books of Fort Worth.

*F*ort Worth, since those early-day cattle trails wound through the dust of its streets, has been called Cowtown, that distinctive place in Texas where the West actually begins. It was a maverick city, hard-nosed and rowdy, carved from rawhide and horn. Yet, Fort Worth has emerged as, perhaps, the most cultured cornerstone of Texas.

Now upon the same grounds where Billy Rose recreated the Old West, Fort Worth has proudly built its refined and elegant Acropolis of the Southwest.

In a land of cattle barns, Rembrandts, Picassos, and Remingtons hang on the wall. It is sophistication in faded blue denim. It is worth millions. It has no price tag at all. It is the work of the masters, put together by masters in the art world

Old San Antonio Barbeque Sauce

1 (16 oz) btl Old San Antonio
Jalapeño Catsup
½ cup Worcestershire sauce
¼ cup Aunt Betty's Tarragon
Vinegar
½ cup Gandy's Butter
salt and pepper, to taste

- Heat all ingredients together until hot. Do not boil.
- Serve with steamy hot tortillas, a big bowl of beans, chopped onions and jalapeño peppers.

Quick Tartar Sauce

Dixieland Chow Chow,
Hot or Mild
mayonnaise

- Mix two ingredients together to taste.

Sinful Shallot Sauce

3 fresh shallots, finely diced
¼ cup water
½ cup Aunt Betty's
Texas Sunset Vinegar
1 oz Take Stock
Glace de Viande
¼ cup Sealtest
Whipping Cream
12 tbsp Vandervoort's Butter

- In small saucepan, combine shallots, water, vinegar, glace and cream.
- Cook down over medium heat to about ¼ cup in volume.
- Slowly add butter over LOW heat.
- Serve warm with the pork, beef or chicken.
- Makes 1 cup of a very creamy sauce.

Best Chili Con Queso

1 lb ground beef or turkey
2 (15 oz) cans Old El Paso
Cheese Sauce
1 (16 oz) can Carole's
Picante Sauce
2-3 tbsp Aunt Betty's
Chili Con Queso Mix
Ricos Nacho Chips

- Cook meat until brown.
- Stir in cheese sauce and picante sauce.
- Add con queso mix.
- Cook 10 minutes on medium heat.
- Serve with chips.

Other Serving Suggestions:

- In tacos, over omelettes, with meat and veggies, on baked potatoes, mixed with pasta or simply smeared over Texas-size hamburgers.

Tex-Mex cuisine has long been a Fort Worth tradition.

Cheryl's Favorite Mushroom Sauce

1 tbsp Borden's Butter
1 medium onion, diced
1/3-1/2 red or yellow bell pepper,
thinly sliced
6 Big State Shiitake
Mushrooms, thinly sliced,
stems removed
8 oz Take Stock Demi-Glace or
Glace de Viande

- Lightly saute in butter the onion, bell pepper and mushrooms.
- Add the glace and heat thoroughly.
- Serve with lamb, beef or roasted chicken.
- Makes 1½-2 cups.

Rosemary Sauce

1/2 cup Walnut Creek Vintage
Texas Port or La Buena Vi
Vineyards Springtown
Red Wine
4 oz Take Stock
Glace de Viande
1 small stalk Herbal Gems
Fresh Rosemary
1/2 tsp black pepper
1-2 tbsp butter, optional

- Heat together wine and glace.
- Add rosemary and pepper.
- After 10 minutes, remove rosemary.
- Remove from heat and swirl in butter.
- Serve hot with roast, grilled meats or poultry.
- Makes 1 cup.

who knew and understood the great work and where to find it. Even though many of the paintings had been lost, they could still be found if you knew who to pay in the dead of night in some lonely, out-of-the-way European village.

The Kimball Art Museum, in fact, has, for its size, probably a higher percentage of discovered and rediscovered pieces of art than any other museum in the nation. It is the legacy of Kay Kimball, an oilman, who for decades matched his earnings with his collections of eighteenth century British portraits and late European Rennaissance paintings. When he died, he left behind a hundred million dollars, give or take an oil well or a corporation or two, to build a museum whose rooms now hold 4,500 years of great works that have become the envy of the international art world.

The medieval "Barnabas Altarpiece," the oldest surviving English painting on wood panel, was created about 1250. A Bellini painting, "Madonna and Child," owned by Napoleon III, had disappeared a century earlier. Peter Paul Rubin's portrait of the Duke of Buckingham had been lost for two centuries. Rembrandt's "Portrait of A Young Jew" had been hidden away in a vault for two decades, and is deemed priceless. "The Three Crosses" is considered to be Rembrandt's crowning achievement. Cezanne's "Peasant in A Blue Blouse" was purchased for $3.9 million. The Kimball paid $4 million for Picasso's "Nude Combing Her Hair" and $4.5 million for Georges Braque's "Girl With A Cross." They are all showcased in courtyards so similar to those found in a European Renaissance villa.

The Kimball, the last creation, the personal masterpiece of architect Louis I. Kahn, salutes the old masters. The Amon Carter Museum of Western Art pays tribute to those sturdy men and women who settled a tough and untamed land, symbolized by Cowtown itself. Amon Carter founded the museum with his own personal collection of Charlie Russell and Frederick Remington bronzes and paintings. Many of Russell's works came from a Montana saloon where the artist would trade them for a drink of whiskey simply because he was thirsty and had no money.

Carter, proud of his Texas heritage, said of the Old West,

Daisy Thousand Island Dressing

1 cup Daisy Brand Sour Cream
1 cup mayonnaise
½ cup ketchup
or, ½ cup chili sauce
(for a tangier dressing)
½ tsp juice from Pickleworks
A.D. Sweet Pickles
½ tsp Fiesta Garlic Powder,
optional
1 tsp sweet pickle relish,
optional

- Combine all ingredients and chill.
- Cover tightly and refrigerate for up to 2 weeks.
- Makes 2½ cups dressing.

Brandied Walnut Orange Sauce

1½ cups chopped Sunshine
Country Walnuts
½ cup Hygeia Butter
1 cup Imperial Dark Brown
Sugar, packed
2 tbsp light corn syrup
½ cup Skweezin's Valencia
Orange Juice
1 (29 oz) can cling peach halves,
drained
¼ cup brandy or
¾ tsp brandy flavoring
Hygeia Super Good
Vanilla Ice Cream, optional

- In a small skillet saute walnuts in butter over low heat for 5 minutes, stirring constantly until walnuts are lightly brown. Cool.
- Combine sugar, corn syrup and orange juice in a saucepan and simmer 15 minutes. Add nuts.
- Pour warm sauce over peach halves.
- Heat brandy and pour over peaches and sauce.
- Add a scoop of ice cream, if desired, before pouring sauce over peaches.
- Makes 1½ cups.

"Its pioneer spirit that peopled the wide spaces and laid the foundation for a happy future came down to me in the strain of the blood, and I wish to share it with others who would make Texas their home and inspiration."

The contemporary works at the Fort Worth Art Center must often be seen through abstract eyes. It is challenging place to experience art, not merely view it, to hike through chrome sculpture and surrealistic glass. The paintings are sometimes a bit odd and often misunderstood, but they are never boring. And the works of Picasso, Kline, and Mondrian alone are valued at more than two million dollars.

The William Edrington Scott Memorial Theater is the plush home for ballet, community theater, symphony, opera, the Texas Boys Choir and the Van Cliburn Piano competition. Casa Manana, an aluminum-domed playhouse, the namesake of Billy Rose's "House of Tomorrow," offers musicals and theater-in-the-round. Nearby, the Botanic and Japanese Gardens add beauty and color to a forest thicket. The Zoological Park puts animals on terrain similar to their natural landscape back home, rare and exotic birds in a rain forest. Within the Museum of Science and History are found dinosaurs from a prehistoric age, meteorites from space, guns from the frontier, and a curious array of artifacts from around the world. Its Noble Planetarium, *The Los Angeles Times* said, "gives you an unmatched look at the world and at space. The Space Theater (now the Omni Theater) is the biggest show in town and you must see it because you have never seen the likes of it." The Omni, with its wide, curved screen, surrounds you with sights and sounds and unforgettable sensations, as you soar into the clouds, plunge over a cliff, ride a rocket toward the stars, or sink slowly into the dark depths of a mysterious ocean floor. You don't merely see what is happening around you. You become part of it.

*Y*et Fort Worth will always be linked realistically and romantically to its frontier roots. Originally an outpost on the Trinity River, it gained notoriety, if not prominence, when cowboys rode to town, pushing their herds of longhorn cattle northward to Kansas along the Chisholm Trail.

Salads

Summer Fruit Salad
With Raspberry Dressing

1 cup Cross Timbers Vineyard
Seedless Grapes
1 Texas Orchard Apple,
cored and cubed
1 cup TIE Brand Cantaloupe,
cubed
1 cup TIE Brand Honeydew
Melon, cubed
1 cup Rio Queen Orange
Wedges, peeled
1 cup TIE Brand Watermelon,
seeded and cubed
1 cup Fincastle Fresh
Strawberries, stemmed
and sliced
1 cup Sunshine Country
Walnuts or Pecans, chopped
mint leaves to garnish

Dressing:

½ cup Imperial Light
Brown Sugar
¼ cup Texafrance Raspberry
Vinaigrette (Basil-Lime
Vinaigrette can be substituted)
1 cup Borden's Fruit Yogurt

- In a bowl add brown sugar to the raspberry dressing whisk until sugar is dissolved.
- While whisking add the yogurt to a smooth consistency.
- Pour over the fruits, toss lightly.
- Serve in wine cup as dessert or light summer salad.
- Decorate with mint leaves.
- Serves 4-6.

A Log Cabin Village, rough-hewn reminders of a day when life was simple, yet precarious on the prairie, is hidden away on a small, timbered corner of the Acropolis. The cabins belonged to a farmer, a minute man who held a plow with one hand and a rifle with the other, a legislator. From rustic homes such as these, from aristocratic Thistle Hill, the last of the mansions built by cattle barons, a town was born.

Beyond the contemporary sculpture of its skyline, the stockyard district has been restored with western-styled stores, restaurants, a hotel, the world-famous Billy Bob's nightclub, and the White Elephant Saloon, where Long Hair Jim Courtright, sometimes a peace officer, sometimes an outlaw, and Luke Short squared off eyeball to eyeball in one of the last great gunfights on the streets of Cowtown. It's a legendary kind of place where the sidewalks are still boarded, jukeboxes sing of broken hearts and cheatin' hearts, saddlemakers and bootmakers are craftsmen of a rare breed, and honest-to-god cowboys still hang onto bucking broncs and bulls—earning big money when they do, dodging flying hooves and slashing horns when they don't—in the Cowtown Coliseum's historic indoor rodeo arena.

Fort Worth survived the rugged life. It endured the good life. And it never forgot the words of early-day publisher B. B. Paddock who wrote of his hometown, when the population had barely topped the two thousand mark: "Scores of the best men in the country are coming to and locating in Fort Worth, and are going to work with energy and determination to build up the place and make it what it is inevitably destined to be—the city of Northwest Texas."

*A*cross the wind-swept North Texas prairie lands blew the winds of greatness. In Denison, they touched Dwight David Eisenhower. He was born there. In Bonham, they bent the grass around the crusty, outspoken Sam Rayburn. Mister Speaker called it home.

Eisenhower's birthplace, a gabled, two-story, white frame house, rests down alongside the Katy railroad tracks where his father worked. It is a quiet reflection of the lifestyles of the

Daisy Ambrosia Hawaiian

1 cup crushed pineapple, drained
1²/₃ cups pineapple tidbits (or chunks), well drained
1 cup miniature marshmallows
³/₄ cup shredded Comanche Golden Coconut
1 small jar maraschino cherries, drained
1 cup Daisy Brand Sour Cream
¹/₂ cup Comanche Golden Walnuts or Almonds, optional

- Mix all ingredients together and place in lightly greased mold or in a bowl. Chill overnight.
- Serve as salad, entre accompaniment or dessert.

Variation:

- Mandarin oranges may be substituted in whole or in part for maraschino cherries.
- Serves 6.

Pears Cardinal

6 fresh Pape Pears
2 cups Rosser Wasser Rock Brand Spring Water
1¹/₂ cups sugar
1 tbsp lemon juice
³/₄ tsp salt
1 (8 oz) jar The Pepper Palate Sweet Pepper Relish, red
¹/₂ cup The Pepper Palate Mild Pepper Jelly, red

- Peel pears, leaving stems on.
- Mix water, sugar, lemon juice and salt in a saucepan. Bring to a boil.
- Add whole pears. Simmer, turning pears occasionally in syrup for 20-25 minutes or until tender.
- Cool pears in syrup. Remove pears.
- Combine relish and jelly in top of double boiler. Melt over low heat.
- Remove from heat and chill.
- To serve, place pears upright either individually or together in flat dish. Spoon sauce over pears.
- Serves 6.

1890s, a State Historic Site that holds tightly to the roots of a man who was destined to leave Denison, fight and win a world war as the commander of all Allied Armies, and one day live in another white house as President of the United States.

Sam Rayburn, tough and tenacious, was an imposing figure in the House of Representatives during the administration of eight Presidents—from Woodrow Wilson to Eisenhower. But he always said, "I served with them, not under them." He weilded the gavel longer than any other Speaker of the House in United States History. And, as leader of the House majority, Mr. Sam was often called "the third most powerful man in the world." It was a description he deserved and liked.

Rayburn's home in Bonham was restored and opened to the public as "a monument in honor of a man who never did forget where he came from." It is a simple frame house, set amidst the town's Victorian elegance, with a front portico supported by four Doric posts, looking much as it did when Mr. Sam was at home. The house showcases almost three thousand reminders of Rayburn's colorful career, and only a few miles away, the Sam Rayburn Library contains every word that the Speaker uttered officially during two decades on the floor of the house, as well as his official correspondence and papers.

The cities of North Texas form a curious blending of the refined and the rough-hewn. It is gingerbread lace, hanging on the eaves, the cupolas of fine Victorian homes. It bears the scars of axes hammered against the historic logs of tiny prairie cabins. Ranchers said they didn't particularly want to own all the land in the world, just the land that joined them. Indian wars stained the soil with blood. Wildcatters stained it with oil. And giant sauropods, sixty feet long and weighing thirty tons, left their footprints deeply embedded in Paluxy River rock at Glen Rose's Dinosaur Valley State Park, tracks that not even time has been able to erase.

Wichita Falls, for years, was known as the capital of the independent oil operators, its refineries taking care of the black gold that flowed from the fields of Burkburnett and Ranger. It was boom time, when North Texas was suddenly choking on money instead of dust, when towns were irrigating their crops, whether they wanted to or not, with oil, not water. Oil was more

Summer Fruit Salad

2 cups cooked Island Girl
Brand Rice, cooled to room
temperature
½ cup **each** quartered
strawberries, grape halves,
quartered kiwifruit slices,
pineapple tidbits, and banana
slices
¼ cup pineapple juice
2 tbsp Gandy's Quality Chekd
Plain Yogurt
1 tbsp Fancy Brand Honey
lettuce leaves

- Combine rice and fruits in large bowl.
- Blend pineapple juice, yogurt and honey in small bowl; pour over rice mixture. Toss lightly.
- Serve on lettuce leaves.
- Serves 4.

Carrot and Raisin Salad

3 medium to large Big State
Fancy Carrots
¼ small onion
½"-1" fresh ginger root
⅓ cup Comanche Golden Raisins
2 tbsp Borden's Fresh
Orange Juice
2 tbsp brandy
1 tbsp raspberry vinegar,
optional
8 oz Gourmet Garnishes Poppy
Seed Dressing

- Shred carrots, onion and ginger root in food processor.
- Heat raisins, orange juice and brandy in microwave on HIGH (or on the stove in a non-aluminum pan).
- Add plumped raisins, with liquid, to carrot mixture (plus raspberry vinegar if desired).
- Add poppy seed dressing.
- Chill at least 1 hour before serving. Keeps 2 weeks in refrigerator.
- Serves 8.

plentiful. Overnight it turned poverty-stricken farmers into millionaires. A granite monument marks the famed McClesky Well that ushered the good times into Ranger, pumping 1,700 barrels of oil a day, and artifacts of the wild and wicked boom are on display in the Roaring Ranger Museum.

The face of Corsicana, too, was splattered by a gusher's oil that fell like rain from the sky. It was all an accident. The city had been drilling an artisian well back in the 1890s, but grew rich instead. Corsicana's frontier years, even before they were smudged with oil, are portrayed in Pioneer Village, a rare collection of log homes, a trading post, slave's cabin, mule-drawn corn mill, blacksmith shop, and general store, with its barrels that once held corn liquor, almost as lucrative and tempting as the oil the boiled beneath the earth.

For those pioneers who staked their dreams in the black land dirt of North Texas, life was promising, but troubled. Fort Parker was a lone sentinel, standing guard beside the Navasota River, and it was to the outpost that warriors came on a spring day in 1836, riding beneath a soiled white flag of truce that became a lie. Five men died in a brief, violent skirmish before the war party galloped madly away, carrying nine-year-old Cynthia Ann Parker, whose fateful odyssey among the Comanche Indians lasted twenty-four years before she was finally rescued by Texas Rangers. It was too late. Her blood may have been Anglo, but the sad, angry tears she shed were for her Comanche home. Within a few tormented years, Cynthia Ann Parker was dead of a broken heart. The reconstructed blockhouses of old Fort Parker, wedged between the towns of Mexia and Groesbeck, are a State Historic Site, appearing as they did on that day when a girl's life was forever ruined, but her name never forgotten, on the North Texas prairie.

The post hospital and wooden barracks of Jacksboro's Fort Richardson are grim relics of an era when stubborn settlers kept pushing their way westward into a hostile land. General Randolph Marcy had ridden the rolling hills and written in his journal: "This rich and beautiful section of country does not contain to-day as many white people as it did when I was stationed here eighteen years ago, and if the Indian marauders are not punished, the whole country seems to be a fair way of

Peachy Surprise Salad

¾ cup Borden's Butter, melted
2¼ cups crushed pretzels
1¾ cups sugar
2 (8 oz) pkgs cream cheese,
softened
1 large (16 oz) ctn whipped
topping
3 cups sliced Brazos Valley
Orchards Peaches
1 (15½ oz) can pineapple chunks
1 (6 oz) pkg peach gelatin
Texas Pride Pecans, to garnish

- Combine butter, pretzels and ¼ cup sugar in 13"x9" pan, mixing and spreading over bottom of pan.
- Blend cream cheese, whipped toppings and 1½ cups sugar in a bowl. Spread over pretzel layer.
- Drain juices from peaches and pineapples, reserving juices.
- Combine juices with enough water to measure 2 cups and heat to boiling.
- Dissolve gelatin in hot juice mixture.
- Stir in 2 cups ice, chill until thickened.
- Fold in fruit. Spread over cream cheese mixture.
- Garnish with pecans.
- Serves 6-8.

Purple Lady Salad

2 (6 oz) pkgs raspberry gelatin
1 cup hot Artesia Sparkling
Natural Mineral Water
1 (15 oz) can sweetened
blueberries
1 (8 oz) can crushed pineapple
1 (8 oz) ctn whipped topping
½ cup San Saba Pecan Pieces

- Dissolve raspberry gelatin in hot water.
- Add sweetened blueberries and crushed pineapple. Do not drain fruits.
- When about half congealed, fold in whipped topping and pecan pieces.
- Chill until firm.
- Serves 8-10.

becoming depopulated." Three chieftains, Satank, Big Tree, and Satanta, would pay for their crimes, standing trial at Fort Richardson. Satank never made it to the remote outpost. In chains, he grabbed a carbine, tried to escape, and was shot down. Big Tree and Satanta—described by prosecutors as "vile creatures" and "tiger-demons" who have "murdered and scalped our people and carried off our women into captivity worse than death"—were sentenced to be hanged. They were later paroled, however, and Satanta recaptured when the Indians rebelled again. He leaped from a prison window to his death. Big Tree had vanished, swallowed up by the prairies.

The trials and tribulations that taunted North Texas left Granbury with its greatest legacy. At the turn of the century, there were seven saloons on the square around the Hood County Courthouse. Sin could be found on the street corners every night, and songs could be heard coming from within the opera house. But, alas, in time, the songs went elsewhere. The stage darkened. The opera house crumbled in ruins. It was a sad, neglected derelict by the time, JoAnn Miller, who had owned the famed Cooperstown Playhouse in New York, and the hard-working people of Granbury finally got around to rescuing and restoring the building. The stage is no longer bare, as JoAnn Miller, a songbird herself, produces theater and musicals within its historic walls. The Opera House has become an architectural and an artistic success, a mirror of the good life that was and is again in Granbury.

In Waxahachie, every building on the downtown square is listed on the National Register of Historic places. Cotton was king upon its black dirt, and wealthy planters invested their riches in the Victorian splendor of gingerbread homes. Lancaster's turn-of-the-century square has been revitalized, capturing the spirit of the days when Sheriff Pat Garrett described it as "a wild and woolly place where everyone wore a gun, unless he had two." Ennis dances to the polka of its old-fashioned Czech traditions, and its tables are filled with kolaches, strudel, and koblase sausage. And the stately Victorian heritage of Hillsboro surrounds the controversial appearance of its courthouse. The building has been labeled "a monstrosity" by some, "an outstanding cathedral" by others. It

Zesty Southwest Cole Slaw

1 small red cabbage, shredded
(about 2 lbs)
1 small white cabbage,
shredded (about 2 lbs)
2 cups red bell pepper, diced
2 cups red onion, diced
1 cup poblano pepper, seeded
and diced
4 tbsp Texafrance Serrano
Pepper Jelly
½ cup white wine vinegar

Dressing:

½ cup Daisy Brand Sour Cream
½ cup mayonnaise
6 oz Texafrance Roasted
Poblano Pepper Pesto
1 tsp salt and white pepper

- Combine cabbages, bell pepper, onion and poblano pepper in large bowl.
- In a separate bowl, mix the serrano pepper jelly and the white wine vinegar until the jelly is dissolved.
- Add the dressing ingredients to the vinegar mixture, mix well.
- Pour over the cole slaw, toss and let stand for at least 2 hours before serving.
- Serves 12.

Baldy's Cole Slaw

1 head cabbage, shredded
1 lb carrots, grated
1 small onion, diced
2 tbsp tarragon vinegar
1 tbsp salad oil
1 tbsp sweetener or ¼ cup sugar
to sweeten to taste
4 tbsp Baldy's™ All-Purpose
seasoning
3-4 heaping tbsp mayonnaise

- Place all ingredients in large bowl and mix well.
- Cover and refrigerate for at least 1 hour before serving.
- Serves 6-8.

has never been ignored.

Waxahachie, Ennis, and Midlothian have all become cornerstones of the revolutionary Super Conducting Super Collider, which will one day be smashing atoms beneath the Texas soil. Buck Jordan, vice president of the Waxahachie Chamber of Commerce, points out, "The rolling prairie around us once formed a frontier that beckoned for settlers with their hopes and dreams to enter into a vast, unknown land. Now it is a new frontier, where research and science will be unlocking secrets to the great unknowns for generations to come. We still have our hopes, our dreams, and our faith that Texas will somehow be able to make them all a reality."

A wandering band of Wacos devoutly believed that the Great Spirit, in its infinite wisdom, had brought them to the banks of the Brazos. And they were convinced that the tribe would live in happiness as long as they continued to drink from the springs at the river's edge.

The springs remain. The Brazos never changes.

Happiness is what Waco is all about.

There was a day when the burgeoning village of Waco was known as Six Shooter Junction. But time tamed it, and the years have polished the rough edges off a city that became the gateway for American expansion across the western plains.

The Armstrong Browning Library, on the Baylor University campus, contains one of the world's foremost collections of the delicate poetry of Robert and Elizabeth Barrett Browning. Theirs were sonnets of love.

Baylor's Strecker Museum offers a vivid portrait of the natural history and early settlement of Texas. Not long ago, a team from the museum excavated the remains of a lumbering herd of fifteen Columbian mammoths who died clustered together on a brushy river bottom some 28,000 years ago. It is the largest known mammoth herd ever to die in a single incident. The reason remains a mystery.

An old suspension bridge became the nation's largest—475 feet long—when it was built across the impetuous Brazos in 1870. It was engineered by the same company that would later

Cornbread Salad

1 pan Ro*Tel Cornbread, cooked
1 pint mayonnaise
2 stalks celery, chopped
1 large bell pepper, chopped
1 (2 oz) can diced pimentos
1 cup chopped green onions
and tops
½ cup Texas Pride Pecans,
chopped
1 large tomato, diced

- Crumble cornbread in bowl.
- Mix all ingredients and stir.
- Place in refrigerator to chill.
- Serves 6-8.

Guacamole Salad

shredded lettuce
4 Old El Paso® Tostaco Shells
2 ripe avocados, peeled, pitted
and mashed
½ cup Old El Paso®
Thick 'n Chunky Salsa
2 tbsp finely chopped onion
2 tbsp lemon juice
½ tsp salt
¼ tsp garlic powder

- Preheat oven to 350 degrees.
- Heat shells 5-7 minutes.
- Line cooled shells with shredded lettuce.
- Combine remaining ingredients and spoon approximately ½ cup of guacamole into each shell.
- Garnish with additional shredded lettuce.
- Break off portions of shell to use for dipping.
- Serves 4.

The elegance of Waxahachie's past is portrayed in its historic courthouse and its lifestyle.

Simple Salad Vinaigrette

1 oz Take Stock Glace de Viande
½ tsp Dijon mustard
3 tbsp vinegar
½ tsp Herbs de Provence
(or thyme)
⅓-½ cup extra virgin olive oil

- Melt the glace de viande.

- With a small whisk, stir together the mustard, vinegar, herbs and glace de viande.

- Blend well and slowly add, whisking, the olive oil.

- Dressing will thicken as oil is blended.

- Serve over greens or vegetables.

- Keeps 10 days in the refrigerator.

- Makes approximately 1 cup.

Asparagus Vinaigrette

1 lb asparagus, washed, steamed and chilled
1 cup Texafrance Basil-Lime Vinaigrette
2 hard boiled eggs, chopped

- Steam the asparagus 10-15 minutes or until tender but do not overcook or they will become limp after marinating.

- Cool for 30 minutes and place them in serving dish.

- Cover with the vinaigrette and seal with plastic wrap.

- Leave in the refrigerator until ready to serve, 2-24 hours.

- Decorate with chopped hard boiled eggs.

- Serves 4.

Normandy Salad

1 head red leaf lettuce, washed and dried
4 Adams Red Delicious Apples, cored and sliced
1 cup Gruyere cheese, grated, or your favorite hard cheese
1 medium onion, thinly sliced
1 cup Texafrance Raspberry Dressing

- Tear lettuce into pieces and place in a large bowl.

- Add the other ingredients and toss with the dressing.

- Serves 6-8.

use it as a pattern to errect the Brooklyn Bridge in New York. The suspension bridge, in time, funneled thousands who drove their wagons determinedly toward the setting sun. It was the place, the one crossing, where the Old South met the New West. With them came prosperity. Riverfront cotton plantations rose regally above the Brazos, grand homes that are typified by East Terrace, a museum house that mirrors the proud and noble face of Waco's antiquity.

It was in 1837 when a band of Rangers established a fort upon the land that would become Waco. One later wrote that the countryside "was in possession of buffalo and only a short time before had been vacated by the Waco Indians; cornstalks were found in the fields...and peach trees were growing where the city now stands...We went back, calling the place we had left Fort Fisher."

Fort Fisher has been reconstructed as the Texas Ranger Hall of Fame and Museum, a stirring tribute to breed of lawmen whose motto was best spoken by William McDonald: "No man in the wrong can stand up against a fellow that's right and keeps on a-comin'." A Ranger had to be able to ride a fast trail, sleep wherever night caught up with him, live off the land, and strike suddenly and swiftly. Men feared him and hated him and prayed for him. But they all learned to respect him. As one outlaw said, "It is easy to see a graveyard in the muzzle of a Ranger's gun."

The Ranger was described as a "quiet, deliberate, gentle person who could gaze calmly into the cold eyes of a murderer, divine his thoughts, and anticipate his action, a man who could ride straight up to death." Their deeds became the stuff of legend, the kind of lawmen who quickly answered the orders of S. P. Elkins in 1870: "There's a fight going on. Everybody get there that can."

*W*aco owes its existence, its life to the Brazos River, and to the Rangers who brought peace to the surrounding hillsides, now thick with the bluebonnets and Indian paint brush. The solitude of Lakes Whitney, Ray Hubbard, Eagle Mountain, Lewisville, Grapevine, Arlington, Lavon, and Texoma is

Antipasto Salad with Wild Mushroom Pesto

8-10 artichoke heart halves
8-10 sundried tomatoes, sliced
8-10 Italian sweet peppers
1 cup black olive halves
½ lb small to medium Kitchen
Pride Fresh Mushrooms, whole
½ lb Mozzarella Company
Fresh Mozzarella Cheese, cubed
1 medium red onion, thinly sliced
fresh grated Parmesan cheese
crusty French bread

Dressing:
1 cup Texafrance Classic
French Vinaigrette
4 oz Texafrance Wild
Mushroom Pesto
1 tbsp Texafrance Roasted
Garlic Essence

- In a large bowl whisk the ingredients for the dressing.
- Add all the other ingredients.
- Toss and allow to marinate for 2 hours.
- Serve on a large platter.
- Sprinkle with fresh grated Parmesan cheese. Serve with crusty French bread.
- Serves 6-8.

Mozzarella and Tomato Salad

½ lb Mozzarella Company
Fresh Dallas Mozzarella
1 ripe tomato
lettuce leaves
salt and
freshly ground black pepper
extra virgin olive oil
Patty's Herbs Fresh Basil
Leaves, torn or cut
into small pieces

- Slice tomatoes and mozzarella into uniform slices, approximately ¼" thick.
- Arrange slices alternately on platter or salad plates atop lettuce leaves.
- Sprinkle with salt and pepper to taste.
- Drizzle with olive oil and sprinkle with fresh basil.
- Serves 2.

interrupted only by the feverish roar of high-powered boats in search of the elusive bass. Dallas is wrapped up in furs and diamonds, Fort Worth in rich denim and exotic-skin boots. Indian war trails have vanished beneath super highways and the dust has settled where Presidents walked. John Wayne is in wax, a white rhino prowls the prairie, a roller coaster takes somebody's breath away, a scream amidst the laughter. And all is well within the land of high cotton and gingerbread lace.

WEST TEXAS

"Nowhere have I found such a wildly weird country. The very silence is oppressive. A man grows watchful for his own safety and becomes awestruck by nature in her lofty moods. Emotions are stirred by the grandeur and beauty of the scenery and the ever-changing play of light and shadow. An old Mexican, who could neither read nor write, stood beside me. I pointed to the Chisos. His countenance lighted up. He exclaimed, 'Bonito.' It was an eloquent tribute."

——U. S. Treasury Agent William Ferguson, who rode across the desert to Boquillas in 1895.

*H*e was sitting in the shady corner of a little country store on the outskirts of Marfa, wiping the sweat from the wrinkles in a face that had weathered too many summer winds. With a wry grin, he solved one of the great mysteries of life.

"Do you know why cowboys always wear the brims of their hats turned up on the side?" he asked.

"No, sir, I don't," I answered.

"It's so they can sit three abreast in a pickup truck." It made sense to me, and he was a cowboy. He ought to know.

West Texas wears cowboy hats, shuffles through a rugged, independent land with scarred boots, and drives pickup trucks as hard as it once rode horses. It breeds mavericks but seldom ties them down for very long. Channing and Dalhart grew up on ground trampled by cattle: rangy, wild, longhorned cattle that grazed the famous 3.5 million-acre XIT Ranch. The sometimes barren, sometimes mountainous landscape bore such brands as the Pitchfork, the Four Sixes, the LS, the JA, and the Matador in an era when all that it took to become a cattleman was a hot running iron and the nerve to use it.

Burkburnett and Ranger, Midland and Odessa were bathed in oil, birthed when the sky was black with gushers of crude, and wildcatters found fortunes on land nobody wanted.

*T*he Texas drought of 1918 had crept into Burkburnett, had caught Old Man Fowler when he was looking the other way. Early one morning he walked out of his house and began packing his wagon. All he wanted to do was get out of town and never look back. "But we can't leave," his wife told him.

"Why not?"

"There might be oil underneath us."

Old Man Fowler laughed. His wife had been listening to too much gossip about all of those gushers over at Ranger, and it had darn near ruined her. Why Ranger was irrigating crops with oil instead of water, or so the rumors went. Farmers in debt for breakfast were millionaires by dinner time. And some drillers even had the audacity to begin digging deep within the sanctified soil of the cemetery. Oil was everywhere.

Old Man Fowler's wife wanted some of it. But all Old Man Fowler could dream about were the cotton fields of Louisiana, where the land was rich and moist, not baked by the sun.

The Fowlers finally reached a compromise. She would go with him to Louisiana, but only if he would drill at least one test well before she bid farewell to Texas.

Old Man Fowler talked a few of his friends into putting up $12,000 to drill a well. He was, indeed, a fortunate man to have friends who had caught the fever and were suffering as badly as his wife. The old man ambled out across the farm land and chose the spot where he would dig the test well. One patch of farm land was as good as another when they were all dry anyway. All he wanted to do was turn the dirt until his money ran out, then hit the road for Louisiana.

On the night of July 26, Old Man Fowler was suddenly awakened by a man whose face was wet and stained the color of oil. "Sir," the driller said, "I hate to wake you, but your well's come in, and we don't know quite what to do. We've already got twelve hundred barrels of storage filled, and now she's runnin' down the cotton rows." Old Man Fowler lay back in his bed and

Marinated Vegetables

1 can baby corn
½ can black olives
1 can artichoke hearts or bottoms
1 can garbanzo beans
1 large onion, sliced
1-2 cloves Fiesta Fresh Garlic, minced
1-2 fresh jalapeños, sliced, optional
1 btl Gourmet Garnishes Original Herb Vinaigrette

- Open first 4 ingredients, drain and rinse 3 times to remove excess salt.
- Combine corn, olives, artichokes and beans in a large bowl, or glass or plastic jar.
- Add onion and garlic. If desired, add fresh sliced jalapeños.
- Cover with herb vinaigrette and let marinate 2-3 days in refrigerator.
- Eat this as is or fix a regular green salad and add the desired amount of marinade to spice up your salad.
- Keeps for at least a month in the refrigerator.
- Serves 20.

Chili Salad

1 pkg Wick Fowler's 2-Alarm Chili Kit, prepared as directed
shredded lettuce
2 tomatoes, chopped
1 onion, chopped
½ cup sliced ripe olives
1 avocado, sliced, optional
1 cup Cheddar cheese, grated
Texas Fresh Tortilla Chips

- Cook chili according to instructions on pkg. (Or heat up leftover chili.)
- On individual plates, place lettuce; spoon hot chili on lettuce.
- Top with tomatoes, onion, olives, avocado and cheese, in that order.
- Serve with tortilla chips.
- Serves 6-8.

tried hard to dream of Louisiana, but, for the life of him, he could not remember where it was or how to get there.

*T*he triumphs, the tragedies, the gambles won and lost in the oil patches of West Texas are graphically displayed at Midland's Permian Basin Petroleum Museum. It is an industry that has been called, with reason, the lifeblood of Texas. Larger-than-life photographs recall the boom years. The world's largest collection of antique drilling rigs, dating back to 1910, are grim reminders of the hard work, the grit, the determination that it took to coax oil out of the ground. Amidst startling displays, you stand side by side with the "shooter," whose job was to free the oil trapped in rock by blasting it out with nitroglycerine. The ground begins to tremble beneath your feet. A 1930 rig shudders. And you can almost feel the fire, the heat as a dreaded "blowout" erupts around you. In Boom Town, you walk the streets of a recreated slice of life from the roaring twenties, visiting a general store, saloon, barbershop, and oil field supply store, just as the wildcatters did when they were risking their lives and their last fistful of dollars on the promise of oil.

A granite monument marks Ranger's McClesky Number 1, the gusher that forever changed the face and pocket book of West Texas, touching off a high-dollar boom with a violent well that poured out 1,700 barrels of oil a day. And the Roaring Ranger Museum houses artifacts from those frenzied years of economic sin and salvation in an old railroad depot.

*W*est Texas, some have said, is God's Country, where the horizon, streaked with pastel threads of purple and pink at sunset, is part of the scenery, where you can drive for miles and miles and see nothing but miles and miles. It is a vast, wide-open country, anchored with ninety mountains that climb more than a mile high, that has just about everything mankind could ever need, with the possible exception of shade.

Lying buried beneath the prairie of Odessa is one of the world's largest meteorites, which came plunging to earth in a ball of fire some twenty thousand years ago. Nature trails now

Salad with Goat Cheese
Apples and Toasted Pecans

½ cup Pape Pecan House
Pecans, coarsely chopped
1 green apple, peeled
1 tsp lemon juice
½ head Romaine lettuce
½ head red leaf lettuce
4 oz Mozzarella Company
Dallas Goat Cheese, crumbled

Dressing:

⅓ cup extra virgin olive oil
1 tbsp balsamic vinegar
1 tsp lemon juice
½ tsp salt
freshly ground pepper

- Whisk together all ingredients to make dressing.
- Toast pecans, slice apples and toss with lemon juice.
- Tear lettuces into pieces.
- Place all ingredients in salad bowl and toss gently with dressing.
- Serves 4.

slip through the crater where impact shattered the limestone bedrock and left explosion pits as large as five hundred feet in diameter. Some even believe that the fierce, blinding light that flashed with the meteor shower across the sky gave birth to the old Indian legend of the coming of the Thunderbird.

Fritch is gateway to Lake Meredith and the Alibates National Monument, where ancient man mined multicolored flint for the tools that tilled his land and the weapons that killed to hold it. And high atop the Hueco Tanks, just outside of El Paso, Indians collected precious and infrequent rain water in a land that seldom quenched their thirst. The natural rock basins are now a state park, painted with tribal pictographs, carved with messages left by the forty-niners, whose eyes were glistening with the lure of gold in California.

The sunswept Llano Estacado, the staked plains, stretches aimlessly from Lubbock to Amarillo and beyond. The timbered Guadalupe Mountains climb to the tallest point in Texas. The Rocky Mountains make their last stand atop the deserts of El Paso. The Davis Mountains wear their rocks like a crown of royalty. The Big Bend hides away in the midst of isolation, down where the Rio Grand cuts the United States away from Mexico, possessing a rare beauty, a haunting reverence for the handiwork of nature that slowly works its way into your skin like a mesquite thorn. The tough came. The tougher stayed and tied the western cornerstone of Texas together with adobe, cowhide, and barbed wire.

*T*he gathering began along about sundown as the shadows crept across the shinnery and reached for the night. They didn't have to reach far. The men rode slowly into Stamford, as rugged as the hills that stretched out behind them, as stubborn as the mesquite that sought water upon a land that had none to give. The men's faces had been shaped by sun and wind. Their character had been molded by working the hind end of a cow at branding time. They had been stomped in stampedes, blinded by blizzards, choked by unforgiving sand storms, and aged by drinking too much stagnant water from too many alkali creek beds. And, God, how they missed it.

Blackeyes and Rice Salad

1/2 cup mayonnaise
2 tbsp lemon juice
1 tsp Menchaca™ Brand Italian
Seasoning
1/2 tsp dillweed
salt and pepper, to taste
1 (16 oz) can sliced carrots,
drained
1 (15 oz) can East Texas Fair
Fresh Shelled Blackeyed Peas,
drained
2 cups cooked Comet Long
Grain Rice
1 stalk celery, sliced
1 green onion, chopped

- Combine mayonnaise, lemon juice, Italian seasoning, dillweed, salt and pepper. Stir to blend.
- Place carrots, blackeyed peas, rice, celery and onion in serving dish. Spoon dressing over and stir gently to coat.
- Cover and refrigerate until chilled.
- Serves 4.

Rice Salad Olé

1 cup cooked Fiesta Brand Rice
(cooked in chicken broth),
cooled
1/2 cup chopped fresh tomatoes
2 jalapeño peppers, minced
2 tbsp red wine vinegar
1 tbsp vegetable oil
1 tsp snipped fresh cilantro
or parsley
1 clove garlic, minced
1/2 tsp Rosehill Culinary Herbs
Fresh Basil
1/4 tsp Rosehill Culinary Herbs
Fresh Crushed Thyme

- Combine rice, tomatoes and peppers in medium bowl.
- Whisk remaining ingredients in small bowl; pour over rice mixture.
- Chill 2-3 hours so flavors will blend.
- Stir before serving.
- Serves 2.

The men had journeyed to Stamford, as they do every year, to hold and old-time cowboy reunion and roundup rodeo on July 4, to remember those seasons past when they rode straighter and taller, perhaps, but never prouder.

J. C. is stooped, and his face is cracked leather now, red against the gray of his brush eyebrows. "It was a rare breed, the cowboy was," he told me. "I've been so cold I couldn't stretch my hands out, so hot my lips turned inner-side outwards. I've had to use cigarette paper over my lips to keep the sun and the wind and the dirt off. You know why God put whiskers on a man's face? It was to protect him. Man just styled it and called it a mustache." J. C. grinned and limped away, the sign of an old bronc rider with age nagging at his heels.

J. C. and the old-time cowboys are the last of a breed, the final witnesses to an untamed West that was finally civilized because of them or in spite of them. Nobody really knows for sure.

The roots of the Old West are still planted deep in Trans Pecos soil, and, like the gnarled mesquite tree, they are too stubborn to wither or die. West Texas refuses to forget the era when cowboys pointed their herds toward the north star and drove more than five million cattle to the Kansas railroads. As one trail boss said, "We placed our faith in God, a pistol, and the chuck wagon, and trailed our cattle to market."

A vivid architectural portrait of the high plains, when those rangy longhorns were wild and cowboys wilder, has been staked to the flatlands on the campus of Texas Tech University in Lubbock. The dirt trail that meanders beneath the windmills of the Ranching Heritage Center faithfully weaves together a hundred years of the good life and the hard life that endured upon the crest of the Cap Rock. It is a tribute to the wealthy cattle baron who lived in the Victorian splendor of the Barton House, to the lonely, sun-toughened cowboy who rode across an endless prairie, earned thirty dollars a month and all the beans he could eat, and found winter shelter in a line camp, keeping cattle fed when blizzards stormed across the plains and shooting flies off the ceiling at night for entertainment. Pioneers

Caviar and Chicken Ring

1½ tbsp plain gelatin
2 cups cold chicken broth
1 cup B.B. Berzette's Lone Star
Caviar, drained
1 cup cooked diced chicken
salt and pepper to taste
1 (8 oz) ctn Borden's Cottage
Cheese
black olives to garnish
mayonnaise to top

- Soften gelatin in ¼ cup of chicken broth.
- Heat remaining broth to boiling and add to softened gelatin.
- When cooled, stir in caviar, chicken, salt and pepper.
- Pour into non-stick ring mold.
- Chill until firm, unmold and place on bed of leaf lettuce.
- Fill center of ring with cottage cheese and black olives.
- Top with mayonnaise.
- Serves 4-6.

Turkey Waldorf Salad

1 cup cooked Island Girl Brand
Rice, cooked in chicken broth,
cooled
1 cup Sunday House Turkey
Breast, cut into strips
¾ cup diced, unpeeled apple
½ cup sliced celery
2 tbsp slivered almonds, toasted
3 tbsp Briannas Poppy Seed
Dressing
lettuce leaves

- Combine all ingredients except lettuce in medium bowl.
- Serve on lettuce leaves.
- Serves 2.

built the El Capote cabin out of pecan and elm logs. A half dugout, from the Matador Ranch, was an outpost for cowboys who formed a living fence around their employer's sacred land, keeping cattle safe from wolves, rustlers, and freedom. The George Jowell House was fashioned by a rancher, who came home after a trail drive to discover that Comanches had burned his home. Defiantly, he rolled his big sleeves up, quarried limestone from a nearby creekbed, and built a fort, one that had gun ports for protection, one that could not be consumed by fire. Las Escarbadas—"the scrapings," named for a scar in the earth where Indians had dug for water—served as headquarters for one of seven divisions on the XIT, a ranch that surrounded itself with six thousand miles of barbed wire. The barn came from the 6666 Ranch. The line cabin stood guard over the Long S whiteface camp. The office is a relic of the Matador, 400,000 acres owned by a syndicate from Scotland. The meat and milk cooler survived the JA Ranch. And the school house, the blacksmith shop, the depot all reflect the stark simplicity of life on the high plains in the 1880s.

The poignant legacy of the Llano Estacado can be found in the Panhandle-Plains Historical Museum on the campus of West Texas State University in Canyon. More than 1.5 million art objects, artifacts, and documents chronicle the nomadic Plains Indian, as well as early-day ranching. The life-size diorama of a campsite is complete with a chuckwagon, loaded down with coffee, spices, and flour needed by the cowboy cook, who ruled over those long trail drives north. It was said, "Only a fool ever argues with a woman, a mule, or a cook." If a cowboy did, he would wind up with gravel in his beans and too much alkali water in his coffee. One cowhand bit into a sourdough biscuit after a tiring day in the saddle and scowled, "Such stinkers! Burnt on the bottom, soggy in the middle, and salty as hell." He suddenly looked up into the frowning face of the cook, smiled, and added, "But that's jes' the way I like 'em."

A reconstructed Panhandle town at the museum provides a turn-of-the-century glimpse at a print shop, bank, general store, barbershop, law office, and millinery, where a dress, trimmed in lace, hangs on the dressmaker's dummy, and plumed hats line the display cases. Inside an old four-room

Hot Pasta Primavera Salad

½ cup no-salt broth
1-2 cloves garlic, minced
½ medium onion, chopped
½ cup frozen Italian cut
green beans
½ cup frozen crinkle-cut carrots
½ cup frozen English peas
½ red bell pepper cut into strips
(or 1 small jar pimentos with juice)
¼ cup Monterey First Harvest
Fresh Mushrooms, sliced
1 small zucchini, sliced in circles
1 cup fresh broccoli flowerettes
8 oz tri-colored rotini, cooked as
directed
¼ cup celery, diced
12 oz Gourmet Garnishes
Italian "Ciao" Dressing
tomato wedges to garnish

- In a large, non-stick fry pan, add broth, garlic, onion, green beans and carrots. Cook 3 minutes.
- Add peas, bell pepper or pimento, mushrooms, zucchini and broccoli.
- Cover and cook 3 minutes.
- Add the vegetable mix to the hot pasta, plus the celery and dressing.
- Decorate with tomato wedges.
- Serves 6.

Lite Wurst Salad

½ lb julienne strips of Hans
Mueller Schinkenwurst,
Jagdwurst and Headcheese
½ bell pepper, diced
½ onion, diced
1 Texas Krispy Dill Pickle,
diced
¼ cup vinegar diluted
with water
1 tsp sugar
1 tbsp oil

- Mix all ingredients together and marinate at least 4 hours. Best when marinated over night.
- Serves 4.

house are a potbellied stove, churn, wire rug beaters, and a tattered teddy bear that lies on a child's trundle bed, waiting for a child who will never hold it again.

The legendary Judge Roy Bean, from his weathered Jersey Lilly saloon, billiard hall, and courtrooms in Langtry, handed down a peculiar brand of justice that became the "Law West of the Pecos." More than once, he fined a horse thief of every cent and valuable he owned, including his gun, then expelled him from town, promising to hang the man if he ever appeared again. The rustic Jersey Lilly Saloon still stands, the last testament of a gambler, a con man, a boozer, a justice of the peace who held court with a six-gun and a copy of the 1879 Revised Statutes of Texas, which he seldom ever consulted.

North of Amarillo, the violent past of Old Tascosa lies unwritten on the tombstones of Boot Hill, twenty-seven graves guard the last memories of a booming Texas trail town that has crumbeld and vanished from the prairies of the Panhandle. All that's left is the courthouse of Judge Scotty Wilson, who once told an outlaw who threatened to take his case to a higher court: "Shut up and sit down. There is no higher court." The old stone building is now the Julian Bivins Museum, containing relics and remnants of the town's forgotten glory days.

Clay Allison, known as "the gentleman gunfighter," spent his last days in Pecos. He lies buried behind the old Orient Hotel, and the epitaph on his tombstone says somberly, "He never killed a man that did not need killing." The Orient was once described as "the finest hotel between Fort Worth and El Paso," and it has been preserved as the West of the Pecos Museum. More than thirty rooms are furnished to portray such historical vignettes as a doctor's office, a bunkhouse, and an early-day school room, back when settlers went out of their way to choose the ugliest teachers they could find. The pretty ones all married within a year and were gone. One corner of the Orient is even dedicated to the Pecos Rodeo, which began in 1883 and claims to be the oldest in the country.

The trappings of the Old West have not faded entirely from the landscape. The Prude Ranch reaches across 8,500 acres of Limpia Canyon, deep within the Davis Mountains, near Fort Davis. It is an oasis on the northern fringe of the Great

Mexican Garden Salad

1 cup sour cream
1 (16 oz) jar Old El Paso® Thick
'N Chunky Salsa, divided usage
3 cups cooked and
shredded chicken
¼ cup water (omit for
microwave preparation)
1 (1¼ oz) pkg Old El Paso®
Taco Seasoning Mix
1 head lettuce, torn in
bite-size pieces
3 cups broccoli florettes
1 small red onion, sliced thin
and separated into rings
1 avocado, peeled, pitted
and chopped
1 carrot, shredded
1 large tomato, chopped
1 (4 oz) can Old El Paso®
Chopped Green Chilies, drained
1 (4 oz) cup shredded
Cheddar cheese
1 (7½ oz) box Old El Paso
Nachips® Tortilla Chips, broken

• Combine 1 cup thick 'n chunky salsa and sour cream; refrigerate until ready to serve.

• In a large skillet combine chicken, remaining salsa, water and taco seasoning mix.

• In a large skillet combine chicken, remaining salsa, water and taco seasoning mix.

• Bring to a boil and let simmer 15-20 minutes.

• In a large serving bowl, layer vegetables.

• Top with chicken mixture, chilies and cheese. Toss to combine.

• Top each salad with broken tortilla chips and salsa and sour cream dressing.

Chihuahuan Desert, where pinon and ponderosa pine shade the tall country, high above the juniper and oak grasslands. The ranch was staked to the rocky knolls in 1898 when Andrew and Ora Jane Prude homesteaded forty sections of land, far from the reaches of civilization. Since 1921, however, it has been one of the state's top guest ranches, headed up by John Prude, offering such traditional activities as horseback rides along hidden canyons trails, as well as hiking and tennis.

Amarillo is proud of its cowboy mornings out on the famous Figure 3 Ranch, where horse-drawn wagons carry you at sunrise to an honest-to-goodness cowboy breakfast, cooked on an open mesquite fire high upon the wind-carved rim of the spectacular Palo Duro Canyon. It's a chance to walk amongst real cowboys, the legacy of the staked plains, and watch them rope and brand cattle on a genuine working ranch.

*A*n old timer once described majestic Palo Duro Canyon as "the collecting ground of everything that has happened here abouts for the last two hundred million years or so." He may not be far from wrong. The forty ton brontosaurus roamed the swampy marshland along with the stegosaur way back before that stubborn Red River wasted away eons carving Palo Duro across the Panhandle of Texas. Their skeletal remains have been found cemented in canyon walls, along with the dry bones of old Tyrannosaurus rex, the 19-foot-tall "King of Reptiles" and the strange pterodactyl: it flew the West Texas skies but had no feathers, only leathery wings. That was the beginning.

A few million years later, Coronado came searching for cities of gold. He stumbled across Palo Duro Canyon. He had prayed for mythical wealth. Instead, he found safety and shelter on the staked plains. Coronado, in his wisdom of 1541, may have been disappointed, but he wasn't ungrateful. He and his men knelt and held the first Thanksgiving in the new world deep inside that rugged, palatial canyon of hardwood.

Coronado had written: "The flat grassy lands stretch so far I never see the end of it." Yet, within that sea wave of golden-tipped grass, Palo Duro Canyon plunges eight hundred feet off the edge of the table-topped plains, a vermilion gorge torn open

Speedy Fajita Salad

1 cup Pace® Picante Sauce
2 green onions with tops,
thinly sliced
¼ cup chopped fresh cilantro
¼ cup vegetable oil
1 tsp lemon juice
1 clove garlic, minced
½ tsp salt
1 (15 oz) can pinto beans, drained
2 medium tomatoes,
seeded and diced
1 ripe avocado, peeled, seeded
and diced
1 lb B3R Beef Sirloin or
Top Round Steak
salt and pepper
4 cups shredded lettuce
12 El Lago Flour Tortillas, heated

- Combine first 7 ingredients; mix well.
- Toss beans with ¼ cup of the picante mixture; chill.
- Toss tomatoes and avocado with ¼ cup of the picante mixture; chill.
- Sprinkle meat with salt and pepper; broil, grill or fry to desired doneness.
- Slice thinly across the grain; toss with ¼ cup of the picante mixture; arrange on platter.
- Arrange beans, tomato mixture and meat on greens.
- Serve with tortillas and add additional picante sauce.
- Makes 6 servings.

Brisket Salad

½ medium size lettuce head,
cut in bite-size pieces
1 large tomato, cut in small pieces
1 small purple onion, cut in rings
½ cup chopped green pepper
½ cup chopped red pepper
1 small cucumber, chopped
coarsely
½ cup black olives
½ lb shredded, cooked and
cooled brisket cooked in
Claude's Barbecue Brisket Sauce

½ cubed Gruyere cheese
Gourmet Garnishes Italian
"Ciao" Dressing
oregano

- Combine first 9 ingredients together, add salad dressing to taste and a dash of oregano.
- Toss and refrigerate till ready to serve.
- Serves 4-6.

The outdoor drama "Texas" unfolds on the dramatic stage of Palo Duro Canyon.

Breads

Pepper Relish Surprise Corn Muffins

1 cup Pioneer Enriched Cornmeal
1 cup Pioneer All-Purpose Flour
¼ cup sugar
4 tsp baking powder
½ tsp salt
1 cup Sealtest Milk
1 egg
¼ cup vegetable oil
½ cup The Pepper Palate Sweet Pepper Relish

- In medium bowl, combine cornmeal, flour, sugar, baking powder and salt.
- Combine milk, egg and oil. Add to dry ingredients, mixing just until dry ingredients are moistened.
- Fill greased, medium-size muffin cups ⅔ full of cornmeal mixture. Place 1½ tsp relish in center of each muffin cup, press lightly into batter.
- Bake at 425 degrees for 15-20 minutes.
- Cool 5 minutes in muffin pans, remove to wire cooling rack.
- Makes 12 muffins.

by the Red River. It slashes its way, painted like the last shadows of the setting sun, for 120 miles across the Llano Estacado.

The Indians found refuge in the canyon, warmth from the winter winds, and hardwood for bows and arrows. They hid there and fought there and died there, did the Kiowa, Apache, Comanche and Cheyenne. For years, after the beginning of the great California gold rush, covered wagons had been attacked by Indian bands that would strike quickly then disappear into the grass, leaving no path to follow, fading from sight when there were no hills and no trees to hide them. Only the Indian knew the entrance to that canyon of escape.

General Ranald Mackenzie and his troops were ordered to stop the hostility. They rode to the rim of Palo Duro on a cold September morning in 1874, then slipped down a narrow switchback trail to the canyon floor. The attack came swiftly and suddenly, and a running gunfight drifted back into the shadows of the cuts in the rock. The troops, on unfamiliar ground, almost panicked. One gazed up at the towering, steep walls above him and asked: "How will we ever get out of here."

Said Mackenzie: "I brought you in. I will take you out."

He did, burning the village, capturing fourteen hundred horses, leaving the Indians on foot. Just before sundown, the chieftain led his people off the bluff and down to the waiting soldiers. The Battle of Palo Duro had ended. It was the last Indian war fought on Texas soil.

A year later, Charles Goodnight rode alone into the wild, vermilion gorge, deciding that it would make a natural shelter for his ranch, the first one staked to the Texas Panhandle. In 1876, Goodnight brought in 16,000 head of cattle, driving the stock slowly down a rugged 700-foot drop. It took two days. His men dismantled the wagons and dropped the pieces down by rope. More than ten thousand buffalo were stampeded out of the canyon to preserve the grass for his herd.

As great cattle trails pointed northward toward Kansas, a railroad began cutting through the Panhandle beside a little tent city called Ragtown. In time, Ragtown became known as Amarillo, the largest, most important industrial city in the Panhandle. Amarillo lies twenty miles northwest of Palo Duro,

Honey-Bran Muffins

½ cup "Feelin' Your Oats!"
Oatmeal
1 cup "Feelin' Your Oats!"
Oat Bran
½ cup White Wings Flour
2 tsp baking powder
½ tsp salt
½ tsp cinnamon
3 egg whites
1 cup Burleson's Honey
2 tbsp vegetable oil
½ cup Hygeia Plain Yogurt

- Preheat oven to 400 degrees.
- Lightly coat muffin tin with oil or place paper liners in tins.
- In a mixing bowl, combine oatmeal, oat bran, flour, baking powder, salt and cinnamon.
- In another bowl, mix egg whites, honey, oil and yogurt until well blended.
- Stir liquids into flour mixture just until blended.
- Pour batter into muffin tins to fill each ⅔ full.
- Bake for 20 minutes.
- Makes 20 small muffins.

Herb N' Wine Muffins©

2 cups Gladiola Biscuit Mix
¼ cup chopped green onion
1 tbsp sugar
1 tsp each fresh dill, basil, oregano from Fredericksburg Fresh Herbs
1 egg
½ cup Borden's Milk
4 oz Cheddar cheese, shredded
¼ cup Borden's Butter
¼ cup Oberhellmann Vineyards Bell Mountain Edelblume Wine

- Combine biscuit mix, onion, sugar and herbs.
- Mix the egg and milk together; beat slightly. Add this, ⅔rds of the cheese, the butter and wine to the dry ingredients. Beat until blended.
- Turn out into a well-greased muffin tin.
- Sprinkle the remaining cheese on top. Bake at 400 degrees until brown and crusty, about 15 minutes.
- Serve with butter.
- Makes 12 muffins.

©1990 Varney's Chermist Laden, Fredericksburg Herb Farm, Fredericksburg, Texas

whose 15,103 acres make it the largest state park in Texas. The park is a colorful range of peaks and valleys of sharp cliffs and gentle slopes, of jagged rock and that tumbling Prairie Dog Town Fork of the Red River. On the canyon floor, mesquite, juniper, and cottonwoods cluster together along the creek bank and spread back in the draws. Sagebrush casts its silver sheen in moonlight. Yucca leaps from the ground like living daggers.

Each summer, the heritage of the Panhandle is vividly portrayed in the outdoor drama **Texas**, presented in the canyon's unique Pioneer Amphitheater. The production pays tribute to the brave men and women who had the courage to settle a hard and bitter land, once called uninhabitable, and make it prosper. It focuses on the people who responded to that 1888 Panhandle editorial that said, "The man we want out here is the man who will roll up his sleeves and produce something."

Texas, the original idea of Mrs. Margaret Harper, was written by the Pulitzer Prize winning author Paul Green. He has used the whole canyon as a stage, believing, "With sight and sound, it will be possible for the audience to experience the blizzards those settlers suffered, the sand storms they endured." Indians perch on rocks. Cowboys ride hell bent for leather across the terrain. And even a train rumbles through the night. Thunder rolls across the gorge. Lightning pierces the sky. A tree is struck and burns. It happens every night. And, according to one official for the Texas Parks Department, "Palo Duro Canyon is the one place in Texas big enough and with the proper setting to tell the story of the development of the great Southwest."

*T*he Guadalupe Mountains knife down from New Mexico into the far western arm of Texas. Their high, wind-chiseled ridges angle southward across a flatland of desert flowers, then stop suddenly at the solemn yellow face of El Capitan.

For centuries, the stone cliffs of the Guadalupes have stood guard over the rugged terrain like an ageless prospector with a cache of hidden gold. Their secrets have remained in the shadows of a wild and beautiful country lying just beyond a rusty red rim, a strange land called home by elk and deer and bobcat. Guadalupe Peak juts upward 8,751 feet. It is the tallest

Glazed Apple Coffee Cake

2 cups Pioneer Biscuit
and Baking Mix
¾ cup Superior Milk
¼ cup butter, melted
1 egg
1 tbsp + ¼ cup sugar
1 tsp cinnamon
2 large Texas Orchard's Apples,
peeled and sliced
Glaze:
½ cup sugar
¼ cup half and half cream
1 Fenton's Egg
1 tsp vanilla

- Preheat oven to 400 degrees. Grease an 8"x8" pan.
- Mix first 4 ingredients + 1 tsbp sugar until well blended.
- Spread batter in prepared pan. Top batter with apple slices. Mix ¼ cup sugar with cinnamon; sprinkle over apple slices.
- Bake 20 minutes.
- Combine all ingredients for glaze. Pour over hot cake.
- Bake 20-25 minutes more.
- Makes 9 servings.

Spinach Bread

2 (14 oz) cans leaf spinach, drained
1 (1 lb) loaf frozen bread dough,
thawed
1½ (6 oz) cups shredded
Monterey Jack cheese with
green chilies
1 egg

- Preheat oven to 400 degrees.
- Lightly grease 2 baking sheets; set aside.
- Squeeze spinach dry; set aside.
- Divide thawed bread dough in half. Roll out each half into 13"x6½" rectangle.
- Spread half of the spinach on each rectangle of dough.
- Sprinkle cheese on spinach.
- Roll up each rectangle, jelly-roll fashion, beginning at long edge. Pinch seams and edges together to seal.
- Place rolls, seam-side down, on prepared baking sheets.
- Lightly beat egg. Brush egg over each roll.
- Bake loaves, 1 at a time, 20 minutes. Serve warm.
- Makes 24 slices.

point in Texas, near Pine Springs, shielding a land that one venerable explorer has called "the most rugged country I've seen on the North American Continent."

In time, goats grazed the foothills, and small ranches dotted the plains where the old Butterfield Stage once rolled from St. Louis to San Francisco. The Guadalupes themselves became the property of Abilene's J. C. Hunter, but he always said: "I own title to the land, but how can anyone consider himself owner of this magnificent country when these mountains have stood here alone more than a million years." He offered the magnificent landscape to the National Park Service for a mere $21 an acre. It was definitely penthouse property at a bargain basement price.

The ground of the national park is covered with golden maple leaves, and a crystal creek descends lazily among the sculptured stone walls of McKittrick Canyon, named for an outlaw. During the 1800s, Kid McKittrick rode New Mexico, robbing banks, then heading south. Lawmen followed, but when the kid reached the canyon, he vanished. No posse ever found him. Some say his stolen loot still is hidden in the caves that pock the Guadalupe cliffs. Geronimo boasted that the world's richest gold mines honeycombed the rocky ridges. Tio Ben, who walked the Guadalupes while his beard grew longer and he grew older, said, "There's tons of gold in these mountains. I know where it all is, but it's hidden. I won't get it, and nobody else will find it. The gold's there, but the world's not ready for it to be found."

The forest-blanketed mountains were brought into being by an ancient ocean that dried of old age. Backpacking and hiking trails cut precariously along the slopes of a strong, defiant citadel that geologists have called the most fragile ecological laboratory in the world. The sheer 1,000-foot cliff of El Capitan, the continent's most significant Permian fossil reef, is visible on a clear day—not forever, but for eighty miles. In Hermit Cave, artifacts have been found that date back more than twelve thousand years. A cremation burial in a McKittrick canyon dugout revealed shells of a marine mollusk that lived during 600 A.D. And bones of the musk ox, four-horned antelope, and extinct mammoth have been dug from their limestone graves.

Lemon Glazed Banana Muffins

½ pkg (6 oz) Texas Tofu, cubed
½ cup Caldwell's Texas Honey
⅓ cup oil
1 tsp vanilla
2 very ripe bananas, sliced
1 cup Flatland Whole Wheat
Flour
1 cup unbleached flour
1 tsp baking powder
1 tsp baking soda
¼ tsp salt
¾ cup chopped Comanche
Golden Pecans, Walnuts
or Almonds
1 tsp grated lemon peel

Glaze:

1 tbsp freshly squeezed lemon
juice
½ cup sifted Imperial 10x
Powdered Sugar

- Combine lemon juice and sifted sugar.
- Preheat oven to 350 degrees.
- Combine tofu, honey, oil, vanilla and bananas in bowl of food processor or blender; process until smooth.
- In a separate bowl, mix the flours, baking powder, baking soda and salt.
- Combine the banana mixture and flour mixture and mix until just blended.
- Fold in chopped nuts and lemon rind.
- Spray mufin tin with non-stick vegetable spray.
- Fill tins almost full.
- Bake for 20-25 minutes or until golden brown.
- Drizzle glaze over tops of muffins before serving.
- Makes 12 muffins.

The rugged peaks of the Big Bend country rise high above both Texas and Mexico.

Main Dishes

Shrimp and Seafood Lasagne

20 each lasagne noodles dry or
1 pkg fresh lasagne noodles,
uncooked
olive oil
1 lb fresh shrimp, size 30-35,
peeled and deveined
1 lb fresh fish, scallops, crab
meat, clams, combined
1 lb Mozzarella Company Fresh
Mozzarella Cheese, grated
8 oz Parmesan cheese
4 oz Romano cheese
8 oz Mozzarella Company
Fresh Ricotta Cheese
24 oz Texafrance Marinara Sauce

- Cook the pasta according to pkg directions, drain, rinse and let dry. Oil your lasagne pan (pan to have at least 4″ side) with a good olive oil.
- Then begin with the layers. First, one layer of pasta. Second, one layer of the sauce then a layer of seafood pieces. The third layer more pasta, then, the fourth layer Ricotta cheese, a layer of Mozzarella cheese and a sprinkle Romano, Parmesan cheeses, and lastly a layer of pasta.
- Repeat as many times as you have ingredients, making sure to finish top with layer of sauce and the remaining Mozzarella.
- Cook at 350 degrees for 45-60 minutes or until top is golden brown.
- Serves 4-6.

The canyons, Frijole Valley, the high bowl mesa, and the great peaks stand bold and wild and rugged. From a distance they appear to be a dark and ragged thunderhead rising up in a pale, sun-bleached sky. Trout and bluegill swim in streams as clear as cut glass. The jackrabbit, gray fox, porcupine, and occasional black bear roam among the maple, the quaking aspen, the ponderosa pine that shade the park's campgrounds.

Former Secretary of Interior Stuart Udall walked its back country ridges and said, without hesitation, "The Guadalupes contain the most diversified and beautiful scenery in Texas, some of the most beautiful landscape in the entire Southwest."

A strange silence pervades the Big Bend country, lost within the barren reaches of the Great Chihuahuan Desert, isolated and unspoiled, a land, old timers said, where you can lose everything and find yourself.

Its mountains are a moonscape, carved from rock, whose grace and beauty have been tortured and molded together with unchained boulders and gaunt, lava-faced peaks that bespeak of another time on earth. The terrain is stark, but not forsaken. In spring the soil becomes carpeted with the bloom from 2,500 varieties of wildflowers. Orchids and fern and honeysuckle find refuge at the foot of slender waterfalls, tumbling like molten threads of silver into stone-encased pools. Yucca, those giant Spanish daggers, are as treacherous as the land itself. The firecracker bush explodes with color, vibrant and red. Pink mistletoe dangles from the trees at Christmas. The century plant is the promise of life upon a harsh desert that is as revered as holy ground.

The sharp contrast between hard rock cliffs and delicate flower petals has, for a long time, created deep feelings for the Big Bend, causing the celebrated author Ludwig Bemelmans to write: "In a lifetime spent in traveling, here I came upon the greatest wonder. The mantle of God touches you; it is what Beethoven reached for in music; it is panorama without beginning or end. It will make you breathe deeply whenever you think of it, for you have inhaled eternity."

Man has touched but not tainted the land. A rustic lodge,

Beef Kabobs Over Lemon Rice

½ lb B3R Beef Boneless Sirloin
Steak, cut in 1" cubes
1 small zucchini, cut in chunks
1 small yellow squash, cut in
chunks
1 small red pepper, cut in
squares
1 small onion, cut in chunks
¼ cup Gourmet Garnishes
Oriental "Ah-So" Dressing
1 cup hot cooked Elco or Fiesta
Brand Rice
2 tsp fresh lemon juice
1 tbsp Patty's Herbs Fresh
Parsley, snipped
¼ tsp Brooke's Seasoning Salt

- Combine beef and vegetables in plastic bag with zippered closing.
- Add salad dressing and marinate 4-6 hours in refrigerator.
- Alternate beef and vegetables on 4 skewers.
- Grill or broil, turning and basting with remaining marinade, 5-7 minutes, or to desired doneness.
- To prepare Lemon Rice, combine rice and add remaining ingredients. Serve kabobs over Lemon Rice.
- Makes 2 servings.

Italian Chicken and Rice

2 whole chicken breasts,
deboned, skinned and sliced
½ lb Big State Fresh Zucchini,
thinly sliced
½ cup chopped green onion
1 (16 oz) can tomatoes,
undrained and chopped
3 cups cooked Texmati Lite
Bran Rice
¼ cup chopped parsley
½ tsp salt
¼ tsp pepper
pinch of dry oregano

- Coat large skillet with cooking spray. Saute chicken till lightly browned.
- Add zucchini; cook until crisp tender.
- Stir in remaining ingredients. Cover, reduce heat, and simmer 15 minutes or until heated through.
- Serves 8-10.

stone cottages, and campgrounds occupy the Chisos Basin, the scenic heart and soul of a national park that sprawls across 789,000 acres down where the unpredictable Rio Grande makes its big bend around the southwestern edge of Texas.

The park lands lie south of Marathon and Alpine, east from Presidio, and nobody simply drops by the Big Bend on his way to anywhere else. Big Bend is not on the way to anywhere else. It is a world apart, haunted by the whispers of legend and veiled by superstition.

In the pale darkness of night, shadows paint their way up the rock walls, where bald outcroppings stand like spectral sentinels in a shroud of white moonlight, hooded figures in golden robes, moving silently but moving nowhere at all. The Apaches called the cliffs chisos, meaning ghost. The Spanish called them hechizos, meaning enchantment. Both were right.

Horseback rides lead down to the window, a great cut in the mountain that opens up vistas to the Chinati Mountains a hundred miles away, and up to the South Rim, where, old timers swear, you can see clear into day after tomorrow. A hiking trail winds sharply to the crest of Lost Mine Peak. It hides tunnels of silver, once dug from its bowels by prisoners from the presidio in San Vicente. At dawn, they were blindfolded and marched up the trail to gouge ore from the vaults of the Chisos. Only the soldiers knew the pathway to the mine. They all died when the Indians came riding beneath that dreaded Comanche moon, and the silver still lies in an unmarked grave. Some say, however, that if you stand in the decaying doorway of the old mission at San Vicente on Easter morning, the first rays of sunlight point out the entrance to the mine.

The crumbling ruins of San Vicente nestle in the mud and sand of the Rio Grande. Raft rides drift lazily and sometimes recklessly down through the red, massive walls of Santa Elena and Mariscal Canyons. Carved by wind and water, they rise dramatically for 1,500 feet above the river, reaching up to those golden eagles that patrol high overhead. There is peace on the Rio Grande, a curious solitude that cloaks the somber abyss of the canyons. The shadows are cool, even when the sun bakes the desert, and the sky is merely a ribbon of blue.

On the western edge of the Big Bend, civilization has crept

Chili Lasagne

8 oz lasagne noodles
oil
4 cups prepared Wick Fowler's
2-Alarm or Family Style Chili Kit
2 cups round zucchini slices,
lightly cooked and drained
2 cups Cheddar cheese, grated

- Prepare noodles according to package directions. Oil 1½ qt rectangular baking dish. Line with noodles.
- Spread noodles with 2 cups chili, 1 cup zucchini and 1 cup cheese.
- Place noodles on top and layer remaining ingredients in the same order.
- Bake in oven at 350 degrees for about 20 minutes or until heated through.
- Serves 4-6.

Microwave Instructions:

- Bake on high in glass baking dish covered with waxed paper for 10-15 minutes, or until casserole is heated through and cheese is melted.

Easy Chili Rellenos

¼ lb lean ground beef
1 onion, chopped
1 clove garlic, chopped
salt, to taste
pepper, to taste
¼ tsp Fiesta Ground Cumino
2 cups shredded Cheddar cheese
2 cups cooked Texmati Rice
12 large fresh poblano peppers,
roasted and peeled
12 egg roll wrappers
oil to deep fry

- Brown ground beef.
- Drain drippings, add onion, garlic, salt, pepper, and cumin. Cook stirring often until onions are golden brown.
- Remove from heat, add cheese and cooked rice, stirring to blend.
- Split peppers lengthwise, remove seeds and pat dry. Stuff with meat mixture.
- Place each filled pepper diagonally on an egg roll wrapper. Bring lower rectangle point over pepper and tuck under. Place right side over center, bring top point down over pepper then roll to left side. Seal edges with few drops of water.
- Deep fry at 325 degrees.
- Makes 12 servings.

into Lajitas, a favorite haunt of the bandidos who rode with Pancho Villa. The wooden walls of the old trading post are scarred by bullet holes, put there by Villa who drank hard whiskey in the shank of the afternoon while General Black Jack Pershing and his army was out chasing the bandit's shadows in the desert. However, a hotel and condominium development has now been nailed to the harsh beauty of the landscape. Yet, it does not seem out of place at all. The hotels look as though they have always been there, reflecting an authentic frontier architecture that even has plank sidewalks and hitching rails. A swimming pool is a rare oasis on the desert, and a golf course is a patch of green that's lost amidst the mountains.

The ghostly ruins of Terlingua form a visual memory of a day when the volcanic rock—sliced by dry, brittle arroyos—was both blessed and cursed with the discovery of mercury. Around the turn of the century, millions of dollars of the rich red ore were dug from the desert floor, and Terlingua's population boomed to 2,000. Howard E. Perry, who found his fortune in the most unlikely and ungodly of places, built a store, a post office, saloon, casino, church, and mansion as a wedding gift for his bride. But, alas, she was a lady of high society. She rode to Terlingua, took one hard look at the forboding land around her, then promptly headed back east to the bright lights of home. The mansion was forever abandoned.

In time, the mines failed, and Terlingua became a ghost on the desert. On the wall of its old general store, I found a weathered sign that read:

"Next time two hours hangs heavy on your heads, spend it on our porch. Along in the cool of the evenin', we present 'sunset on the Chisos' in natural color and on the widest screen on earth. It's pure beauty gone plumb loco in thin blue air. A million pair of 20-20 eyes can't take in all its beauty. All props ten times older than the pyramids. All sunsets painted personally by the Lord."

El Camino del Rio, the river road, leads on west toward Presidio, and it passes the ruins of an old fortress, now restored as a state park. For years, the red adobe walls of Fort Leaton crumbled atop a barren knoll, overlooking the same Rio Grande that it once chose to protect.

Enchiladas

3 Fiesta Brand Chili Pods or ½
tbsp of Chili Pepper
1 tbsp Fiesta Brand Paprika
2 cloves Fiesta Fresh Garlic,
chopped
¼ tsp Fiesta Ground Comino
½ cup flour
¼ tsp Fiesta Whole Oregano
1 qt chicken broth
¼ tbsp salt, or to taste
⅜ cup oil
¾ lb Cheddar cheese, grated
¾ lb Monterey Jack cheese,
grated
1 onion, chopped
additional oil
2 dozen tortillas (red tortillas
are traditional)

Sauce:

- If using ancho chilies, remove stems and seeds from pods, simmer in hot water until skin loosens, and put through sieve to separate the skin from the chili pulp.
- Fry the paprika, comino and garlic, in ⅜ cup oil for 1 minute.
- Add the flour, and cook until just brown.
- Add the chili pulp or chili pepper, the oregano and the chicken broth, bring to a boil, and simmer until thick.

To Assemble Enchiladas:

- Mix the 2 kinds of cheese and the chopped onion.
- Heat ¼″ of oil in a pan.
- With tongs, dip a tortilla briefly in the hot oil until soft.
- Put 1 tbsp of the sauce in the tortilla, stuff with cheese and onions, roll up, and place side by side in a baking or microwave pan. Stuff all of the tortillas.
- Sprinkle top with cheese, onions, and sauce.
- Bake in 425 oven, or microwave until cheese is melted.
- Serves 8-10.

Golfers find their refuge in the shadow of El Paso's Franklin Mountains.

Chicken/Spinach Sour Cream Enchiladas

1 Pilgrim's Pride Chicken, whole
1 onion, chopped
2 cloves garlic, minced
dash cumin
dash coriander
1 (12 oz) pkg fresh spinach
2 tsp white vinegar
12 El Galindo Flour or Corn Tortillas
1 (16 oz) can Hygeia Sour Cream
1 lb Monterey Jack cheese, grated
paprika
sliced jalapeños

- Boil chicken with onion, garlic, cumin and coriander 2 hours, remove bone, retain broth.
- Cook spinach 30 minutes with vinegar; strain.
- Mix chicken and spinach; chop finely.
- Dip tortillas, one at a time, into hot chicken broth, then roll chicken/spinach mixture in tortilla 1½" thick. Place flap down in enchilada dish.
- Gently beat sour cream with 2 tbsp chicken broth until creamy. Pour over enchiladas.
- Heat in oven 350 degrees for 30 minutes. Garnish with cheese, paprika and sliced jalapeños.
- Serves 6-8.

Cheesy Enchiladas

8 Old Mexico Bakery Corn Tortillas
1 (15 oz) can Wolf® Brand Chili
2 cups shredded Colby or Monterey Jack cheese
1 (4 oz) can chopped green chilies, drained
½ cup water

- Preheat oven to 350 degrees.
- Spoon about 2 tbsp chili, 1 tbsp cheese and 1 tsp green chilies onto each tortilla; roll up.
- Place seam side down in 13"x9" baking dish.
- Combine remaining chili with green chilies and water. Spoon over tortilla; sprinkle with remaining cheese.
- Cover with foil; bake about 30 minutes or until heated through.
- Serves 4.

The forts of Texas played a key role in the settling of the frontier. Among the best preserved of the military sentinels is San Angelo's Fort Concho, built mostly of stone by skilled German craftsmen from Fredericksburg. Sixteen of the structures remain, links to a turbulent time when troops, both black and white, escorted the mail and stood guard on the passage west for stagecoaches and wagon trains.

Albany's Fort Griffin was a hardscrabble outpost, never glamorous, always on the threshhold of ruin. But it offered protection for settlers who were slowly beginning to homestead the western prairies. And its troops helped supervise the transferral of Kiowas and Comanches from their homes on the plains to reservations in the Indian Territory. When warriors almost killed General William T. Sherman, he angrily ordered that Indian hostilities in Texas be brought to an end in the quickest manner possible. Beneath the rock walls of Palo Duro Canyon, General Ranald Mckenzie carried out those orders to a grim finality. Each summer, the Fort Griffin Fandangle, a rip snortin' outdoor drama, relives the raucous 1800s, when soldiers, buffalo hunters, ranchers, drovers, outlaws, saloon girls, and gamblers crowded into the settlement, all rubbing elbows with such notorious characters as Wyatt Earp, Doc Holliday, Bat Masterson, Big Nose Kate Elder, and, of course, Lottie Deno, "The Poker Queen."

Abilene's Fort Phantom Hill rises in jagged columns from the prairie floor. About all that's left are a couple of stone buildings and a few chimneys. One soldier stationed there in 1851 wrote: "Everybody is disgusted. Like the Dove after the Deluge, not one green sprig can we find to indicate that this was ever intended by man to inhabit." Shortly after the troops marched away, the fortress mysteriously burned. Some said that Indians lit the torch. Others swear that an enlisted man tried to destroy the post so that no one else would ever have to serve there again.

Fort Davis, on the other hand, was referred to by Colonel Benjamin H. Grierson as "the most luxurious quarters in the Southwest." It was built in a little box canyon near Limpia Creek at the base of the Davis Mountains. There were thirteen houses for married soldiers, a hospital, an adjutants office, a

Black Bean and Goat Cheese Enchiladas

³/₄ cup chicken broth, divided
4 or 5 tomatillos (husk removed), rinsed and chopped (or substitute green tomatoes, canned or fresh)
3 cloves Fiesta Fresh Garlic, peeled, divided
¹/₂ cup chopped yellow onion
2 serrano chilies, stemmed and seeded
1 tbsp Big State Fresh Cilantro, chopped
1 cup cooked black beans
4 tbsp fresh Comanche Golden Mango or Papaya, diced
2 scallions, white part only, thinly sliced
¹/₄ cup (about 2 oz) Texas Chevre Goat Cheese
salt, to taste
¹/₄ cup corn oil
4 corn tortillas (6" size)
red and/or yellow bell peppers, cut in thin strips, to garnish

- To make salsa, in a medium-sized saucepan, cook ¹/₂ cup chicken broth, tomatillos, 2 cloves garlic, onion and 1 serrano chili over medium-high heat for 10 minutes, stirring frequently.
- Place mixture in blender with cilantro and puree until smooth. Reserve salsa.
- Mince remaining garlic and serrano.
- In a medium saucepan, place black beans, remaining ¹/₄ cup broth, minced garlic and serrano chili, mango or papaya, and scallions. Bring to a boil and whisk in goat cheese.
- Season with salt, remove from heat, and keep warm.
- In a medium-sized skillet, heat the corn oil until just smoking.
- Pass each tortilla through the oil to moisten and seal. Place between paper towels to drain.
- To assemble, place ¹/₄ of the bean and goat cheese mixture down the center of each tortilla. Roll tortillas and place, seam-side down, on plates.
- Spoon the salsa equally over the filled tortillas and sprinkle with red and/or yellow pepper strips.
- Serves 4.

stable, sawmill, sutler's store, "billiard room," corral, and graveyard. For a time, Confederate troops occupied the post. But Federal soldiers returned two years after the War Between the States ended. For them, life at Fort Davis was an easy life, occasionally interrupted by skirmishes with Indians who raided wagon trains that trekked the Trans-Pecos.

According to the National Park Service, "The remains of Fort Davis are more extensive and impressive than those of any other southwestern fort." So they are. The haunting sounds of history ricochet sharply off the walls of Limpia Canyon when, periodically, park rangers play a recorded reenactment of an historic retreat ceremony. You hear the National Anthem as it was originally scored, flat and mournful, bugles piercing, drums ruffling, the clank and rattle of horses and caissons as ghostly troops—heard but never seen—more slowly down the parade field. In June of 1891, the order came which finally closed the doors on the frontier outpost. It said simply: "Fort Davis has outlived its usefulness."

In El Paso, Fort Bliss remains as strong, perhaps even stronger, than it ever was during the chaotic era of Indian wars that strangled an unknown land. It is now the U. S. Army Air Defense Center for rocket research. a training ground for combat troops and missile batallions. But more than a century ago, it was an important defense post, the center of strategic planning for the last confrontation with the Apache Chieftain Geronimo. Museums on base trace military history from the Mexican War and Indian campaign era to present-day air defense and artillery displays.

El Paso, the legendary El Paso del Norte, lies at the foot of the barren Franklin Mountains, the southern tip of the Rockies. Only a river away sprawls the foreign shopping flavor of Mexico and Juarez. For centuries, the pass to the north has been rich with the legacy of priests who searched for an Indian tribe to save and settlers who looked westward for a home.

Overlooking the lower valley of El Paso are the missions at Ysleta, Socorro, and San Elizario, all fashioned between 1682 and 1777. Ysleta is the oldest community in Texas, and the chapel was put together by Franciscan monks in an attempt to civilize and Christianize the Tigua Indians. The mission still

King Ranch Chicken

1 (2½-3 lb) Buddy's Natural
Chicken
salt, to taste
pepper, to taste
1 bay leaf
1 cup chopped green pepper
1 cup chopped onion
1 stick margarine or butter
2 (10¾ oz) cans cream of
chicken soup
2 (10¾ oz) cans cream of
mushroom soup
1 (10 oz) can Ro*Tel Tomatoes
and Green Chilies
12 soft corn tortillas, torn in
bite-size pieces
1½ cups shredded
Cheddar cheese

- Stew chicken with salt, pepper and bay leaf. After cooking, bone and cut chicken into bite-size pieces.
- In a large saucepan, cook green pepper and onion in butter until tender.
- Stir in soups on tomatoes and green chilies.
- In a 3 qt shallow baking dish, 13"x9", arrange alternate layers of tortillas, chicken, soup mixture and cheese, using ⅓ of all ingredients. Repeat layers 2 more times.
- Bake at 325 degrees for 40 minutes.
- Serves 10-12.

Zesty Fajitas

1 (12 oz) jar Claude's Fajita
Marinating Sauce
1 cup Gourmet Garnishes
Mexican "Ole" Dressing
2 lb skirt or flank steak
1 large tomato, cut in
small wedges
1 medium onion, cut in small
wedges
1 stick Gandy's Butter
4-6 flour tortillas
1-2 avocados, sliced
1 (8 oz) ctn Gandy's Sour Cream
Miguel's Gourmet Salsa

- Blend marinating sauce and dressing together. Add fajita meat, tomatoes and onions, toss to coat with sauce. Marinate for at least 5 hours in refrigerator.
- Remove meat, tomatoes and onions from sauce.
- Melt butter in large skillet over low heat. Add meat, tomatoes and onions.
- Fry for about 10 minutes or until meat is cooked.
- Serve with hot flour tortillas, avocado slices, sour cream and salsa.
- Makes 4-6 fajitas.

stands, but the Tiguas almost became a forgotten tribe, a lost nomadic band of Pueblos from New Mexico. They were overlooked when other Indians were given reservations, and, like the Seminoles in Florida, never officially signed a peace treaty with the United States. Their descendants cling to the tiny community of Ysleta, and, after being stranded for three hundred years, their culture and tribal heritage are at last being restored on the mission grounds. The Tiguas perform tribal dances and serve tribal bread, baked in ovens as it was during the 1600s.

Nearby, the Socorro Mission is the oldest continuously active church in Texas. Once a chapel, it became, out of necessity, a fortress during Indian uprisings. Many of the parishioners call the church San Miguel because of the legend of the ox cart. It seems that the cart was carrying a statue of St. Michael to New Mexico when it became stuck in the mud near the village of Socorro. Wrought with superstition, the Mexicans believed that Divine Providence had sent them a sign. So they promptly unloaded the statue, adopted the saint as a patron on the spot, and built the mission in the mud that had trapped their cart and ended their journey.

Although the San Elizario Mission was not built until 1777, the military garrison around the chapel was established by Juan de Onate in 1598.

Much of the region's natural and historical past can be seen in the Centennial Museum on the campus of the University of Texas at El Paso; dinosaur bones from the Big Bend, fossils from Ice Age deposits, pottery, stone tools, and shell jewelry from the prehistoric ruins of Casas Grandes in Mexico. And the city's culture is couched regally in the Museum of Art, which boasts pieces of antique furniture that once sat in the homes and offices of old El Paso, as well as the third finest Kress Collection in the nation, including Gilbert Stuart's famous portrait of George Washington.

The Magoffin Home State Historic Structure is a monument to the lifestyle of 1875. The Border Patrol Museum honors the lawmen who ride the Rio Grande. A Bullfight Museum focuses on those who duel raging horns. The greyhounds race in Juarez. The horses run at Sunland Park.

Fixin' Fajitas

2½-3 lb flank, skirt or sirloin
steak or chicken
1 (12 oz) jar D.L. Jardine's®
Fajita Marinade
1 jar D.L. Jardine's® Fajita
Seasoning and Tenderizer,
Original or Mesquite
12 flour tortillas

Your choice of garnishes:
1 jar D.L. Jardine's®
Chile Con Queso
1 jar D.L. Jardine's® Santonio
Hots Jalapeño Slices
1 jar D.L. Jardine's® Brand
Texacante Salsa, Cactus Salsa,
or Texas Picante
lettuce, chopped
tomatoes, diced
onion, diced
sour cream
guacamole

- Pour fajita marinade over beef or chicken; refrigerate for up to 24 hours, turning meat occasionally.
- Remove meat from marinade; sprinkle with fajita seasoning.
- Char-grill meat over hot coals.
- When cooked, slice meat diagonally into strips.
- Place meat in the center of a warm flour tortilla.
- Garnish with your choice of salsa, lettuce, tomato, onion, sour cream and guacamole.
- Makes 12 fajitas.

Tru-Tex Casserole

2 lb ground hamburger
1 (16 oz) jar Tru-Tex Picante
12 oz noodles
2 cups water
1 cup grated Cheddar cheese

- In dutch oven, brown meat.
- Add picante, noodles and water. Cover. Simmer until noodles are done.
- Remove from heat. Top with grated cheese and serve.
- Serves 6-8.

El Paso has much to offer. But then, it should. After all, mankind has left its footprints in the sands of the pass that led north for more than four centuries.

*H*igh atop Mount Locke in the Davis Mountains, at 6,701 feet, McDonald Observatory scans the sky with a 107-inch telescope. The site was chosen back in 1932 because of the highland's clear air and high ratio of cloudless nights. The experiments there are definitely high tech, as astronomers probe the heavens and beyond. But the large dome is open to the public. And the Caverns of Sonora possesses a brilliant, sometimes spectacular, array of delicate crystals and formations that have been called both "unbelievable" and "impossible," particularly in the Valley of the Ice. The past president of the Speleological Society said, "This is the most indescribably beautiful cavern in the world."

Stinnett and Spearman remember the Battle of Adobe Walls and the day a band of Indians attacked twenty-eight buffalo hunters. Billy Dixon crouched low, carefully measured the ferocity of the wind, raised his rifle, took aim, and shot a warrior on horseback almost a mile away. The Indians, shocked at the accuracy of his amazing sharpshooting, fled from the plains. Fort Stockton proudly celebrates its heritage with the Annie Rigs Hotel Museum, Grey Mule Saloon, and Tunis Creek Stagecoach Stop. Vernon's museum caters to the Waggoner Ranch and the Red River Valley. Perryton's museum applauds those who conquered the plains with covered wagons and barbed wire. San Angelo's Miss Hattie's Museum is a restored "Ladies of the Evening Saloon and Parlor House," which entertained soldiers, cowboys, and ranchers until the Texas Rangers, with more might than heart, closed it down in 1946.

Upon the Llano Estacado, the cactus is abloom. Cattle graze off mesquite beans when the buffalo grass is gone. A windmill reaches high to catch the wind. An oil rig reaches deep to search the earth for crude. The desert beckons. The mountains are a purple bruise in the sky. And all is well within the rugged, independent land of sourdough and pickup trucks.

Central Texas

"There is no other place that can do for me what this land and what this water and what these people and what these hills and these surroundings can do."

——*President Lyndon B. Johnson*
on the Texas Hill Country, his home

*H*e walked out of the valley, as lean as a mesquite fence post and just about as gnarled, his eyes harsh and stubborn like the land around him. He paused to kick at a clump of prickly-pear cactus that held on selfishly to a patch of dirt that had washed down among the rocks. He looked out at the bluebonnets, the Indian paintbrush, the clover, the purple, orange, and red haze that ran up and down the gentle hillsides without going anywhere at all, the beauty amid the bristles.

In the rugged valley from whence he came, he saw the face of Texas the way the mythical Texas is supposed to be: big and empty, delicate yet defiant, tough as boot leather and just about as polished.

"This land ain't worth a plugged nickel," he explained, a definite German accent rolling off his tongue. "I've seen cows walk for ten miles just tryin' to find an acre of grass to chew on. 'Bout all you can raise on it is rocks, and a little cain now and then."

He paused and sighed.

"It's poor, useless, good for nothin' and too dadgummed

hard to even leave a footprint.

"But ain't it purty?"

And so it was. The old man grinned again, bent low into the wind, and slowly shuffled away. I looked close. There were no footprints behind him to even prove he had ever come to or from the valley that separated Kerrville from Medina.

Central Texas is a blessed land, tempting and taunting. The Germans draped their gingerbread architecture from the balconies of Fredericksburg and New Braunfels. The French left a trace of the Alsace at Castroville. Forts, which once protected a troublesome frontier, lie scattered like weathered gravestones on the plains. And a President called it home.

The hills rise up with broad, strong shoulders above the backbone of Texas, rolling and rugged, a chunk of the old-time Western legacy that's as solid as the pink granite beneath its scrawny soil. Severe canyons cut down into the juniper flats. Wide, sweeping meadows hover around little towns, many still harboring the customs and traditions of those old settlers who found their way into the hills, then never tried to find their way back out. It is a world of wurst and beer, mariachis and tortillas, bluegrass and barbecue, with hot sauce dripping off elbows and onto a sawdust dance floor.

Winding rivers—sometimes peaceful, sometimes raging with white water—slip reverently beneath the arching, aching limbs of the knock-kneed cypress, beckoning the canoes, the rubber rafts. And the scenic Highland Lakes—Travis, Buchanan, LBJ, Inks, Marble Falls, Austin, and Canyon—hide within the hills, reaching out, quenching the thirst of a sun-spackled land. The silence is interrupted only by the sounds of nature. A spring-fed waterfall cascades like lace for a hundred feet down a limestone cliff. Goats graze slopes that are too steep for man to stand upon. An armadillo scurries along the water's edge. A whitetail buck darts back into the cedar. Wild pigs tramp the marshes. And far above, a blue heron, an egret reach out with their wings to grab hold of the wind.

The Vanishing Texas River Cruise boat has left all vestiges of civilization behind as it moves for eighteen miles up the Colorado River from Silver Creek Village on the northern shore of Lake Buchanan. Ed Low, who began the service, pointed out:

Old San Antonio Fajitas

2 lb skirt or flank steak
"Old San Antonio Style" Fajita
Seasoning
1 cup oil
1/4 cup "Old San Antonio Style"
Salsa Tampiquena or Salsa
Mexicana Green
2 cloves Fiesta Fresh Garlic,
smashed
2 limes, juiced
4-6 flour tortillas, warmed
"Old San Antonio Style"
Picante Sauce
guacamole
1 onion, chopped, optional

- Rub steak with fajita seasoning.
- Combine oil, salsa, garlic and lime juice.
- Marinate meat for 6-8 hours in the salsa mixture.
- Cook outside over charcoal or bake in oven for 3 hours at 275 degrees.
- Cut into strips and serve in hot flour tortillas with picante sauce, guacamole and onion.
- Serve 2-3.

Tamale Pie

2 lbs ground beef
2 pkgs Wick Fowler's
Taco Seasoning
1 1/2 tsp Texas Gunpowder®
Ground Jalapeño Powder,
divided
2 (6 oz) pkgs Gladiola Corn
Bread Mix
2 (15 oz) cans Old El Paso®
Pinto or Mexican Beans
2 (17 oz) cans corn, drained
2 (8 oz) cans tomato sauce
2 cups water

- Preheat oven to 400 degrees.
- Brown hamburger meat.
- Add taco seasoning and 1/2 tsp jalapeño powder, heat 5 minutes.
- In a mixing bowl combine corn bread mix and 1 tsp jalapeño powder.
- In a 9"x13" baking dish combine beans, corn, tomato sauce and hamburger mixture. Cover with corn bread mixture.
- Carefully cover corn bread mixture with water, trying not to pour a hole through the corn bread.
- Bake 1 hour.
- Serves 6-8.

: "I studied the history of the area, the German land grants, the Indians who hunted and fought on this land, the legends of gold mines that catacomb the hills. It was fascinating. And I wanted to share what I had found with others." He does in a rare, isolated wilderness riverway. It's an unspoiled land, rarely touched, seldom seen, lost amidst rock formations that have been guarding the curious Texas granite hills for more than 400 million years.

*E*nchanted Rock rises out of the valley, 16 miles north of Fredericksburg, like a great granite blister, sculpted—then polished—by winds and rain since time began. It dominates the landscape as it did during the days when Indians looked upon it with fear and amazement. To them, the pink bald rock was sacred. Some even referred to it a "holy mountain."

Samuel C. Reid wrote in 1848: "The Indians had a great awe, amounting almost to a reverence for it and would tell many legendary tales connected with it and the fate of a few brave warriors, the last of a tribe now extinct, who defended themselves there...as in a strong castle, against the attacks of their hostile brethren. They were finally overcome and totally annihilated, and ever since, the "Enchanted Rock" has been looked upon as the exclusive property of these phantom warriors."

Charles Moss, who was guardian of the hunk of granite for twenty-five years, understood the superstitions. He told me, "There are a lot of indentions up near the top we call dinosaur tracks. They would trap rainwater, then reflect the light of the moon at night. The Indians became frightened of the mysterious lights shining from a mountain that groaned. For, you see, there are a lot of cracks in the rocks up there. The cold and heat cause them to contract, then expand. And the noise makes it sound like the whole mountain is in pain."

Enchanted Rock is a state park, covering 460 acres and rising up for five hundred feet. The climb to the top is relatively easy—though slippery in places—and usually takes about forty-five minutes. But, as a Houston backpacker told me, "Walking from one side of Enchanted Rock to the other is like moving from one century to another."

Layered Turkey Florentine Loaf

1 lb Plantation Ground Turkey
¼ cup seasoned dry bread
crumbs
2 tbsp milk
⅛ tsp pepper
1 egg
2 tbsp finely chopped onion
½ tsp salt

Florentine Layer:
1 (10 oz) pkg frozen chopped
spinach
1 cup Mozzarella Company
Fresh Ricotta Cheese
1 egg
¼ salt
¼ cup grated Parmesan cheese
½ tsp Menchaca™ Brand Italian
Seasoning
⅛ tsp pepper

Toppings:
1 (10 oz) can Ro*Tel Whole
Tomatoes, drained, cut-up
⅓ cup Pedro Gatos
Spaghetti Sauce

- In medium mixing bowl, combine all turkey layer ingredients; mix well; set aside.
- Unwrap spinach and place on plate. Microwave at HIGH for 4-5 minutes, or until defrosted. Drain thoroughly, pressing to remove excess moisture.
- In small mixing bowl, combine spinach and remaining Florentine ingredients; mix well; set aside.
- Press half of turkey mixture into 8"x4" loaf dish.
- Spread Florentine layer over turkey.
- Spread evenly with remaining turkey mixture. Cover with wax paper.
- Place on saucer in microwave oven. Microwave at HIGH for 5 minutes. Rotate dish half turn. Reduce power to 70% (Medium-High). Microwave for 15-23 minutes, or until center registers 150 degrees, rotating dish once or twice.
- In 2-cup measure combine topping ingredients. Spread topping over loaf.
- Reduce power to 50% (Medium). Microwave for 2 minutes to heat through.
- Let stand for 5 minutes before serving.
- Serves 6.

The eastern cornerstones of the region are Austin and San Antonio, two destination cities that runneth over with culture and history—and enough nightlife to make you forget both. Austin has the Capitol. San Antonio has the Alamo.

Ironically, it was a Texas Hill Country blind man who suggested pink granite for the state capitol in Austin as a last-ditch effort to rekindle his own dwindling city. Adam Rankin Johnson journeyed to Central Texas shortly after his twentieth birthday, searching for and finding the great falls of the Colorado River. He dreamed of carving a town out of the granite valley and setting it on the shores of a crystal lake. But his dream was shattered by Civil War. As he led the charge at the Battle of Grubbs Crossroad in Kentucky, a bullet slammed into Johnson's face, forever blinding him.

Almost twenty-two years later, Adam Johnson designed and platted the town of Marble Falls. A cotton and shoe factory, a schoolhouse, and finally a power plant were built, but the blind architect was facing a new problem. A railroad was needed if his town was to grow and flourish, even survive. He headed to Austin to plead his case. When Johnson arrived, he found that the state capitol had burned, and he heard of plans to construct a new statehouse. The legislators were saying, "We'll build a capitol of which Texas can be proud, fashioned of true, native Texas stone." Johnson grinned, remembering Granite Mountain, its slopes blanketing 540 acres with rich, pink granite above his town of Marble Falls.

"Why not pink granite for the capitol?" he asked. The legislature agreed it was a fine suggestion, but wondered, "How do we transport the stone? There is no railroad."

Adam Johnson merely shrugged and said, "Gentlemen, to promote a railroad to Marble Falls, I'll give seven miles of right-of-way through my holdings at Burnet. I'm sure others along the way will do the same." They did. And the Texas State Capitol was built of pink granite quarried from Marble Falls, a town that did not die simply because its founder, a blind man, had more vision than anyone else around him.

*I*t was on a crisp spring day in 1838 when Mirabeau B.

Turkey Cheddar Rice Bake

¼ cup Borden's Butter
¼ cup Light Crust All-Purpose Flour
3 chicken bouillon cubes, crumbled
2 cups Superior Milk
3 cups cooked cubed Sunday House Turkey
½ lb Monterey First Harvest Fresh Mushrooms, sliced
4 cups cooked Texmati Rice
1 cup grated Cheddar cheese

- Melt butter in a 3 qt saucepan.
- Blend in flour and chicken bouillon cubes. Gradually stir in milk. Cook over medium heat, stirring constantly, until mixture comes to a boil.
- Remove from heat. Stir in turkey and mushrooms.
- Spread cooked rice in buttered 8″ square baking dish; spoon turkey mixture over rice.
- Sprinkle with cheese.
- Bake at 350 degrees for 30 minutes or until casserole is hot and bubbly.
- Makes 6 servings.

Turkey and Avocado Sandwich

4 slices Heart Bakery Cholesterol Free Bread
4 oz Ranch House Turkey Breast
1 avocado, thinly sliced
1 cup Fresh from Texas Alfalfa or Zesty Sprouts

- Layer bread with turkey, avocado, and top with sprouts.
- Makes 2 sandwiches.

Caviar Con Jamon

1 jar B.B. Berzette's Lone Star Caviar, undrained
2 cups Ranch House Ham, cubed
black olives to garnish
lettuce leaves

- Combine caviar and ham in covered dish and refrigerate at least 2 hours before serving.
- Garnish with black olives, if desired.
- Serve on lettuce leaves with garlic bread or cornbread.
- Serves 4.

Pepper Steak Stir-Fry

½ cup Pace® Picante Sauce
½ cup water
2 tbsp soy sauce
1 tbsp cornstarch
½ tsp ground ginger
3 tbsp vegetable oil, divided
1 lb B3R Beef Round Steak, cut into 1½" x ¼" x ¼" strips
1 medium red or green pepper, cut into short thin strips
1 cup Kitchen Pride Fresh Mushrooms, sliced
6 green onions, cut into ¼" pieces
1 garlic clove, minced
hot cooked rice

- Combine first 5 ingredients in small bowl, set aside.
- In large skillet or wok over high heat, heat 2 tbsp of oil until hot but not smoking.
- Add meat and stir-fry 1-2 minutes; remove with slotted spoon and set aside.
- Drain skillet, if necessary. Heat remaining tbsp oil in skillet.
- Add peppers, mushrooms, onions and garlic to skillet; stir-fry 3 minutes.
- Return meat to skillet.
- Stir picante sauce mixture and pour into skillet.
- Cook and stir about 1 minute or until sauce thickens.
- Serve over rice with additional picante sauce.
- Makes 4 servings.

The famed Texas longhorns amble past the State Capitol, celebrating the state's sesquicentennial.

Peach Jambalaya

1 green pepper, diced
1 onion, sliced
2 tomatoes, chopped
2 cloves garlic, minced
1 tsp Patty's Herbs Fresh
Thyme
¼ lb Farm Pac Brand Ham,
diced
¾ lb Farm Pac Brand Smoked
Sausage, sliced
2 tbsp oil
1 tbsp tomato paste
1 cup chicken broth
8 fresh Brazos Valley Orchards
Peaches, sliced
¼ lb Hillman Shrimp, shelled,
deveined
salt and pepper, to taste
3 cups cooked Comet Long
Grain Rice

- Saute green pepper, onion, tomatoes, garlic, thyme, ham and sausage in oil about 5 minutes.
- Add tomato paste and chicken broth; simmer 5 minutes.
- Add peaches and shrimp; cover and simmer 5 minutes until shrimp turns pink.
- Salt and pepper, to taste.
- Serve over hot rice.
- Serves 4.

Old Grouch Casserole

2 cups cooked Adolphus Rice
2 tbsp Aunt Betty's Old Grouch
Fixings
3 H&H Chorizo or Paisano
Italian Sweet Sausages

- Mix in fixings with the rice.
- Cook sausages quickly in a hot iron skillet. Drain fat. (An iron skillet cooks hotter and faster.)
- Add the rice and fixings to the meat. Cook quickly, fluffing the rice with the meat.
- Mix, stir, and serve hot.
- Serves 4.

Lamar, president elect of the Republic of Texas, rode into the valley where the Colorado River was breaking through its last barrier of cedar-topped hills. He looked around proudly and told the band of rough-hewn Rangers riding with him: "Gentlemen, this should be the seat of a future Empire."

It was a glorious land, full of hope and full of promise, possessing a rugged beauty where rulers, Lamar reasoned, ought to rule. Within a year, a surveyor was back in the valley, designing the city that would be Austin.

Sam Houston was not impressed. Houston ran for the presidency, promising, "If elected, I will see that Austin is no more than a watering hole for cattle in three years."

He wanted the capitol moved.

Houston thought that the statehouse should be located in, of all places, a city to the east called Houston.

Austin had it. Austin never let go of it. Austin built its capitol from Adam Johnson's mountain of granite—making sure that the dome was taller than the U. S. Capitol—paying for the statehouse by giving contractors three million West Texas acres, which eventually formed the famed XIT ranch.

The University of Texas has eight colleges and eight schools spread across three hundred acres. And its 307-foot tower has long been a Central Texas landmark. Exhibits on anthropology, zoology, geology, and history are displayed at the school's Texas Memorial Museum, and the University Art Museum, a teaching gallery, brings in great paintings and sculpture from major museums throughout the world. However, the University's most noble monument is the memorial to a President who took his oath of office aboard Air Force One in one of America's most unforgettable moments.

The Lyndon Baines Johnson Presidential Library houses in its archives thirty-one million pieces of the massive Johnson manuscript collection. Most will never be seen. For others, it contains the poignant memories of LBJ himself: the copy of the television speech, with handwritten corrections, that stunned the world the night President Johnson announced he would not seek re-election; a Model T, given LBJ by Henry Fort II; woodcarvings, boots, spurs, and walking sticks from the American people, the common, every-day man and woman for

Cajun Style Seafood Gumbo

4 tbsp Doguet's Roux
3 qts water
1 large onion, chopped
1 bell pepper, chopped
2 cloves Fiesta Fresh Garlic, chopped
2 stalks celery, chopped
2 lbs Hillman Fresh Shrimp, cleaned and deveined
1 lb Hillman Fresh Crabmeat
1 lb Dad's Crawfish, if desired
1 pt Hillman Fresh Oysters
1/2 cup chopped green onion
1/4 cup chopped parsley
2 cups Doguet's Extra Fancy Fine Rice

- Dissolve roux in water over medium heat, then let boil 1/2 hour.
- Add onion, bell pepper, garlic and celery, and cook over low heat for 1/2 hour.
- Add all seafood, green onion and parsley and simmer for 20 minutes.
- Serve over cooked rice.
- Serves 4-6.

J-B Sausage Stir-Fry

6 slices Texas Smokehouse Bacon
4 potatoes, thinly sliced
1 bunch broccoli, trimmed and sliced
3 carrots, sliced
1/2 cup celery, sliced
1 medium onion, chopped
salt and pepper, to taste
1 lb J-B Smoked Sausage, cut into 6 portions

- In non-stick skillet, fry bacon until crisp. Remove bacon and drain, reserving 1 tbsp bacon drippings.
- Heat drippings in skillet over medium heat, add vegetables and salt and pepper. When vegetables are tender, place sausage on top. Heat covered for 15 minutes.
- Top with crumbled bacon before serving.
- Serves 4-6.

whom Johnson devoted his life.

The LBJ Library is a bold new look at the past. Austin, in general, prefers an old look at the present. It is a city that would rather fight than lose any piece of its colorful history. Austin, however, is not particularly interested in preservation merely for the sake of hanging on to memories. Austin puts life into its restorations.

For years, East Sixth was a street in disarray, held together solely by pool halls, pawn shops, two-bit bars, and stores that hawked second-hand clothing in their windows. But a new day has dawned for the old neighborhood. The Driskill Hotel showed the way. It had been elegant, but decrepit, ornate and doomed, tagged for the wrecking ball. But preservationists drew a battle line, pointing out that every President who ever visited Austin kicked off his shoes in the Driskill. Their loud, agonized cries of dismay were heard, and, amidst the classy sounds of renovation, the hotel's grand old name was added at last to the National Register of Historic Places.

East Sixth, its neighbor, then shook the cobwebs from its own dreams. It has, at last, become an avenue of fine clubs and restaurants, art galleries and theaters, all occupying aged stone buildings. And the maverick music that ricochets down its back alleys defies description. It's country, and it's progressive. But it's also rock and roll and jazz, and there's even a little of the blues that keeps weaving its way into the songs."

But then, Austin has always been the home of mavericks. As early as 1890, it was a fertile ground for O. Henry. He published a newspaper here, the original **Rolling Stone**. Also a bank teller, William Sidney Porter, alias O. Henry, was imprisoned for embezzling. He began writing and became one of the greatest short story authors this country has ever produced. The small home he lost for a cell is open for tours.

The oldest house in the city is the French Legation, a keepsake of 1839, the residence of Alphonse de Saligny, King Louis Philippe's charge d'affaires to the Republic. The Legation has a distinct foreign flavor in its architecture and furnishings, but Austin remembers Saligny with more than a little disdain. The French diplomat stayed just long enough to print his own supply of money, then deny Texas a badly needed loan from

Spring Stir-Fry

1 tbsp sesame oil
1 tbsp vegetable oil
1 lb Plantation Turkey Breast
slices, cut into thin strips
2 cloves garlic, minced
2 tbsp soy sauce
1 cup Monterey First Harvest
Fresh Mushrooms, sliced
4 green onions with tops, sliced
2 medium zucchini or yellow
squash, sliced
1 pkg Fresh From Texas Bean
Sprouts
1 green pepper, cut into strips
1 cup Sunshine Country
Cashew Nuts, toasted
2 cups cooked Comet Long
Grain Rice

- Place sesame oil and vegetable oil in wok or deep skillet over high heat. Add turkey and garlic; stir-fry for about 3 minutes.
- Add soy sauce, mushrooms, scallions, zucchini or yellow squash, bean sprouts, pepper and cashews.
- Stir to combine; cover and cook over medium-low heat for 8-10 minutes. Stir occasionally, and test turkey and vegetables for desired doneness.
- Serve with cooked rice.
- Serves 6.

Thai-Style Drunken Spaghetti

—from SATAY, the Asian Cookery, Austin, Texas

1 tbsp minced garlic
2 tbsp jalapeño or serrano,
chopped
1 lb lean ground beef
2 cups spaghetti, cooked
1/2 cup cherry tomato, halved
1 tbsp sweet soy sauce
2 tbsp regular soy sauce
1 tbsp vinegar
1 tbsp sugar
1/4 cup vegetable oil
3/4 cup water or beef stock
1/4 tsp ground black pepper
1/2 cup fresh basil leaf

- Heat oil in wok or deep sauce pan until hot. Add garlic, jalapeño and ground beef; stir-fry until meat is cooked.
- Add all ingredients, except basil leaf, and spaghetti; saute thoroughly at medium heat until excess liquid disappears.
- Stir in basil leaf and serve on spaghetti.
- Serves 2.

France just because a pig trespassed on his property.

The most beautiful home in Austin open for tours is the Governor's Mansion, as stately today as it was when built for a mere fifteen grand in 1855. Its white columns loomed with elegance above the frontier landscape, scarred by Indian wars, prompting one admirer, General George Armstrong Custer, to write: "The governor's mansion looked regal to us, so long bivouacking in the forest and on the uncultivated prairies." Custer rode away from Austin, his yellow hair blowing in the wind, and headed north where he would bivouack for the last time on the uncultivated prairies of Little Big Horn.

The past is sacred. The land is revered. Jogging and bicycle trails slip alongside Town Lake. Canoes and sailboats crease the calm river waters that slice through Zilker Park.

And Mount Bonnell, the most scenic of places, overlooks Austin from a limestone outcropping 775 feet above the valley. Purple mountain laurel, cedars, and live oak form the crown atop the city that, as Lamar wished, did, indeed, become the seat of the future empire of Texas.

*S*an Antonio has been molded in the spirit of the padres, baptized by a river that winds, twists, and meanders through the city—as the Indians used to say—like a drunken old man going home at night. The river is, as it has always been, the key to the heart of San Antonio. Legend persists that Spanish missionaries were lost in a dry and barren land. They thirsted and they prayed. One padre tore a mesquite tree from the sun-baked earth, and from the depth of a parched soil flowed the San Antonio River. It's still flowing.

During those hardship days of the eighteenth century, the river became the lifeline for five missions that stand, even today, with the pride and dignity of their Spanish heritage. Four of the chapels are located along the well-marked Mission Trail, all serving as parish churches.

There are the twin towers of Mission Concepcion, with rare and original frescoes still visible in the red, blue, and ocher colors that an unknown and unamed artist chose so many decades ago. It's the oldest unrestored stone church in the

Meats & Seafood

Honey-Glazed Ribs

2 slabs (5-6 lbs) pork spareribs
½ cup ketchup
½ cup pineapple juice
1 tbsp soy sauce
¼ cup Burleson's Honey

Broiled Pineapple:
1 pineapple, peeled and cut
into ½" slices
¼ cup vegetable oil

- Preheat oven to 350 degrees.
- Place a wire rack on a baking sheet, arrange ribs on top and bake for 1 hour.
- In a small bowl, stir together the remaining ingredients.
- Increase the heat to 375 degrees.
- Baste the ribs with the marinade and bake for 30 minutes, basting every 10 minutes.
- Turn ribs over and continue to bake and baste for 30 minutes more, until ribs are dark, glazed and fork-tender.
- Cut ribs apart and serve with broiled pineapple (see below).
- Lightly brush pineapple slices with oil.
- Arrange in 1 layer on baking sheet.
- Broil for 15-20 minutes, until golden.
- Serve immediately.
- Serves 6-8.

United States, having changed very little from that day in 1755 when the last dab of adobe was plastered into place. At one point, the mission lay abandoned for almost seventy-five years, and, in the 1840s, U. S. troops were even stationed at the compound. Cowboys later used it for a cattle pen.

Mission San Jose has been restored to recapture the feel, the essence of another time. But then, it should have been. For San Jose was, without doubt, the most elegant and ornate, most prosperous, and best fortified mission within Texas. The years have not dimmed its grace nor its beauty, and Mission San Jose has been declared a National Historic Site. The sacristy was described by Father Lopez in 1785 as "the most beautiful room this side of Saltillo." You can still walk beside the mission's granary, its five cloisters, its Indian pueblo of eighty-four compartments, and pause beside the Rose Window, carved by hand in the memory of a lost love. Inside San Jose, the queen of missions, the choir loft was for reverence, the portholes for rifles.

An open bell tower looks down from Mission San Juan Capistrano. The chapel itself was never fully completed, but it houses rare and ancient figures of Christ and the Virgin Mary made of cornstalk pith, a process perfected by the Indians of central Mexico before the days of Spanish conquest. It is a lost art that has yet to be rediscovered.

Services are still held at Mission San Francisco de la Espada, located about a mile away from the defiant Espada Dam. The dam, fashioned from adobe mixed with goat's milk, is an engineering paradox. It curves the wrong way, yet has withstood every flood for the past two centuries. No one really knows why the chapel was called the mission of the sword. Some say that it refers to St. Francis's vision of a sword in the sky. Others merely believe that it was affected by a ghostly image seen long ago within the mission itself, one that held a cross in one hand and a sword in the other.

The fifth mission is San Antonio de Valero. But most know it, with respect, as the Alamo. During the turbulent years of the 1830s, it was a fortress of death and a battle cry. Today it is a shrine, a monument to the 188 men who fought and died there in pursuit of Texas independence. David Crockett came

Peach Glazed Pork Ribs

4-4¼ lbs pork ribs, cut into serving pieces
1-1½ cups New Canaan Farms Pedernales Picante Sauce
1½ cups Hill Country Farms Texas Peach Preserves
¼ cup soy sauce

- Place ribs in shallow roasting pan with meaty side up. Bake uncovered in 350 degree oven 45 minutes.
- Heat picante sauce, preserves and soy sauce to boiling, stirring constantly.
- Brush pork with about ½ cup of the sauce, bake until tender, 45-60 minutes.
- Baste ribs several times while baking.
- Serves 4-6.

Sweet and Sour Pork Ribs or Chicken

Smoked Cap Ranch Pork Ribs or Chicken
Carole's Jalapeño Jam

- Warm ribs or chicken as directed.
- About 10 minutes before serving, spoon jalapeño jam over all surface, or warm jalapeño jam and mop it on.

Smokey Pork Chops

6 (1" thick) pork chops
1 (8 oz) can tomato sauce
½ cup catsup
⅓ cup Claude's BBQ Brisket Sauce

- Brown pork chops in skillet, drain excess fat.
- Combine rest of ingredients in small bowl.
- Add to pork chops. Cover and simmer for about 1 hour, turning occasionally.
- Serves 6.

with his band of Tennesseans, smarting from a political defeat. He had angrily told his constiuents: "You can go to hell. I'm going to Texas." Commander William B. Travis wrote to the people of Texas: "I am besieged by a thousand or more of the Mexicans under Santa Anna. I have sustained a continual bombardment & cannonade for 24 hours...& our flag still waves proudly from the walls. I shall never surrender or retreat." And James Bowie, clutching his famous knife, died, lying on his sickbed. His brother would only remark, "I'll wager they found no wounds in his back." The Alamo is a solemn place, a hallowed place, and a sign on the door whispers: "Be silent, friends, here heroes died to blaze a trail for other men."

During the daylight hours, the river walk is a quiet and tranquil place, soothed by fountains, waterfalls, and tropical vegetation. Artists prop their paintings against stone walls. A senorita tries to sell you a hand-carved San Antonio Rose. Clubs and pubs, tucked away back beyond sidewalk cafes, lie sleeping, waiting for the night. The neon pales, as though afraid to compete with the sunshine.

But when night tumbles over San Antonio, the river is no longer a tranquilizer. It comes alive. It throbs. It rocks. It swings as though it never intends to sleep again.

San Antonio has become one of the nation's largest and most important cities, rising from the prairie in steel and glass, not just adobe, topped by the Tower of the Americas, a revolving restaurant perched 622 feet above street level. It was once the landmark for a world's fair, HemisFair.

Yet, adobe remnants of that first eighteenth-century village remain in a cluster of downtown dwellings known as La Villita. Those tiny cottages, cloaked with antiquity, now house galleries and craft shops. Within them, you can find glassblowing, hand weaving, leather working, jewelry making, mosaics, and sculpture. One is know as the Cos House. Inside those walls, on a December day in 1835, Mexican General Cos signed the articles of surrender, giving up San Antonio to a small band of Texas rebels. The news outraged Santa Anna, and he marched toward a chapel known as Alamo.

San Antonio offers a variety of activities. Dolphins, otters, and the walrus perform at the spectacular Sea World of Texas.

Peach Teriyaki Pork

3-4 lbs boneless pork loin
salt and pepper
Herbal Gems Fresh Rosemary
½ cup ketchup
½ cup soy sauce
¼ cup Texas Duet Wildflower Honey
1 clove garlic, crushed
Brazos Valley Orchard Fresh Peaches, sliced or halved

- Place a pork loin on a rack in a shallow pan. Rub with salt and pepper.
- Sprinkle on rosemary.
- Roast at 350 degrees for 2-2½ hours.
- Mix ketchup, soy sauce, honey and garlic. Use as basting last 45 minutes.
- Transfer to a heated platter. Surround meat with peach slices and/or halves.
- Serves 6-8.

Ham with Champagne and Oranges

1 thick ham slice
2 onions
2 Rio Queen Fresh Oranges
¼ cup brown sugar
1 small lemon
Moyer Texas Champagne

- Place ham in casserole dish. Score around edge of ham.
- Chop onions and place on top of ham.
- Peel oranges and cut in medium thick slices and place on top of onions.
- Sprinkle brown sugar on top of oranges.
- Slice lemon without peeling and place slices over brown sugar.
- Pour ¼ to ⅓ bottle of champagne over all.
- Bake in 350 degree oven for 45 minutes.
- Serves 3-4.

But the undisputed star is Shamu, the killer whale, leaping with grace and beauty above a $140 million tropical isle showplace. The Hertzberg Circus Collection highlights two centuries of the Big Top in America, typified by the tiny violin, the pipe, walking cane, and horsedrawn coach of P. T. Barnum's famous Tom Thumb. There is a reflection of history, a chilling touch of horror displayed in the Plaza Theater of Wax. Ripley's Believe It or Not offers more than five hundred artifacts and oddities from around the world. The Lone Star Brewery has its Hall of Texas History and Wax Museum, as well as the Buckhorn Hall of Horns, an eccentric aggregation of mounted animals, antique firearms, and relics of old Texana that were originally crammed in the nooks and crannies of the notorious old Buckhorn Saloon. On the grounds is another home of O. Henry, who penned 381 stories, many while locked away in prison. The courts said O. Henry stole some money. If he did, his wife used it to warmly furnish the homes that he could not enjoy. He was in a cold, bare cell. It's the kind of tale with an odd twist that O. Henry himself might have written.

The McNey Art Institute—San Antonio's manor of modern art—is a gallery for the works of both European and American masters. Its walls are lined with the paintings of Cezanne, van Gogh, Gauguin, Toulouse-Lautrec, Picasso, Degas, Goya, and Renoir. They are worth millions. They no longer have a price tag, only a home that itself is a work of art, a grand and esthetic blend of Mediterranean and Spanish Colonial Revival architecture. The sprawling Witte Memorial Museum, devoted to the natural history and science of the state, is surrounded by early Texas homes and log cabins. And the Governor's Palace is a sculpture of white adobe, the home of thirty-two Spanish governors from 1722 to 1821, when San Antonio was still the capital of the Spanish Province of Texas.

San Antonio has a definite Spanish flavor. Yet, the flags of five other countries have flown over it. Many cultures contributed to the growth of Texas, and their influences are vividly brought to life in the Institute of Texan Cultures, located in HemisFair Plaza. It is more than a mere museum. It has historical artifacts, to be sure, but primarily the institute deals with the struggles, the battles, the journeys of those twenty-six

Honey Glazed Ham Slice

1 slice, 1-1½" thick fully cooked
Plantation Turkey Ham

Glaze:
¼ cup Weaver's Pure Country
Honey
2 tbsp Borden's Fresh Orange
Juice
1 tbsp vinegar
1 tsp cornstarch

- Combine glaze ingredients in a 2 cup glass container. Microwave on HIGH 1½-2 minutes, or until slightly thickened, stirring after first minute. Set aside.
- Slash fat on turkey ham slice.
- Place turkey ham in 12"x8" dish; cover with wax paper.
- Microwave on MEDIUM (50% power) for 10 minutes; drain.
- Pour glaze over turkey ham; do not cover. Microwave on MEDIUM (50% power) 7-10 minutes, or until turkey ham is hot.
- Serves 6.

Peachy Keen Ham

1 (10-12 lb) ham
2 (5.5 oz) jars Fischer & Wieser
Original Peach Honey

- Prepare ham for cooking according to directions.
- Place in shallow baking pan, uncovered.
- Baste ham with peach honey.
- Cook in 325 degree oven for 3 hours, or until ham is fully cooked, basting every 30-45 minutes.
- Serve with additional peach honey on the side.
- Serves 16-20.

ethnic groups, of real people who settled the land.

The contributions of each ethnic group are featured in a separate exhibit area of the $10 million museum. Background music, sound, and slides emphasize and embellish the factual story told by pictures, relics, and documents. The late R. Henderson Shuffler, who developed the institute, once escorted Prince Ranier of Monaco through the displays, pointing to the picture of Count de Polignac, who commanded a renegade band of Texas troops during the War Between the States.

"His soldiers were a little irreverent," Shuffler said. "They changed his name and called him Polecat."

Prince Ranier only smiled. "I know," he said. "He was my great uncle."

$\mathcal{M}$any of those early settlers came to Texas to find jobs at the dusty end of a cattle herd. They drove longhorns, cursing them in many languages, and ate at the chuckwagons of ranches that were scattered amidst the mesquite and buffalo grass. The heritage of the cowboy, too, has threaded its way into the Hill Country, particularly into Bandera, the dude ranch capital of Texas. Accommodations usually range from rustic to modern, and they are just about as close to old-time ranch life as you would ever want to come. Bandera offers a choice of the Twin Elm Guest Ranch, the Mayan Dude Ranch, and the Flying "L" Ranch. A few miles further west, in Medina, there is the Circle R Resort Ranch. And Wimberley's 7-A Resort Ranch hitches its ties to the past with Pioneertown, a recreation of the Old West, where you amble nostalgically along a street lined with saloons, a post office, hotel, and a log fort. A medicine show barker livens up the surroundings. Early-day melodramas—a time to pray for the heroine and boo the villain—unfold within the Opera House.

At the dude ranches, you can ride horseback and even have breakfast on the range during an early-morning trail ride back into the juniper and cedar thickets. When you're tired of the cowboy life, you can play golf and tennis, or ride canoes, maybe even inner tubes, down the chilled, rushing waters of the Medina River. The Mayan Guest Ranch has a Texas Night, a

Osso Buco

2½ lbs veal shanks, cut in 1-1½" pieces
salt
pepper
flour
virgin olive oil
1 onion, diced
1 carrot, diced
1 stalk celery, diced
1 cup Wimberley Valley Chardonnay Wine
½ lb tomatoes, diced
1½ cups Take Stock Brown Veal Stock
risotto alla milanese (recipe on page 182)

For Gremolata:
½ cup parsley, minced
2 cloves garlic, minced
grated peel of 1 whole lemon

- Lightly dust shanks with salt, pepper and flour.
- Brown slightly in olive oil. Remove shanks to a plate.
- In same pan, saute the vegetables lightly.
- Place the shanks and vegetables in an ovenproof casserole.
- Add wine, tomatoes and brown veal stock.
- Cook in a 325 degree oven for 1½ hours (cover if liquid reduces too much).
- Serve with risotto alla milanese.
- Top with a sprinkling of "gremolata," the combination of the parsley, garlic and freshly grated lemon peel.

Marinated Chicken

1 cup Texafrance Classic French Vinaigrette
½ cup Guadalupe Valley Winery River Valley White Wine
1 cup water or increase white wine
1 tbsp Texafrance Roasted Garlic and Raspberry Vinegar Mustard
1½-2 lbs Pilgrim's Pride Chicken Breast

- Blend the first 4 ingredients well.
- Place chicken in a shallow pan; pour sauce over the chicken.
- For best results, marinate for 2 hours before grilling, broiling, baking, etc.
- Serves 4-6.

Ranch Style Brisket

1 large beef brisket, trimmed
3 btls Figaro Hickory
Liquid Smoke

- Pierce several holes in brisket with fork.
- Place the brisket in a plastic bag and add bottles of liquid smoke.
- Tie end of bag and place in sink to marinate for 3-12 hours or overnight.
- When ready to cook, remove brisket from bag and place in cooling pan fat side up.
- Place the pan holding brisket on the middle rack of oven at a temperature consistent with desired cooking time: 275 degrees for 6 hours is perfect or 350 degrees for shorter cooking times.
- Cook until tender and slices easily.

The Hill Country is cowboy country, with chuckwagon cooking and down home barbecue.

BBQ Brisket

1 large beef brisket, boneless chuck or shoulder clod
1 cup salad oil
1 can Shiner Beer
4 tbsp Fiesta Black Pepper
2 oz Fiesta Fresh Garlic, chopped or
1 tbsp Fiesta Powdered Garlic
6 Fiesta Bay Leaves
1 tsp salt, optional
Heart of Texas Mesquite Country Wood for fire

- Trim the fat off of the meat. Mix all ingredients together and pour over the meat. Refrigerate 24-28 hours; turning morning and night.
- BBQ meat 6-10 hours to the side of a moderate wood fire.
- Turn meat occasionally, basting with the reserved marinade.
- Add wood to the fire as needed.
- This can be baked in the oven, covered on 250 for 6-10 hours until tender.
- Fiesta Brand Brisket Rub can be used in place of the spice mix listed above.
- Serves 10-12.

Heat 'N' Sweet Barbecued Chicken

1 jar B.B. Berzette's Heat 'N' Sweet Bar-b-Que Sauce
½ cup dry sherry or Rosser Wasser Rock Brand Sparkling Water
6-8 pieces Signature Foods of Texas Natural Chicken

- Place bar-b-que sauce in blender, add sherry or water. Blend enough to combine well and break up tomato pieces.
- Clean and pat chicken dry.
- Place chicken in dish and pour sauce over chicken, coating both sides.
- Cover and refrigerate about 1 hour.
- Remove chicken from sauce (reserve sauce) and cook slowly on grill or in the oven until tender.
- Turn and baste often.
- Serves 4-6.

happy-go-lucky time to test your talents at horseshoe throwing, gunny-sack racing, washer pitching, and even enter a good, old-fashioned, down home cow chip tossing contest. The table is spread with a moveable feast of fried chicken and German sausage, jalapeno corn bread and *posole*, an Indian concoction of hominy, lean pork, and tomatoes.

The nights mourn the sad, heart-broken confessions of country music at the Mayan's Wrangler's Rose Saloon and Yellow Belly Bar, or down at Bandera's Silver Dollar Saloon, with owner Arky Blue doing most of the singing. Throughout the Hill Country, honky tonks line the backroads, with jukeboxes belting out such classics as "If You Want to Keep Your Beer Cold, Put It Next to My Ex-Wife's Heart" and "I Gave Her My Heart and She Stomped That Sucker Flat."

*F*redericksburg remains forever linked with its German ancestry. Throughout the community are fascinating Sunday Houses, once used by German farmers as their weekend homes, places to sleep when they left their fields and came to town. One of them is now the Pioneer Museum, which showcases the early tools, rustic furniture, and sparse lifestyle of those immigrants who plowed the new ground and planted seeds of hope in the rocky Hill Country soil. Vereins Kirche, a decorative and distinctive downtown landmark, is an eight-sided building that is called, with affection, the Coffeemill Church. And the Admiral Chester Nimitz State Historical Park, housed in the old Nimitz Hotel, is a naval museum, a long way from the sea, that honors Fredericksburg's favorite son, who served as Commander in Chief of the Pacific Fleet during World War II.

Wimberley, overlooking the crystal-clear rapids of the Blanco River, has has become an antique mecca. Route 32, slipping quietly out of Wimberley, is easily the most spectacular drive in the Hill Country, a winding razorback ridge where the craggy terrain drops abruptly into timbered canyons and hidden lakes. It is breathtaking and tortuous and called, appropriately, the Devil's Backbone.

And it leads you on to San Marcos and Aquarena Springs,

Meat Loaf

1½ lbs lean ground beef
½ cup bread crumbs
¼ cup Adams Parsley Flakes
1 egg
1 tsp Baldy's™ Original
All-Purpose Seasoning
dash Adams Malabar Ground
Pepper
1 (8 oz) can tomato sauce
with onions
1 cup shredded Cheddar cheese
½ cup Dixieland Hot
Chow Chow

- Combine first 6 ingredients with ½ can tomato sauce.
- Pack ½ of mixture in loaf pan, top with cheese and chow chow.
- Bake at 350 degrees for 1 hour.
- Unmold into shallow baking pan. Remove excess fat.
- Pour on remaining tomato sauce.
- Bake 15 minutes longer.
- Serves 4-6.

Gourmet Beef Patties

½ cup Wimberley Valley Celler
Select Red Wine
1 cup water
3 tbsp Menchaca™ Texas Style
Barbecue Seasoning
12 Clamon Beef Patties
½ tsp salt
1 cup diced onions
1½ cups Kitchen Pride Fresh
Mushrooms, chopped
2 tbsp minced green pepper
¾ cup Cheddar cheese, grated

- In saucepan, pour in wine, water and barbecue seasoning.
- Heat over medium heat until sauce boils and

thickens. Set aside.
- Sprinkle patties with salt; then brown in skillet. Pour off excess fat.
- Add onions, mushrooms and green pepper.
- Pour in barbecue sauce; then cover.
- Heat for about 15 minutes on low heat until meat is done and vegetables are tender.
- Sprinkle beef with cheese and replace the cover for a few minutes to let the cheese melt.
- Serve as an entree or on a hot open-face sandwich.
- Serves 6-8.

spreading over ground that held the camps of primitive Indians more than thirteen thousand years ago, or so their artifacts claim. Franciscan monks trekked here to the banks of the San Marcos River in the 1750s to establish a church. At the park itself, an aerial tramway carries you to the hills beyond the river, to a Mexican market, old mill, and mission ruins, all enveloped within colorful gardens that hang onto a rock-faced hillside. Glass-bottom boats slip across the lake, opening up a strange world beneath the water, still clear at depths of fifty feet. And in the Submarine Theater, beautiful mermaids perform an underwater ballet, without being weighted down by cumbersome air tanks. They are poetry amid the bubbles of the springs. Ralph, the swimming pig, isn't. But he splashes along for laughs anyway. The hellfire-and-brimstone past of the frontier is portrayed in Texana Village, a collection of historic buildings that were found throughout the Hill Country.

Wonder World, in San Marcos, features an anti-gravity house, a miniature train for children, and tours through a dry cave created long ago by the anger and confusion of an earthquake. Natural Bridge Caverns, near New Braunfels, is a living cave that wanders for more than half a mile past twenty-eight chambers with such alluring names as Castle of White Giants, Sherwood Forest, and Hall of the Mountain King. Georgetown's Inner Space Cavern is a massive vault for the fossilized remains of such prehistoric creatures as the ground sloth, saber-toothed cat, and mastodon, whose fragile tusk measures thirteen and a half feet in length. And Longhorn Cavern State Park, near Burnet, is the world's third largest cave, once a hideout for outlaws and a secret manufacturing depot for Confererate gunpowder.

Burnet grew up around old Fort Croghan, built in 1849 as the army tried to keep up with the settlers hurrying to free land in the west. The outpost now includes a museum, encircled with log cabins. One belonged to Logan Vandeveer, hired by the government to provide food for Indians in the region. One day he ran across a band of renegades attacking his herd of cattle. Vandeveer rode his mule up to Yellow Wolf, grabbed the chief by his throat, and demanded, "Stop it." Yellow Wolf did. Therefore, Indians traveling near Burnet would often ask, "You

Mexican Steak Ranchero

2 lbs B3R Round Steak
1 tbsp olive oil
1 large onion, sliced
1 garlic clove, mashed
1 (16 oz) can sliced mushrooms
4 tbsp Borden's Butter
1 cup beef bouillon
1 (8 oz) jar Old San Antonio Picante Sauce
1/2 cup La Buena Vida Vineyards Centennial White Wine, optional
2 cups cooked Comet Long Grain Rice
salt and pepper, to taste

- Cut steaks into individual servings.
- Brown in oil; in heavy skillet saute onions, garlic and mushrooms in butter, just until onion becomes soft.
- Add bouillon, picante sauce and meat. Cover and allow to simmer about 1 hour.
- Add wine the last 10 minutes of the cooking time.
- Serve over rice.
- Serves 4-6.

Tamale Dressing

8 oz seasoned sausage
1 large onion, chopped
1/2 stick margarine
36-48 Pedro's Tamales, broken into pieces
2 (6 oz) pkgs Gladiola Cornbread Mix, prepared
1/2 (10 oz) can Old El Paso® Green Enchilada Sauce
1/4 tsp Menchaca™ Brand Cayenne Pepper
1/2 tsp Fiesta Ground Cumino
salt and pepper, to taste

- Brown sausage and drain.
- Saute onions in margarine.
- Crumble tamales and cornbread into a large bowl.
- Add sausage, onions and remaining ingredients. Mix gently.
- Loosely stuff turkey, or place in casserole and heat separately.
- Makes about 2 qts.

know him, Logan Vandeveer? Him heap big brave, skeer Yellow Wolf." But to Vandeveer, it was a land worth the gamble, worth risking his life to protect.

*T*he settlers came in droves, and one of their descendents became President. Lyndon B. Johnson always said of those burly hills, "It is impossible to live on this land without being a part of it." The land around Johnson City and Stonewall are interwoven with the heritage that was so much a part of LBJ.

Just east of Stonewall is the Lyndon B. Johnson State Historical Park, showcasing the Sauer-Beckmann living history farm, a graphic portrait of the hard times that became known as the good old days. Buffalo, deer, and those rangy Texas longhorns prowl the terrain that holds two pioneer homesteads in its unforgiving clutches. Bus tours amble down Ranch Road 1, past the old Junction School; the storied Ranch House which once served as the Western White House; and the quaint country cemetery, shaded by live oaks, where Johnson lies buried. The tour stops at a small, unpretentious "dog-trot" cabin, the LBJ birthplace, furnished with mementos from the family's early days, including a rolling pin, which, perhaps, hastened the naming of the boy who became President.

For several days after the lad was born, his parents did not choose a name. Finally, his mother turned to her husband and snapped, "I'm not getting out of bed to roll your biscuits until you decide what to call your son." Before the morning had ended, Lyndon Baines Johnson had a name.

Near downtown Johnson City is the LBJ Boyhood Home, a national historic site. Horse-drawn wagons carry you out to the cabins, barns, and chuckwagon for a glimpse of the Hill Country as it appeared in the nineteenth century. In those days, cattlemen would gather their longhorn herds at the ranch before heading out toward Kansas, biting the wind and chewing the dust that blew in their sun-wrinkled faces. And when the Indians attacked Deer Creek, the wounded were brought to hide in the shadow of the stone buildings.

On the steps of his boyhood home, Lyndon Johnson, in a

Terrific Tostadas

*1 (16 oz) can Amigos
Refried Beans
4-6 Clamon Beef Patties (Lite,
Deluxe or Rancher)
1 onion, sliced
1 pkg El Lago Corn Tortillas*

Optional Toppings:
*lettuce, chopped
tomatoes, chopped
Daisy Brand Sour Cream
Monterey Jack and/or Cheddar
cheese
Texas Sting Hot Sauce*

- Heat beans.
- Cook patties on one side, then add sliced onions and cook both until patties are done.
- Heat tortillas.
- Put pattie on a tortilla, cover with beans and top with onions.
- Add choice of toppings.
- Serves 4-6.

Escargots Southwest

*6 escargot snails
1 tbsp clarified butter
½ tsp garlic, minced
1½ oz Messina Hof Chardonnay
1½ oz fish stock
1 tbsp chopped green onions
1 oz tequila
1 tbsp whole butter
1 blue corn tortilla
sprig cilantro, chopped*

- Saute escargots in clarified butter with garlic just long enough to brown garlic. Use medium heat.
- Deglaze with white wine and fish stock.
- Add green onions and finish with tequila and butter.
- Serve on blue corn tortilla shell and garnish with chopped cilantro.
- Serves 1.

loud, firm voice, made his first speech to launch his first campaign for national office. And it was on the same porch where President Franklin D. Roosevelt stood to congratulate him after LBJ had won his first election. Perhaps it was an omen, perhaps it was merely a promise of things to come.

Johnson spent most of his life in Washington. But he never forgot the hills of home, writing: "It was once barren land. The angular hills were covered with scrub cedar and few live oaks. Little would grow in the harsh caliche soill. And each spring the Pedernales River would flood the valley. But men came and worked and endured and built." No better eulogy could ever be given them.

*T*he brasada—the brush country—is a land of thorns, bristling with cactus and catclaw and Spanish daggers. Historian Paul Horgan described it as "either swept with gray dust borne on blistering winds or beaten by deluges that hissed as they first struck the hot ground or raked by blizzards that came whistling out of the north." The brasada is a place of extremes, much like the men and women who chose to nail their homes amidst the thorns.

Uvalde holds the roots of tobasco-tempered Cactus Jack Garner who went to Washington in 1903, became Speaker of the House, then agreed to serve as Franklin D. Roosevelt's vice president, a decision he always regretted. "I gave up the second most powerful job in the nation to become a whipping boy for the President," he said. He left Washington, feuding with Roosevelt, believing that no man, not even the celebrated FDR was fit to be President four times. His house in Uvalde is the Garner Museum, each room containing vibrant memories of the crusty politician's life.

The harsh brasada has been christened by Lake Amistad, a joint project between the United States and Mexico, spreading across the Pecos and Devil Rivers. Del Rio is gateway to the great body of water that brings life to a baked and thirsty land, covering 138 square miles of the brush country. The countryside itself looks much as it did when soldiers rode among the thorns in the 1840s, establishing the stone quarters

Presto Parmigiana

4 Clamon Beef Patties
8 oz Di Franco's Spaghetti Sauce
4 oz grated Parmesan cheese

- Cook 4 patties in skillet until lightly brown.

- Heat spaghetti sauce.
- Place patties separately on dish.
- Spread sauce on patties.
- Sprinkle Parmesan cheese on top.
- Serves 4.

Chicken Breasts with Caciotta on Fettuccine

3-4 tbsp Borden's Butter
4 boned chicken breasts, butterflied
2 cloves Fiesta Fresh Garlic, cut in half
½ cup Messina Hof Fume Blanc Wine
salt and freshly ground pepper
½ lb Mozzarella Company Black Pepper and Garlic Caciotta, sliced
water and salt to cook fettuccine
1 lb freshly made fettuccine
1 lb creme fraiche

- Melt butter in pan and saute chicken breasts with garlic until chicken is golden brown on both sides.
- Splash with white wine and let simmer briefly, less than a minute.
- Season with salt and pepper, to taste.

- Place slices of caciotta on top of chicken breasts and allow cheese to melt.
- Set chicken breasts aside to keep warm and leave pan juices in saute pan.
- While cooking the chicken breasts, bring salted water to a boil in a large pot. Gently stir in fresh fettuccine and cook for a minute or two.
- While cooking fettuccine, add creme fraiche to pan juices and simmer to desired thickness.
- Toss drained fettuccine well with creme fraiche sauce, add any left over caciotta, coarsely chopped, and toss again briefly.
- Adjust seasoning with salt and pepper. (Use pepper liberally!)
- Arrange fettuccine on platter or individual plates and top with chicken breasts. Serves 4.

of Fort Clark, the lonely sentinel of the plains. They knew that somewhere beyond the far mountains, the fierce, angry eyes of the Comanches and Lipans, were upon them, watching, waiting to see if the army could stand up to the austere land or buckle beneath the agony of its solitude. The distance between landmarks was overwhelming. The miles staggered the men. Fort Clark fought its wars, its troops battling Indians, Pancho Villa's bandits, and Germany during two World Wars. Now its stark stone quarters, beside the cold spring-fed swimming pool built by General Jonathan M. Wainwright, are a guest ranch on the eastern edge of Brackettville, a town that owes its very life to the existence of the lonely sentinel.

*E*very hungry eye in town stared at Happy Shahan, and the eyes were as hollow as the deserted buildings along the dust-tarnished streets of Brackettville. The place was dying, no doubt about it, and the mourners had all packed up and were looking for the road out of town. Shahan was the last hope they had—him being mayor and all—and they were all tired of waiting for a miracle. Shahan kept bidding for new industry, but nobody in 1950 cared about putting down new roots in a brush country where only the thorns grow well.

One night at a city council meeting, Shahan leaned back in the mayor's chair, propped his boots up, and said simply, "What we ought to do is try and get into cowboy movies." The next day he was in Hollywood, his mind on the desert, the ragged hills, the dry arroyos of his homeland. Why, it was classic cattle country, and he even had black angus herds grazing a ranch to prove it.

Shahan told one executive producer's executive secretary: "You don't know me, but somebody in Hollywood is bound to be lookin' for a good location to make cowboy movies, and I've got one of the best, and I'm not goin' home until somebody listens to me."

She picked up the telephone and made a call. "Go to Paramount," she told him.

Nat Holt, a producer at Paramount, was, indeed, searching for the right location for "Arrowhead." He found it in

Lemon Garlic Turkey Tenders

1 tbsp grated lemon peel
1/2 cup lemon juice
2 cloves garlic, diced fine
1/4 cup cooking oil
1 tbsp soy sauce
6 (8 oz) Plantation Turkey
Tenderloins
1/2 cup Morrison's Peter Pan
All-Purpose Flour
2 tsp paprika
2 sheets heavy duty aluminum
foil 24" long

- Mix peel, juice, garlic, oil and soy sauce, marinade turkey tenders 3 hours or longer (overnight is ideal).
- Save marinade; coat turkey tenders with flour and paprika.
- Place 3 turkey tenders on each piece of foil, brush with marinade. Fold foil seal tightly.
- Bake 30 minutes at 350 degrees.
- Open foil, turn turkey tenders; brush again with marinde. Continue cooking 30 minutes longer at 300 degrees.
- Serves 6.

Ranger Luke's Open Pit Doves

12 Signature Foods of Texas
Doves or Quail
1 (5 oz) jar Shotgun Willie's®
Jalapeño Stuffed Olives
12 small onion slices
12 slices bacon
1 (16 oz) jar Ranger Luke's®
Fajita Marinade
1 cup Ste. Genevieve Texas
Red Wine
4 dashes Shotgun Willie's®
Hot Pepper Sauce
Pek O'Wood Mesquite
Wood Chunks
salt and pepper, to taste

- Cut a 3/4" slice just beside each bird's breast bone. Stuff each opening with 1/2 of a jalapeño stuffed olive and an onion slice.
- Wrap each bird with bacon and secure with a toothpick.
- Combine fajita marinade, red wine and hot pepper sauce.
- Place the birds in the marinade and let stand for 1 hour.
- Grill the birds over mesquite coals, while basting with the remaining marinade, for 45 minutes to an hour depending on the heat.
- Salt and pepper, to taste.
- Serves 4.

Brackettville, and he brought a few unknowns in '51 to the brasada: Charleston Heston, Brian Keith, and Jack Palance, and they all left behind enough money for Brackettville to catch its second wind. It was about time.

John Wayne was wanting to spend millions to make a blockbuster called "The Alamo," and he called Shahan from California.

"I need to rebuild San Antonio exactly the way it looked in 1836," he said, "who's gonna make 'em?"

Shahan grinned. "You're talkin' to him," he said.

The project lasted two years, and John Wayne got a city of 1,250,000 adobe bricks, made from mud that was dug out of Shahan's own ranch land.

To Alamo Village would come such major motion picture productions as "Two Rode Together," "Bandolero," "The Code of Josey Wales," and "Barbarosa," as well as hundreds of smaller films, documentaries, and commercials. Dean Martin was almost hanged beside the church. Raquel Welch fought valiantly for her chastity in one on the adobe buildings. And Jimmy Stewart and Richard Widmark woke up the prairie with gunfire. Alamo Village—with its daily shootouts on the street at high noon and country music down at the cantina—has since become one of Texas's destinations. And Producer Bob Jacks has called it the most authentic western set in America.

*T*he hills fade into a blue mist. The rivers thread the valleys. A lost stand of maples hides away in Sabinal Canyon. Indian pictographs paint the walls of Seminole Canyon. The thorns are softened by the beauty of the wildflowers that lie like a rich carpet around them. And all is well within the harsh, solemn land of cowboy boots and bratwurst.

South Texas

"I've always heard that there was a fortune in gold and silver hidden away in these dunes, but I've never seen any of it lying around on the beach. But that's all right. I've found the sun, and I've found the sea, and maybe that's all I was really looking for anyway."

——A beachcomber on the sands of Padre Island

$\mathcal{A}$s she looked across the restless, wind-battered dunes of Padre Island the day it finally became a national seashore, Lady Bird Johnson began to reminisce. "Lyndon and I used to walk the beach and feel a sense of timelessness that envelopes one like rolling waves," she said in her dedication speech.

"Someone once observed that wilderness is the miracle that man can tear apart but cannot reassemble. I have high hopes that this dizzying dome of sky and these white sands will be here in all their freshness to be savored year after year. For everyone has a thirst to leave their footprints on an untrammeled sand."

South Texas walks barefoot in the sand, its face turned toward a sun that seldom lets it down, its smile as carefree as the coastal winds that tease the tides at sundown. Its beaches have seen the fury of the sea and laughed in its face. It has borne the brunt of hurricanes and was still standing proudly on the water's edge long after the turbulence had passed on by. It is the land of the indomitable beachcomber who finances his life a sand dollar at a time, a country so big that the King Ranch is intertwined with enough fence wire to stretch all the way from Kingsville to Boston, a tropical world that is shaded by palm trees, a barren world that sometimes has no shade at all.

South Texas reaches down across the Rio Grande to embrace Mexico, dancing to a hard-driving flamenco beat that is as hot as the jalapenos on its nachos. At the tip of the Rio Grande Valley, the river of great water, as the Indians called it, finally completes its 1,248-mile long journey, one that begins in the mountain glaciers of Colorado and doesn't end until it touches the sea. Only an international bridge separates Eagle Pass from Piedras Negras, McAllen from Reynosa, Laredo from Nuevo Laredo, and Brownsville from Matamoros. The countries are so close, their lifestyles so different. North is north and south is south, and never the twain shall meet, not as long as the Rio Grande keeps on flowing, and it is always flowing, even when it is nothing but an embarrassed trickle in the mud. Across the border, great open air markets are lined with colorful pottery, leather goods, statuary, tapestries, paintings, and jewelry.

Until 1904, the Valley was a dry, bramble bush jungle of cactus and mesquite, shut off from the rest of civilization. There were no highways, of course, and not even a railroad dared venture across the forsaken land. But developers suddenly discovered a rich soil beneath their feet, and they began building irrigation systems, clearing the brushland, and bringing down wagonloads of Northern farmers who were searching for a climate that would produce crops year around.

They found what they wanted in a flat delta that would be known as the Magic Valley. Seeds began to grown as soon as they touched the ground, and its fields became green with vegetables, white with cotton. Sugar cane sprouted. And the landscape was crowned with 75,000 acres of commercial citrus trees, an industry of grapefruit, oranges, and lemons that is presently valued at more than $40 million a year.

Along the Gulf Coast—from Galveston to Rockport, from Corpus Christi to Port Isabel—charter boats leave the docks daily, combing the deep waters for, tarpon, tuna, red snapper, mackerel, and sailfish. The barracudas are mean. The marlin are huge, sometimes weighing as much as 250 pounds. Fishermen wade the bays, catching redfish, speckled trout,

Barbecue Fish Bake

6 Hillman Fish Fillets
oil
1 tsp salt
2 tbsp sweet vermouth
1 btl D.L. Jardine's® Margarita Bar-B-Q Sauce
½ cup minced celery, sauteed
¼ cup slivered Comanche Golden Almonds
¼ cup minced green onions, for garnish

- Place fish fillets in oiled baking dish and sprinkle with salt.
- In a bowl, mix wine, bar-b-q sauce, celery and almonds. Pour mixture over fish.
- Bake at 350 degrees for about 20 minutes, or until fish flakes.
- Garnish with onions.
- Serves 6.

Shrimp and Broccoli

1 lb medium shrimp, size 36-40
Baldy's™ All-Purpose Seasoning
1 bunch broccoli
¼ cup olive oil
4 cloves Fiesta Fresh Garlic, sliced
1 red bell pepper, sliced

- Peel and devein shrimp, pat dry and put into baggie.
- Sprinkle generously with seasoning and shake, tumble, or whatever it takes to cover shrimp with seasoning.
- Cut flowerettes off broccoli stem and place into pot. Cover broccoli with water and sprinkle with seasoning. Bring to a boil, lower heat and cook until tender, then pour into the colander and run cold water over broccoli to stop cooking.
- Pour oil and garlic into skillet. Place skillet on burner and cook garlic over low to medium heat. Cook until garlic is tender.
- Remove garlic and add red pepper; cook until pepper turns brown around the edges. Remove and save.
- Add shrimp to skillet. Cook until tender (shrimp turns pink).
- Reduce heat, add cooked pepper and broccoli, toss or stir in skillet until broccoli is warm.
- Serves 2-4.

Goliad's Presidio La Bahia bears the scars of Texas' fight for independence.

Cajun Lobster

4-6 *live lobsters*
1 *gal water*
½ btl Muzzy's Magic Cajun
Seafood Seasoning

- Select live lobsters.
- Boil water.
- Add seasoning.
- Add live lobsters.
- Cover; return to a boil. Boil 15 minutes.
- Remove pot from burner and allow lobsters to soak 5 minutes so seasoning can be absorbed.
- Drain and eat.
- Serves 4-6.

Cajun Shrimp

3 *doz fresh Hillman Shrimp*
1 *gal water*
½ btl Muzzy's Magic Cajun
Seafood Seasoning

- Shrimp, either headed or deheaded, should be washed in cool water before they are cooked.
- Boil water. Add seafood seasoning.
- Add shrimp, cover; return to boil. Boil shrimp for 4 minutes.
- Remove pot from burner and allow shrimp to soak 10 minutes so seasoning can be absorbed.
- Drain and eat.
- Serves 4-6.

Cajun Crab

1 *doz fresh Hillman Crabs*
1 *gal water*
½ btl Muzzy's Magic Cajun
Seafood Seasoning

- Boil water.
- Add seasoning.
- Add crabs. Cover the pot with a lid and wait for the water to return to a boil. Boil 15 minutes.
- Remove pot from burner and allow crabs to soak 20 minutes so that seasoning can be absorbed.
- Drain, but keep crabs in pot.
- Sprinkle seasoning over crab shells for that great Cajun flavor.
- Serves 4-6.

sand trout, flounder, and skipjack. And thick beneath the great sprawling waters of Falcon Lake are the elusive crappie, catfish, and largemouth bass.

The Queen Isabella Fishing Pier, linking Port Isabel to South Padre Island, arches for 5,844 feet over the restless waters of Laguna Madre Bay. Merton Wheeler had driven down from Missouri, and he said, "I come twice a year and fish every day the weather says I can." His reason was a simple one. In a single week, Wheeler had caught nineteen varieties of fish, weighing from one to forty pounds.

Dan Geffert, who operated the pier, told me, "This is a beautiful place by day. But under the lights at night, it's a whole 'nother world.

"Those lights draw the little bitty microscopic bugs. And they draw the larger bugs that draw the shrimp and minnows that draw the bigger fish such as flounder, speckled trout, and redfish. It's a vicious life cycle that sometimes brings as many as seven hundred fishermen crowding around those twenty-eight lights when the sun goes down. It gets pretty thick, but there's plenty of fish down there for all of 'em."

And most are disappointed, downright disgusted, if they go home at night without at least fifty or sixty pounds of fish in their tubs. Geffert had come out early that morning and found Clarence Miller sitting and casting at the exact spot where he had started fishing the afternoon before.

"You still here?" Geffert called.

"Yeah," Miller shouted. "By the time I got through fishing last night it was too late to go home, so I thought I might as well stay."

His decision was probably a wise one.

*A*cross the parched flatlands of South Texas, General Santa Anna came marching with his army to conquer the Texas rebels who kept demanding their independence from Mexico. His greatest victory lay behind him in the smoke-blackened ruins of the Alamo. Ahead lay the shame of Goliad.

Colonel James W. Fannin and his 342 men waited behind the thick stone walls of Presidio La Bahia, built in 1749 to

Cajun Crawfish

2-3 doz fresh Texas Crawfish
Farmers Crawfish
salted water
1 gal water
½ btl Muzzy's Magic Cajun
Seafood Seasoning

- Soak (purge) crawfish in a salt water solution for 15 minutes before cooking them.
- Drain and rinse them for 5 minutes in clear water.
- Boil water. Add seasoning.
- Add crawfish.
- Cover pot with lid and wait for the water to return to a boil. Boil 8 minutes.
- Remove pot from burner and allow crawfish to soak 15 minutes so seasonings can be absorbed.
- Drain and eat.
- Serves 4-6.

Cajun Fried Catfish

4 lbs Texas Tender
Catfish Fillets
1 tsp salt
2 tbsp Muzzy's Magic Cajun
Seafood Seasoning
½ cup Morrison's Peter Pan
All-Purpose Flour
½ cup Morrison's Stone Ground
Yellow Corn Meal
cooking oil

- Wash fish and cut fillets into 2″ strips. Place in large bowl.
- Add salt and seafood seasoning. Mix thoroughly with pieces of fish.
- Combine flour and cornmeal together and roll fish pieces in mixture.
- Fill a frying pan half full with cooking oil.
- Let the oil get hot without smoking.
- Fry the fish until golden.
- Serves 4-6.

protect the old mission Espirtu Santo, founded when proud Conquistadores trampled the soil for "God, Gold, and Glory," not particularly in that order. From the Alamo, Commander Travis had begged Goliad for reinforcements. Fannin refused. And, unlike Travis, Fannin would not hold out to the last man. He quickly weighed the odds, saw that they were heavily against him, and promptly surrendered to the Mexican forces. Santa Anna was not in a gratuitous mood at all. On Palm Sunday in 1836, Fannin was executed, and his men were led away from the presidio, crowded into the trees, and massacred.

Goliad's Presidio La Bahia has been faithfully restored by the Kathryn O'Connor Foundation and now serves as a museum of the Texas Revolution. A monument, a hundred yards away, marks the final resting place for Fannin and his men, guilty of trusting a Mexican general who could not be trusted.

*S*outh Texas had a hard life. Galveston toasted the good life. South Texas had sand in its pockets. Galveston had gold. South Texas was the outcast, Galveston the aristocrat. South Texas was blessed by the sea. Galveston was cursed.

Cowboys were battling the brasada, rounding up stray cows and driving them north to market, glad to have a job that kept beans in their belly, even if the cattleman ran out of money. Galveston was sipping French wine.

Galveston was holding fancy-dress balls in fancy $250,000 houses, calling itself the New York of the Gulf, obviously the largest and most important port city in Texas. Why, down upon the Strand, cotton barons ruled over a high-finance world of international shipping, and the sidewalks were crowded with traders and bankers and statesmen, and they were all doing business together. The waterfront commercial district had even become known as the Wall Street of the Southwest.

While the rest of Texas was carving out a niche of rough hewn civilization, Galveston was paving its streets with shell, and its businesses were already lit by gas. In time, the regal city by the sea had the state's first electric lights, first telephone, first hospital, first country club, and, of course, first golf course. Sarah Bernhardt performed on stage of the first opera house in

Picante Shrimp

1 jar Texas Duet Prairie Fire
Hot Sauce
1 can condensed tomato soup
1 lb shrimp, peeled
and deveined
1 stick Borden's Butter

- In saucepan, mix picante sauce and tomato soup, bring to a boil.
- Add shrimp and cook 3-5 minutes or until shrimp is pink. DO NOT OVERCOOK.
- At serving time, melt butter and pour over shrimp.
- Serves 2-4.

Grilled Catfish with Avocado Mayonnaise

6 Texas Tender Catfish Fillets

Marinade:
1 tbsp garlic, minced
2 tsp minced basil or cilantro
1 cup safflower oil

- Mix marinade and soak fillets for 1 hour.

- Remove fillets from marinade to hot greased grill.
- Grill for 4-5 minutes each side, being careful not to overcook.
- Salt and pepper lightly.
- Serve hot with avocado mayonnaise.
- Serves 6.

Avocado Mayonnaise

1 ripe avocado
1/2 tsp salt
1 tbsp lime juice
1 tsp minced basil
1/2 tsp minced garlic
1 tbsp Shadowfox Farms
Herbal Vinegar
1 tsp Dijon mustard
3 eggs yolks
remaining marinade (strain
basil and garlic from oil and
cool oil in pan)

- Puree avocado, salt and lime

juice in food processor.
- In saucepan, simmer basil and garlic in vinegar until almost completely evaporated.
- Add remains of pan to blender with mustard and egg yolks. Blend until smooth and, with motor running, add remaining oil from marinade. Blend until creamy and thick.
- Then add avocado mixture to blender and blend.
- Keep warm in top of double boiler.

Texas. And Galveston's Tremont Hotel was being described as the most luxurious place to spend the night between New Orleans and San Francisco. The island's stores sold French China, English carpets, and rosewood pianos.

The wealthy, the noble aristocrats, built fine three-story Greek Revival homes with turrets and spires, balustrades, and columns crowned with the carved heads of rulers from Europe. Ashton Villa, an Italianate Villa, was the glittering social center for Galveston. It has been elegantly restored and is open for tours. So is the Bishop's Palace, once the home of Col. Walter Gresham, who spent a quarter of million dollars to build what he called the most elaborate house in Texas. He had master designer Nicholas Clayton incorporate the entire history of architecture into the massive red sandstone and Texas granite structure. The home, now valued at more than five million dollars, has touches of Italian Romanesque and French Renaissance styles, wrapped with iron balconies and encircled with towers and turrets and chimneys that reach unabashedly for the sky. Inside are a crystal chandelier from Venice, damask wall coverings from London, and a marble fireplace from Italy. The mantle in the front ballroom won first prize at the Philadelphia World's Fair in 1876.

But, alas, Galveston had anchored itself insecurely to a fragile sandbar, and it sat naked before the sea. On a grim September day in 1900, a hurricane, a sudden, unexpected force of nature, stormed ashore, leaving Galveston buried in its own ruin.

From the rubble, from the mud, from the tides, Galveston slowly began to rebuild itself, still as beautiful, but never again as prosperous as before. The East End, silk stocking row, is a historical district, a wrought-iron reminder of Galveston's "Gilded Age." The Grand Strand has the country's largest collection of restored iron-front Victorian commercial buildings. It has been restored with more than seventy shops, art galleries, boutiques, restaurants, nightclubs, museums, and theaters. And its menus reflect the dockside heritage of Galveston: black lumpfish, icelandic caviar, smoked baby clams, and escargots au natural. The Grand Opera House, an opulent keepsake from 1894, hosted such celebrities as Lillian Russell, Anna Pavlova,

Vegetables

Pasta with Yellow Squash, Sun-Dried Tomatoes and Fresh Ricotta

2 lbs yellow squash, sliced
1 small onion, sliced
1 clove garlic, minced
¼ cup extra virgin olive oil
¼-½ lb sun-dried tomatoes,
sliced into strips
1 lb dried pasta
water and salt to cook pasta
1 lb Mozzarella Company Fresh
Dallas Ricotta
Small bunch Rosehill Culinary
Herbs Fresh Basil Leaves
¼ lb Mozzarella Company
Montasio, grated

- Saute squash with onion and garlic in olive oil until slightly limp.
- Cut tomatoes into narrow strips.
- Cook pasta in rapidly boiling, salted water until al dente and drain.
- Toss pasta with ricotta, then add vegetables, tomatoes and fresh basil leaves, and toss briefly.
- Sprinkle with grated Montasio. Toss again briefly.
- Serves 4-6.

Risotto Alla Milanese

2-3 cups Take Stock Brown Veal Stock
2 cups water
1 onion, diced
4 tbsp butter, melted
1 generous cup Italian Arborio Rice
1 cup Ste. Genevieve Chardonnay or Chenin Blanc Wine
¹/₄ tsp saffron
1 cup freshly grated Parmesan cheese

- Simmer brown veal stock in water, and keep on low heat.
- Saute onion in melted butter.
- Add rice and stir to coat grains.
- Add white wine and saffron. Cook over medium-high heat (do not boil!) until rice absorbs the wine.
- Then, 1 cup at a time, add brown veal stock with water to rice. Allow each cup to absorb before adding next. When ready, the risotto will be thick and loosely creamy.
- Stir in ¹/₂ cup Parmesan cheese before serving. Pass remaining cheese. Serve immediately.
- Serves 4-6.

Galveston's Historical District mirrors the grandeur of another era.

Green Rice

¼ cup Hygeia Butter
½ cup chopped onions
1 (15 oz) can Popeye or
Sunshine Chopped Spinach,
drained
1 cup cooked Doguet Extra
Fancy Fine Rice
¾ (3 oz) cup grated sharp
Cheddar cheese
1 (10¾ oz) can condensed cream
of mushroom soup, undiluted
¼ cup Hygeia Milk
⅛ tsp pepper
2 tbsp grated Parmesan cheese

- Preheat oven to 325 degrees.
- Melt butter in small skillet over medium-high heat.
- Add onions and saute 5 minutes until tender; set aside.
- Squeeze spinach dry. Combine spinach, onions, rice and Cheddar cheese in medium bowl.
- Add soup, milk and pepper, and stir until well combined.
- Spoon into 1½ qt casserole. Sprinkle with Parmesan cheese.
- Bake 30 minutes until set.
- Serves 4.

Oriental Vegetables and Rice

2 tsp sesame oil
1 tsp vegetable oil
1 (16 oz) pkg frozen broccoli, red
sweet peppers, bamboo shoots
and straw mushrooms
2 cups cooked Elco or Island
Girl Brand Rice
reduced-sodium soy sauce

- Heat oils in large skillet over medium-high heat.
- Add vegetables; stir-fry several minutes.
- Add rice and 1 tbsp soy sauce; cook and stir until rice is heated, gently separating grains.
- Serve with additional soy sauce, if desired.
- Serves 4.

and William Jennings Bryan. A survivor of those days—when Galveston was a bastion of culture and commerce—is the Elissa, meticulously restored and berthed at Pier 21. The Elissa called on Galveston from her home port in Liverpool, loading up with cotton, before dueling the oceans on her way back to Britain. She has been called "the finest example of Victorian naval architecture in existence."

Galveston is serious about maintaining the city's link with a gulf that brought both wealth and destruction. At Seawolf Park, you can scramble around the U. S. S. Cavalla, one of World War II's most distinguished submarines, a combat veteran that battled the Japanese Navy, sending one destroyer, two freighters, and the mighty aircraft carrier Shokaku to the graveyard of the Pacific. Nearby, also open for tours, is the U. S. S. Stewart, which served under the flags of two nations. She was a rugged U. S. destroyer escort that the Navy frantically tried to scuttle when it became apparent that she could no longer outrun the ships of Hirohito. The Japanese refloated the Stewart and sent her back into the heat of battle. Throughout the war, the Navy kept getting strange, uneasy reports about an enemy ship "that looks a lot like one of ours." At long last, the Stewart has come home again.

Galveston has always found ways to showcase its beaches. As early as the twenties, the city was holding contests for bathing beauties down on the seashore, promoting them proudly as an International Pageant of Pulchritude. Beauties still catch the sun that tans its beaches. At the west end of the ten-mile seawall, built to hold back the waves when an ocean grows angry, is SeaArama Marineworld, home of thousands of exotic and aquatic animals. The daily shows and attractions feature a killer whale, an elephant seal, porpoises, penguins, sea lions, sharks, sea turtles, and hundreds of species of fish, all in their natural setting. There is even a trained bear, a piano-playing kangaroo, a snake and alligator show, and precision skiers who perform a water ballet that sometimes makes you laugh and often takes your breath away.

Galveston's Victorian depot harkens back to the golden era of railroading, especially when the palatial Anacapa, once described as "the most elegant private car on the rails,"

Rice Cornbread Bake

1 cup Lamb's Stone Ground Mill Yellow or White Cornmeal
½ tsp salt
½ tsp baking soda
2 cups cooked Texmati Rice, white or brown
1 cup Gandy's Low Fat Milk
1 (8¾ oz) can cream-style corn
2 Pilgrim's Pride Eggs, beaten
½ cup chopped onion
2 tbsp finely chopped Galante Jalapeño Pepper
1 tbsp vegetable oil
¾ cup shredded Monterey Jack cheese

- Combine cornmeal, salt and soda in bowl, stirring well.
- Add remaining ingredients except cheese.
- Pour into 12"x8"x2" baking pan that has been coated with cooking spray.
- Bake at 350 degrees for 45 minutes or until lightly browned.
- Sprinkle cheese on top, and return to oven until cheese melts.
- Serves 8-10.

Curried Rice Stuffing

1½ cups precooked rice
1½ cups Dr Pepper
½ tsp curry powder
½ cup chopped Sunshine Country Pecans or Almonds
2 tbsp butter

- Cook rice according to package directions except substitute Dr Pepper for the water.
- Add curry powder to the Dr Pepper before cooking.
- Toast nuts in butter and add to cooked rice, mixing lightly.
- Use as stuffing for game or fowl, or serve separately with game or fowl.
- Makes 4-5 servings or stuffings for 1 roasting chicken.

occupies its historic track. A five-acre museum, a Center for Transportation and Commerce, surrounds the ten-story Art Deco Santa Fe Union Station, a landmark that ties Galveston to those days when it tried to stockpile all the wealth of Texas on a single, scimitar of sand.

The years of hardship, when pirate Jean Lafitte, the most cursed name on the sea, tormented unsuspecting ships, stealing their gold and bringing it back to the beaches of Galveston, is vividly recaptured in Paul Green's stirring outdoor drama, "Lone Star."

*F*or Corpus Christi, the good life came late, but it came just in time. In 1913, someone noted that Corpus was nothing more than "an ill-lighted, poorly served, sandy and run-down tourist resort," whose frontier soldiers once fired kegs of bourbon from their cannons when they ran out of shells.

But times changed. And they changed in a hurry.

Later that year, a wildcatter's drill bore far beneath a farmer's plowed field and tore into a petroleum pocket that bathed Corpus in black crude, turning it virtually overnight into a booming port city.

Although oil brought new life to the resort city, few visitors ever pay close attention to the petroleum industry. Corpus Christi was careful to see that nothing, not even oil, would taint or destroy the beauty of its natural environment. Even as hopeful fishermen wade into the shallow waters of Laguna Madred Bay, they remain unaware that beneath them are gas and oil reserves valued at almost $100 million.

With this financial foundation deep in the ground, the city could afford to go first class. And it has. In 1967, the patrons of the Art Museum of South Texas decided a new edifice was needed to house its treasures. Someone suggested that world-renowned architect Philip Johnson might be just the man to design it. After all, Johnson was known as "the man who builds monuments." So board member Patsy Singer approached the New Yorker. Johnson was interested, he said, but very busy, too busy to worry about devoting any of his precious time to some

Stir-Fry Brown Rice

6 slices Farm Pac Brand Bacon,
chopped
½ cup chopped onions
1½ lbs Signature Foods of
Texas Natural Chicken, boned
and skinned cut
1 (4 oz) can sliced mushrooms,
drained
1 cup snow peas
3 cups cooked Texmati
Brown Rice
¼ cup pimentos, diced
1 tsp salt
1 tsp pepper
1 tbsp soy sauce

- In large skillet, fry bacon and onions until transparent.
- Add chicken and cook 5-10 minutes until chicken is slightly browned.
- Stir in remaining ingredients. Heat thoroughly.
- Serves 6.

Spanish Rice

½ cup water
1½ cups tomato juice
1 tbsp Texas Fun Feed South of
the Border Dip Mix Seasoning
½ tsp Texas Fun Feed Red Chili
Pepper Dip Mix Seasoning
1 cup Comet Long Grain Rice
1 tbsp butter

- Put water and tomato juice in a large sauce pan.
- Add seasonings, rice and butter to liquid.
- Cook over low heat covered with a lid for 18-20 minutes.
- Stir gently before serving.
- Serves 4.

little museum down on the gulf coast. He knew how to get rid of the lady from South Texas. He looked up from his work-cluttered desk, so the story is told, and snapped, "Come back when you have a million dollars."

Less than three months later, Patsy Singer marched into Johnson's office, placed a check for one million dollars on his work-cluttered desk, and replied, "When can you start?"

After Johnson designed the Art Museum of South Texas, he called it, "the most exciting building I have ever done." It stands starkly in the curve of the bay, looking like a white contemporary sculpture, carved with simplicity, elegance, and purity. Its windows, like paintings come to life, frame the sky, the sea, the boats that fade in and out of the distance.

Bathed by the tides of the gulf, nourished by the profits from oil, Corpus Christi has learned to take life in carefree stride. Its downtown business district is anchored solidly to a modern marina, to a broad, winding boulevard lined with towering palms and aristocratic mansions. From waterfront piers, sport fishermen can hire party boats, while others catch the warm breezes with a sail boat, and the daring duel Laguna Madre bay astride jet boats. Some prefer to explore the historic coast by showboat, aboard the paddlewheeler **Flagship** or **Gulf Clipper**, water ski on calm, yet tricky, bay waters, meet the shrimp boats coming home to port, or simply toss popcorn to sea gulls that play in the gentle skies above the city.

Corpus boasts the largest Japanese art collection ever shipped to America, thanks to the efforts of Billie Trimble Chandler. She marched unafraid down the lonely roads of both Corregidor and Bataan. There was a time when she worshipped as the only woman among ten thousand Mohammedans in Kashmir. And she traveled 7,500 miles, sleeping in a different Shinto and Buddhist temple every night, just so she could fully learn and understand the religions of Japan. And the fascinating Museum of Oriental Cultures, with its paintings, sculpture, furniture, and handcrafted Hakata dolls, is her legacy.

Corpus has a healthy cultural climate—a professional symphony orchestra, a community theater, ballet performances, and the wild, frenzied sounds of the Texas Jazz Festival. Beto

Double-Baked Potatoes

2 large rather flat
baking potatoes
¹/₂ tsp salt
2 cups (16 oz) Daisy Brand
Sour Cream
dash of paprika
¹/₂ cup shredded
Cheddar cheese

- Wash and dry potatoes.
- Bake in preheated 450 degree oven for 45 minutes, or until soft.
- Remove from oven and allow to cool enough to handle.
- Cut potatoes in half lengthwise. Scoop out potatoes from skins very carefully to keep from tearing potato skins.
- Mash potatoes well and add salt. Mix sour cream into potatoes until potatoes are light and fluffy.
- Spoon potato mixture into the 4 potato skins and place filled potato skins on cookie sheet or in a shallow pan.
- Sprinkle on paprika, then add cheese on top as desired. Bake in preheated 350 degree oven 45 minutes until lightly browned.
- Serves 4.

Chili Stuffed Potatoes

4 large baking potatoes
1 (15 oz) can Wolf® Brand Chili
1 cup shredded Colby or
Cheddar cheese
1 cup Sealtest Sour Cream
4 green onions, chopped

- Bake or microwave potatoes.
- Heat chili over medium heat.
- Slice open hot potatoes and fluff with fork.
- Top potatoes with chili, cheese, sour cream and green onions.
- Serves 4.

The Gulf of Mexico sweeps past a line of catamarans and onto the shoreline of Corpus Christi.

Candied Sweet Potatoes

2 lbs sweet potatoes
(about 4 medium potatoes)
1 cup Dr Pepper
3/4 cup Imperial Granulated
Sugar
1/4 cup Vandervoort's Butter
1/2 tsp salt

- Parboil potatoes 10 minutes. Place in cold water for 5-10 minutes. Remove from water, peel and slice crosswise into casserole.
- Combine Dr Pepper, sugar, butter and salt.
- Bring to boil. Boil 10 minutes.
- Pour over potatoes.
- Bake at 375 degrees about 45 minutes.
- Baste potatoes several times with syrup as potatoes bake.
- Serves 6.

J-B Baked Beans

1 (31 oz) can pork and beans
1/2 lb or more J-B Sausage, sliced
1/3 cup chopped onion
1/4 cup brown sugar
1 tbsp prepared mustard
1 tsp Worcestershire sauce
1/8 tsp hot pepper sauce

- Heat oven to 350 degrees.
- In 1 1/2 qt lightly greased casserole, combine all ingredients.
- Bake 40 minutes.
- Serves 4-6.

Garcia, the genius behind the festival told me, "We blow the same hot jazz here as they do on the West Coast, and then the rhythm men throw in a Latin beat. And, man, before you know it, you got yourself a whole new brand of music." So you do.

Heritage Park allows the city on the bay to gracefully step back architecturally and historically to its growing up years. White picket fences and old-fashioned street lamps light the brick pathways that wander through a rare collection of old homes, saved from destruction by the heroic efforts of the Junior League of Corpus Christi.

First and, perhaps, foremost, is the gracious house built by Charlotte Scott Sidbury. She was not typical of the Texas women who were supposed to be seen and not heard back in the strict, straight-laced Victorian era of the 1880s. She was tough and assertive. She broke traditions. She spent more time in the boardroom of her businesses than in her kitchen. Charlotte Sidbury was, indeed, a woman far ahead of her time.

The project to preserve Corpus Christi's heritage began with the restoration of the Sidbury House in 1975. It was the last example of high-Victorian architecture left in the city, wrapped by lavish gingerbread-trimmed galleries.

Since then, more than three million dollars have been invested in six other pastel-colored homes that are clustered together on four acres of the city's Old Irishtown, just north of the Bayfront Arts and Science Park. They include the Lichtenstein House, a Colonial Revival residence with an elliptical porch; the Galvan House, tucked inside a walled courtyard; the Guggenheim House, trimmed with gingerbread and lattice work; the Grande-Grossman House; and the Greek Revival Merriman-Bobys home, built in 1851, one that served as a hospital during the War Between the States.

*B*eyond, toward the sunrise, stretches the longest barrier island in the United States—the legendary Padre, beautiful in its austere isolation, haunted by the secrets that it silently keeps to itself. It bends raggedly for 113 miles around the Texas coastline, a long ladyfinger of sand whose dunes have been carved and sculptured and made restless by the gulf breezes—

Quick and Easy Baked Beans

1 (16 oz) can pork and beans
½ cup Hill Country Farms
Special Gourmet Sauce
¼ cup chopped onion
¼ cup chopped bell pepper
2-3 drops Hill Country Liquid
Mesquite Smoke
2 strips Cap Ranch Bacon

- Drain beans.
- Place all ingredients, except bacon, in oven-proof dish (one you can serve from); blend well.
- Place bacon strips across top.
- Bake 45 minutes to 1 hour in preheated 300 degree oven.
- Serves 6-8.

Texas Caviar

1 lb blackeyed peas
2 slices Cap Ranch Smoked
Pepper Bacon
salt, to taste
¼-½ jar Carole's Green
Tomato Relish

- Cook peas as directed, seasoning with bacon and salt.
- When peas are cooked, remove from heat, drain and spoon green tomato relish on top.

Tenderfoot Jalapeño Hominy

¼ cup Borden's Margarine
3 tbsp process cheese spread
¼ cup White Wings Flour
1 cup Superior Milk
2 (15 oz) cans hominy
1 tsp Baldy's™ Original Seasoning
1 tsp Worcestershire sauce
2 tbsp sliced pimentos
1 tsp Texas Fun Feed
Tenderfood Jalapeño Dip Mix

- In a saucepan, melt margarine and process cheese spread.
- Slowly add flour and milk.
- Drain hominy; add to mixture.
- Add seasoning, Worcestershire sauce, pimentos and dip mix.
- Pour into 1½ qt baking dish and bake at 350 degrees for 30 minutes or until thick.
- Serves 6-8.

shaped, molded, then ultimately destroyed by the unpredictable whims of an angry sea wind.

Ghost crabs scurry along the beaches. Jackrabbits and coyotes hide back behind the protection of the sea oats that barricade the dunes. And the white pelicans, herons, snowy egrets, rare sooty terns, and laughing gulls hover like tiny sailplanes above a land called "civilization's last outpost."

Five miles on the northern edge and five miles on the southern tip of Padre have been developed with fine hotels and condominiums that brag about their golf and tennis. But eighty miles have been set aside as a National Seashore, a place where mankind can, indeed, leave his footprints on an untrammeled sand. The beaches hold the spoils and salvage of centuries. Seashells—sharp eyes, sea pansies, baby's foot, angel's wings, and periwinkles—are thrown aside by the tides, along with driftwood, sculpted during their long journey to shore.

When the winds blow just right, and the tide is in an amiable mood, the sands of Padre sometimes do give forth their secrets. For hidden beneath those majestic mounds is a scrap heap of the damned. Ships died off Padre's coastline. Seamen vanished. Gold and lives were lost. The sea claimed them both. But on rare occasions, it gives back a fragment of gold.

A woman in the 1930s was scraping away dune sands with a broken seashell, and she dug out a small gold casket crammed with precious gems and old-fashioned jewelry. Hurricane Carla spit its wrath and fury on the slender, fragile isle of Padre, tearing open forgotten hiding places. And many a beachcomber was seen trotting amidst the sea oats, filling buckets with scattered Spanish coins.

The island is quiet and full of peace, a sanctuary whose dunes are landmarks that can neither be still nor trusted, monuments that lead you on, then mislead you to places you have never walked before. Jean Lafitte left the ashes of bonfires that lured wayward ships at night onto shallow sandbars to be wrecked and looted. He also left a treasure beneath a millstone that bore the inscription: "Dig Deeper." Nobody has. They are all still looking for the millstone.

Castaway John Singer, brother of the sewing machine inventor, was so taken by Padre that he started a cattle ranch

Athens Marinated Blackeyed Peas

2 (15 oz) cans East Texas Fair
Fresh Shelled Blackeyed Peas
1/2 cup chopped onion
1/2 cup chopped bell peppers
1/2 clove Fiesta Garlic, chopped
1/4 cup cider vinegar
1/4 cup Imperial Granulated
Sugar
1/2 cup vegetable oil
1/2 tsp salt
hot pepper sauce, to taste

- Drain blackeyed peas in colander.
- Combine onion, bell pepper and peas.
- Mix remaining ingredients together and pour over pea mixture.
- Cover and refrigerate overnight.
- Will keep in refrigerator up to 2 weeks.
- Makes about 5 cups.

Pecan Croquettes

1 tbsp minced onion
1 tbsp chopped green pepper
2 tbsp shortening
3 cups unseasoned mashed
potatoes
2 cups Comanche Golden Pecan
Pieces
1 tbsp chopped parsley
1 egg, beaten
1 tsp salt
1/8 tsp pepper
1/2 tsp Worcestershire sauce
1 egg
1 tbsp water
fine dry bread crumbs

- Saute onion, green pepper and shortening over medium heat for 5 minutes.
- Add mashed potatoes, pecans, parsley, 1 beaten egg, salt, pepper, Worcestershire sauce to vegetables and shape into croquettes.
- Beat together 1 egg and water.
- Roll croquettes in fine bread crumbs.
- Dip in egg mixture, then roll in crumbs again. Let stand 10 minutes to form slight crust.
- Fry in deep hot fat (375-400 degrees) until golden brown.
- Serve hot with mushroom or cheese sauce, if desired.
- Makes 16 croquettes.

on the island after he was shipwrecked there prior to the War Between the States. When Union troops overran the island and drove him from his home, Singer stuffed the $85,000 family fortune in a screw-top jar and buried it beneath the ever shifting dunes. Singer was too clever for his own good. Not only did he foil the Union soldiers, he stumped himself as well. He never found the money, and neither has anyone else.

In the year of our Lord 1553, a fleet of twenty Spanish galleons, laden with stolen Aztec gold and silver, sailed away from Veracruz, Mexico, and insanely into the growling throat of a Gulf-fueled hurricane. The storm, a raging churn, pulled the boats apart and scattered eight hundred people, as well as fifty million dollars in misbegotten gold and silver upon Padre.

Only two would survive. One, a priest, trekked the Sahara-like sands back to Mexico and safety. The other hid for months among the dunes and waited for help, watching while the Karankawa Indians, described as "tatooed ghouls reeking with alligator grease, mud, and shark oil," killed the others.

The King's soldiers came with help, not for him, but for the gold and silver stolen by the storm. Some was recovered. No one really knows just how much. Records only reveal that the King was sorely and "bitterly disappointed" with the amount that finally reached him and his vaults.

*C*aptain Richard King found his fortune in an empty land that vaqueros swore "Dios gave to the devil." To them, it was the Desert of the Dead. To King, the brittle grasses would be his home, his ranch, stretching further than the eye could see from the banks of Santa Gertrudis Creek, a desolate country that demanded he journey for 124 miles before even finding another flowing stream.

Capt. King slowly began buying up land for less than two cents an acre and building a herd. He rode throughout northern Mexico, buying cattle, usually thin and starving. He believed that the grasses of the Santa Gertrudis would fatten them up again. In the dry, hot hills of Tamaulipas, the elders of a little village offered their herd for sale simply because the cattle were dying, and there was nothing left in the desert to feed them.

Creamy Baked Vegetables

1 cup (8 oz) DaisyLight Light
Sour Cream or Daisy Brand
Sour Cream
1 tbsp dry onion soup mix
1 (16 oz) pkg frozen vegetables,
cooked and drained
(peas, spinach, broccoli,
asparagus or carrots*)
grated cheese or bread crumbs

- Mix sour cream and onion soup mix together.
- Fold sour cream mixture into vegetables and simmer on range, or bake in a 350 degree oven for 25 minutes.
- Top with grated cheese or bread crumbs.
- Serves 6.

*Substitute 1 tbsp brown sugar for onion soup mix if preparing carrots.

Vegetables with Jalapeño Mustard Sauce

1 lb vegetables (preferably fresh
broccoli, asparagus, green
beans, brussel sprouts,
cauliflower)
½ medium onion, chopped
½ stick Borden's Butter
or Margarine
¼ cup Texas Pride
Jalapeño Mustard

- Microwave or boil vegetables until tender.
- Saute onion in butter until tender (if Yankee) or crispy (if Texan).
- To onion, stir in jalapeño mustard quickly and remove from heat.
- Pour over vegetables and serve hot.
- Serves 4-6.

Palm trees silhouetted in sunset are a memorable symbol of the Lower Rio Grande Valley.

Desserts

Texas Traditional Pecan Pie

3 tbsp Borden's Butter
1 tsp vanilla
¾ cup Imperial Granulated Sugar
3 Fenton's Eggs, well beaten
½ cup Great San Saba River Pecan Pieces
1 cup dark corn syrup
⅛ tsp salt
¾ cup Great San Saba River Pecan Halves
1 (9") pie crust shell, unbaked

- Cream butter with vanilla, gradually adding sugar.
- Add eggs in thirds, creaming well after each addition.
- Thoroughly blend in pecan pieces along with syrup and salt.
- Turn into unbaked pastry shell.
- Bake at 450 degrees for 10 minutes; then reduce heat to 350 degrees.
- Arrange pecan halves to cover top of filling. Continue baking 30-35 mintues until set. Cool before serving.
- Serves 6-8.

King sadly looked into the famished faces of the townspeople and realized that when the last herd was gone, the hamlet would no longer be able to sustain itself. It, too, would die. If the villagers followed him back to Texa, King said, they could have a home, a job, and earn regular wages paid in cash. Down the road the ragged prossession came, men and cattle, wagons and burros, dogs and chickens, women and children, walking and squalling in the heat, choking in the dust, barefoot and bareheaded, an abandoned life behind them, a new one somewhere ahead in a strange land, promised by the Senor Capitan, the patron. They became the Kinenos, King's men, and their roots would be buried as deeply in the soil as his. Together, they would build the great King Ranch.

A twelve-mile loop, open to visitors, winds through the thick grasslands and mesquite thickets of the Santa Gertrudis division, just outside of Kingsville. It is a vital part of the ranch that sprawls for 825,000 acres across South Texas. Two thousand miles of fence hold together 60,000 cattle and 1,200 horses. Cotton covers 37,400 acres. And 2,730 oil and gas wells rise up alongside 350 windmills.

*F*or more than a century, the Port Isabel Lighthouse has stood in the brisk winds that sweep the Texas coast. It once guided ships through Brazos Santiago Pass as they crossed to Point Isabel, then headed up the Rio Grand to Fort Brown and Fort Ringgold. During the War Between the States, Confederates and Union forces both used the lighthouse as an observation post, waiting for a war that should not have come at all. News traveled slowly in May of 1865, too slow to stop the dying on the fields of Palmito Hill Ranch, near Brownsville. Confederates routed their Federal adversaries, only to discover that, a month earlier, General Robert E. Lee had surrendered at Appomattox. They were not victors after all. The Rebels became prisoners of the forces they had just defeated.

The old lighthouse is open daily, and you can climb the winding stairway to an observation deck atop the tower for a view of a flat, barren land that is a part of two nations.

At Isla Blanca Park, on the tip of South Padre, Pan American University's Marine Biology Laboratory harbors

Aunt Muriel's Pecan Pie

2 Pilgrim's Pride Eggs
3/4 cup milk or water
1 (10 oz) pkg Aunt Muriel's
Pecan Pie Mix
1 (9") pie crust shell, unbaked

- Blend eggs with milk or water.
- Add pie mix. Stir briefly.
- Pour into unbaked pie shell and bake at 350 degrees for 45-50 minutes.
- Cool before cutting.
- Serves 6-8.

Texas Twister Pie

1 (12 oz) ctn soft cream cheese
1 env unflavored gelatin
1 pkg Texas Topper Mix
1 (8 oz) ctn non-dairy whipped
topping
1 graham cracker pie shell

- Beat cream cheese with a mixer until smooth, add gelatin and package of topper mix; blend well.
- Stir in whipped topping.
- Put in pie shell and chill 4-6 hours or until pie is set.
- Serves 6-8.

Easy Chewy Pecan Squares

1 1/4 cups Pioneer Biscuit
and Baking Mix
3 Twin Rivers Eggs
1 1/2 cups firmly packed
brown sugar
3/4 cup chopped Sunshine
Country Pecans
powdered sugar to sprinkle
on top

- Preheat oven to 350 degrees. Grease a 9"x13" baking pan.
- Blend all ingredients until just moistened.
- Spread mixture into prepared pan.
- Bake 20-25 minutes. Cool. Cut into squares and sprinkle with powdered sugar.
- Makes 24 (2") squares.

exhibits of such creatures as electric rays, sea catfish, sea urchins, sea turtles, and crabs, all pulled from the waters of the nearby gulf. Beyond the causeway, Brownsville is always abloom with bougainvillea and poinciana. Palms and banana trees line its streets. And more than 1,500 mammals, birds, and reptiles from Tropical America, Indo-Australia, Asia, and Africa prowl a natural habitat in an unspoiled environment at the Gladys Porter Zoo, created because Mrs. Porter was deeply concerned about the abundance of wildlife that was vanishing around the globe. Elephants, big cats, gorillas, and rhinos get along in the South Texas tropics just fine. And so many endangered species have found a home in Brownsville, the zoo is often referred to as a survival center for the wild.

*T*he skies can be just as wild.

On a blistering summer day in 1957, Lloyd Nolen, a Texas crop duster, swaggered into Litchfield Park Naval Air Station, near Avondale, Arizona, to bid on an old F8F Bearcat, a naval fighter plane that spread death amid the turbulent clouds of World War II. The Bearcat had been declared surplus and put up for auction, and Nolen thought he just might go home with a good deal. After all, he had already bought a P-40 Warhawk, and he felt a deep affection and admiration for the old relics that had flown so defiantly, so proudly across war-torn skies.

At Litchfield, he grew numb, then angry. Dozens of vintage aircraft—fighters, bombers, patrol planes, trainers—were all being stripped, chopped up by bulldozers, and shoved into a huge smelter. The military was doing what the enemy had not been able to do: destroy the very planes that had so faithfully defended their homeland. They deserved a better fate.

"It's a disgrace, a waste, an affront to history," Nolen said to anyone who would listen to him. A few former Navy and Air Force pilots did. And they got mad, too.

They discovered that very few aircraft from World War II remained intact. The P-47 Thunderbolt was already gone. Of the 15,000 "jugs" built, none were in flying condition. F4F Wildcats, P-40 Warhawks, and P-39 Airacobras were facing the threat of extinction. From Nolen's anger, his dispair, his frustration was

Devilish Honey-Pecan Pie

1½ cups coarsely chopped Southern Gourmet Pecans
1 (6 oz) pkg chocolate chips
1 (9") pie shell, unbaked
3 large Jake's Finer Eggs
1 cup Burleson's Honey
½ tsp vanilla
¼ cup (½ stick) Vandervoort's Butter, melted and cooled

- Sprinkle pecans and chips over bottom of pie shell.
- In medium bowl, whisk together eggs, honey and vanilla.
- Blend in butter and pour mixture into pie shell.
- Bake at 325 degrees 50-60 minutes or until firm.
- Serve slightly warm or at room temperature.
- Serves 6-8.

Mighty Oatie Cake

1½ cups boiling water
1 cup rolled oats
1 cup Sealtest Skim Milk
2 tsp "Adams Best" Vanilla
4 egg whites
½ cup margarine
1 pkg Mighty Muffin Mix

- Mix boiling water with rolled oats and let stand 10 minutes.
- Blend next 5 ingredients; add to oats mixture.
- Add muffin mix; blend until moist.
- Pour into a 9"x13" greased pan.
- Bake 35-40 minutes at 350.
- Makes 20-24 servings.

Honey Cheese Cake

1 (3 oz) pkg lemon gelatin
½ cup boiling water
8 oz cream cheese
½ cup Lone Star Honey
2 tsp lemon juice
1 tsp "Adams Best" Vanilla
1½ cups evaporated milk, chilled
1 (9") graham cracker pie shell

- Mix gelatin with boiling water. Cool. Do not let set.
- Mix cream cheese with honey, lemon juice and vanilla.
- Whip chilled milk. Fold into cream cheese mixture.
- Pour into pie shell.
- Serves 6-8.

birthed the Confederate Air Force, now headquartered in Harlingen. He and a group of battle-scarred pilots became rebels, all right. They were rebelling against the wanton destruction of aircraft that, by every right, should be preserved, not lost forever.

First, they purchased a P-51 Mustang. It was as good a place as any to start. After all, the Mustangs had knocked more than ten thousand enemy planes out of the sky. They learned that a P-47 Thunderbolt could be bought down in the jungles of Nicaragua for eight grand, and a B-17 Flying Fortress carried a Central American price tag of $30,000. It was barely flyable, but it just might be the last one able to get off the ground at all. Their mission may have been impossible, but it had been launched anyway.

The Confederate Colonels have raised a million dollars to buy and fully restore nearly sixty planes, now graced in combat colors and on display at Harlingen's Rebel Field. In essence, the rebel pilots had one stated mission: "the spirit in which these great planes were flown for the defense of our Nation." In South Texas skies, the mission is being completed. But the quest never ends.

*T*he growling engine of a Flying Fortress never misses a beat as it circles Brownsville and banks slowly to the east. Its bomb bays are empty. There are no more wars to fight. The skies are empty and as peaceful as the shafts of sunlight that knife across blue gulf waters, turning purple in the late shadows of afternoon.

Below us, the unspoiled dunes of Padre Island are losing their battle with a restless, reckless wind. A windmill catches the wind. An oil well stands silent. A lighthouse stands guard. And a beach guards its secrets. Cattle run wild amidst the cat claw and mesquite of the Desert of the Dead. Mexico beckons from afar. Corpus Christi keeps its eye on the bay. And Galveston keeps its eye on the past. Both cities revel in what they see. And all is well in a land that walks with the beachcomber and leaves its footprints on an untrammeled sand.

Power Oat Bran Brownies

½ cup low-calorie margarine
½ cup Imperial Light Brown Sugar
2 egg whites (or 1 egg)
1 tsp "Adams Best" Vanilla
1½ cups John Chambers' Power Pancake Mix
1 (6 oz) pkg chocolate chips

- Blend margarine, sugar, egg whites, and vanilla until fluffy.
- Add in pancake mix.
- Stir in ½ cup of chips.
- Spread in ungreased 9" square pan.
- Sprinkle with remaining chips.
- Bake at 350 degrees for 20-25 minutes.
- Cool 5 minutes before cutting into squares.
- Makes 24 squares.

Cranberry Cream Pie

2 cups Messina Hof Johannisberg Riesling, divided
1¼ cups sugar, divided
12 oz fresh or frozen cranberries
1 tbsp fresh grated orange rind
4 Pilgrim's Pride Eggs
1 env unflavored gelatin
2 cups Gandy's Fresh Whipped Cream, chilled, divided
2 (9") deep dish pie shells, baked

- In saucepan, combine 1 cup Johannisberg Riesling with 1 cup sugar. Stirring, bring to a boil.
- Add cranberries and orange rind, return to a boil. Immediately lower heat and cook, stirring for 10 minutes.
- Soften gelatin in remaining cup of Johannisberg Riesling.
- Stir in eggs one at a time, and add gelatin.
- Add 1 cup cream, and stir until mixture thickens.
- Pour into pie crusts and refrigerate.
- Whip the remaining cup of cream with ¼ cup sugar.
- Add dollop of whipped cream before serving.
- Serves 12-16.

A Time for Jubilation

"During my growing up days down South, we were always getting together for a peanut roasting or watermelon cutting or hog killing. And that's what these Texas festivals are all about. They're reasons for people to get together again."

—*O. T. Baker, founder*
Texas Folklife Festival

*T*exans are an eccentric breed. They have their own creed. They believe strongly in God, motherhood, guitar picking, chili dipping, and jalapeno peppers, and Texans hold celebrations every chance they get to pay homage to everything from cow chip tossing to goat pill flipping to a genuine old-fashioned, down-home, backyard duck pluck.

Their festivals are as unusual as the Muleshoe Pitching Contest up in Muleshoe, as unnerving as the Rattlesnake Roundup in Sweetwater, as wild as the Turkeyfest and Great Gobbler Gallop in Cuero, and as tasty as the Watermelon Thump in Luling, corn shuck tamales in Port Arthur, black-eyed peas in Athens, and wurst in New Braunfels. Texans pay tribute to Shakespeare in Odessa, jazz in Corpus Christi, and the polka in Ennis. But that is what you would expect from people who still cry at fiddling contests in Burnet or Turkey because they can't forget Bob Wills, and who always judge a restaurant by the number of pickup trucks out front.

Such out of the ordinary, sometimes out of the way, festivals provide a chance to trade off a three-piece suit for a pair of faded jeans again; lock the door on a closed-in, artificial

206

Dixie's Peach Ice Cream

2 tbsp lemon juice
2 cups Brazos Valley Orchards Peach Pulp
1 cup milk
1 cup sugar
2 tbsp flour
1/2-1 tsp Adams Almond Extract
1 pt Gandy's Fresh Whipping Cream

- Stir lemon juice into peaches, let stand.
- Cook milk, sugar and flour until thick. Cool.
- Stir in peaches and almond extract.
- Fold in whipping cream.
- Freeze.
- Makes 2 qts.

Herbal Peach Dessert Butter©

1 lb salt free butter, softened
3 tbsp Fredericksburg Herb Farm Lemon Balm or Lemon Verbena, minced
1 tsp lemon zest
2 tbsp peach preserves
1 tbsp peach brandy
2 tbsp chopped almonds, toasted
fresh fruit slices and herb sprigs

- Blend well all of the ingredients, except garnishes.
- Perfect on croissants, homemade biscuits or scones.
- Garnish with fresh fruit slices and fresh herb sprigs.

© 1990 Varney's Chemist Laden
Fredericksburg Herb Farm
Fredericksburg, Texas

Moyer Champagne Peaches

2 cups Moyer Champagne
2 tbsp framboise
1/2 cup brown sugar
1 Menchaca™ Brand Vanilla Bean, cut lengthwise
12 prunes
6 Ambrosia Orchards Peaches
lemon slices, to garnish

- Combine first 4 ingredients and bring to boil.
- Add prunes and peaches, lower heat; cook about 8 minutes.
- Spoon into dessert dishes.
- Garnish with slices of lemon.
- Serves 6-8.

world; return to the hound dog-howling traditions of rural America, wandering back to a time when communities knew how to entertain themselves; and find applause instead of frowns for public displays of tobacco spittin', armadillo racin', or jalapeno gobblin'.

No one ever did it better than Hondo Crouch, who became owner, mayor, foreign minister, guitar picker, chief whittler, and self-made imagineer of Luckenbach, hidden away deep in the heart of the Hill Country.

He bought the whole town of Luckenbach, which consisted of four buildings if you count the outhouse, because he was thirsty, saying, "I'd come by from the ranch every day about five o'clock in the afternoon, needin' a beer. But the town closed down at three o'clock. I bought Luckenbach because it had a doggone good beer joint, and I wanted to be able to get a beer anytime I wanted one. Besides, the ad for the town said it already had an established egg route that would bring in enough money to make the monthly payments. It sounded like a steal to me."

Luckenbach, population 3, had a new owner.

And Hondo Crouch promptly discovered, through extensive scientific research, that Luckenbach sat perched in the exact center of the earth.

"How did you figure that?" I once asked him.

"Well, I got an old globe out of the school house in Fredericksburg," he told me. "Then I took a piece of string and cut it the same size as the circumference of the globe. I put one end on Luckenbach, wrapped that string around the globe, and, shoot, the other end fell on Luckenbach, too."

It was, as far as Hondo was concerned, manifest destiny. The whole world slowly began turning its bloodshot eyes toward Luckenbach. And he and his partner, Guich Koock, promptly opened those eyes a little wider, celebrating the invention of plywood, the return of the mud daubers each spring, and the first ladies-only chili bust—the Amelia Earhart Memorial Hell Hath No Fury Like A Woman Scorned Chili Cook-off.

One winner, Aligani Jani, also took the world's chili championship title in Terlingua, a ghost town in the Texas Big Bend country. And she recalled, "I suddenly felt like a cross

Pecan Cherry Cream Cheese Dessert

1½ cups White Wings Flour
2 tbsp sugar
1¾ sticks Borden's Margarine
¾ cup San Saba Pecan Pieces
1 (8 oz) pkg cream cheese
1 (12 oz) ctn whipped topping
2 cups powdered sugar
1 can cherry pie filling

- Mix by hand flour, sugar, margarine and pecans and press into bottom of 9"x12" cake pan.
- Bake at 350 degrees for 20 minutes. Cool.
- Beat the cream cheese with the whipped topping, then add the powdered sugar. Spread the mixture over the cooled crust.
- Spread cherry pie filling over the cream cheese mixture.
- Chill before serving.
- Serves 6-8.

Ricotta-Filled Angel Food Cake

2 lbs Mozzarello Company
Fresh Dallas Ricotta
1 tbsp dark-roasted coffee
beans, finely ground
(espresso grind)
2 tbsp sugar (or to taste)
1 Gladys' Angel Food Cake
½ lb semi-sweet chocolate
½ cup espresso coffee

- Mix ricotta with ground coffee and sugar in food processor until very smooth. Taste, and add more sugar or coffee if you like.

- Cut angel food cake horizontally into 3 separate layers. Spread ricotta mixture between layers and reassemble cake.
- Then frost entire cake with ricotta mixture. Cover with plastic wrap and refrigerate until serving time.
- Melt chocolate and espresso together in microwave oven, stirring frequently. Sauce will thicken as it cools.
- To serve, slice cake and drizzle chocolate and espresso sauce over cake.
- Serves 8-10.

between Miss America, Lady Bird Johnson, and Aunt Jemima."

Hondo was an innovator, an authorized distributor of imagination. He created the Almost-Annual Luckenbach World's Fair, a buffet of the bizarre that offered such outlandish madness as intergalactic chicken fly offs, armadillo races, free cowboy kisses, reptile handling demonstrations, and such gourmet dishes as chicken-fried rattlesnake.

It grew so long that the Almost Annual World's Fair was soon moved on to the fairgrounds of Fredericksburg.

Such audacity from Luckenbach would forever change the Texas style of celebrations. The old fashioned arts and crafts fairs—though still popular—weren't really in vogue anymore. Festivals had to be different, border on the absurd, and be ridiculous enough to be remembered.

And such it was at Victoria's International Armadillo Confab and Exposition. There, between Houston and Corpus Christi, the World's Championship Body Painting Contest was held, even though the art was never framed for hanging in anybody's gallery. Judges also chose Miss Vacant Lot. One year's winner was able to stand on her head and hum John Philip Sousa's "Stars and Stripes Forever" with a mouthful of pennies. And that display, surprisingly enough, was just her talent portion of the contest.

New Braunfels held its own personal run for the roses, the Armadillo Olympics, honoring those tough, cranky little mammals that look much like leftovers from some prehistoric age, animals whose biggest goal in life is getting from one side of a highway to the other while dodging as many wheels of an eighteen-wheeler as possible. Few make it. In fact, most think that armadillos are simply born dead by the side of the road. At New Braunfels, as many as sixty thousand show up to watch the armadillos run.

The little Texas armored tanks race for forty feet, with their trainers down on hands and knees behind them, screaming, stomping, kicking the ground, jumping up and down, pitching cold beer, or blowing in the armadillo's ear—anything to start them running and keep them running, sometimes even in a straight line. The record time is 3.5 seconds.

Armadillos race, too, at Fort Worth's Chisholm Trail

Honey Party Rice

1 cup *Hygeia Whipping Cream*
⅓ cup *Lone Star Honey*
½ tsp *vanilla*
1 cup *cold cooked rice*
1½ cup *crushed pineapple,
drained*
8 *marshmallows, cut up*

- Whip cream stiff.
- Beat Lone Star Honey in gradually.
- Stir in vanilla.
- Fold in remaining ingredients.
- Spoon into individual dessert dishes. Chill.
- Serves 6-8.

Peach Bread Pudding

2 cups *thinly sliced bread,
torn into pieces*
½ cup *toasted Ramage Farms
Pecans, chopped*
2 cups *sliced fresh Madden's of
Texas Peaches*
2 cups *Hygeia Half and Half*
½ cup *Hygeia Milk*
½ cup *Hygeia Sour Cream*
5 *Twin Rivers Eggs, beaten*
¾ cup *white sugar*
¼ cup *brown sugar*
⅛ tsp *salt*
2 tbsp *lemon juice*

- Butter souffle dish and arrange bread pieces evenly on bottom.
- Sprinkle pecans on top of bread.
- Pour peaches on top of pecans, then sprinkle with ¼ cup white sugar.
- In top of double boiler, whisk together half and half, milk, sour cream and lemon juice. Heat just to boiling.
- Beat eggs with ½ cup white sugar, brown sugar and salt.
- When milk liquid is almost boiling, add eggs and cook until slightly thickened.
- Bake in hot water bath at 325 degrees for 1 hour.
- Serve with lemon sauce.
- Serves 8-10.

Roundup Days in June. This festival sprawls across the stockyard district of Cowtown, where cowboys still come regularly to get their buckles, boots, belts, and beer. And quick-draw artists square off against balloons and the clock for shootouts on the dusty streets at high noon. As Bob Graham, world champion, says, "You know, there's a little gunfighter in all of us."

The only thing hotter than the pistols is the chili. But then, that's typical. In Texas, these days, about all it takes to have a festival is a pot of chili and a few spoons. And none of it ever comes out of a can. Chili in Texas is definitely home brew.

I met Brother John ambling across the dusty grounds of the famed Republic of Texas Chilympiad in San Marcos, and he was preaching and pushing his patented "One Way" chili. He kept explaining to anyone who would listen to him, "What this country really needs is a return to God, love, compassion, and a steaming bowl of big red." He just may be right. After all, Harry James, the great trumpet player, once proclaimed, "Next to jazz music, there is nothing that lifts the spirit and strengthens the soul more than a good bowl of chili." Early-day ministers were known to preach against partaking of a dish that was as hot as the brimstones of hell. One even called it the soup of the devil. Yet, Kit Carson's dying words were, "I wish I had time for just one more bowl of chili."

The pepper pod pandemonium began when H. Allen Smith squared off with Frank X. Tolbert in the first World Chili Championship Cookoff down in the forgotten little ghost town of Terlingua. David Witts, the self-appointed mayor of Terlingua always maintained, "The cookoff was really just a spoof that sort of got out of hand."

The next thing you knew, folks were concocting such dishes as Chili Con Coon. I even tasted Burning Memories Chili, guaranteed to ward off attacks of "hectic-flush, scours, blind staggers, anthrax, and mild cases of chili fever." T. Tom T. Chili, according to its maker, was more potent than Polish Ambrosia. Perriman's Powerful Panic Stricken Panther Potion would "pucker your palate, pickle your pancreas, and pulverize your pelvis. It ain't passive," the brewmaster said. Others were swearing that Pancho Villa's men used chili powder when they

Smiling Tummy Chocolate Pie

¾ *stick Vandervoort's Butter*
1 (4 oz) bag Naomi's Kitchen
Deluxe Candy Pecans
9 oz semi-sweet chocolate
⅓ cup coffee or espresso
4 Pilgrim's Pride Eggs,
separated
2 cups heavy cream
¼ cup powdered sugar

- To make the crust, first melt the butter and set aside.
- Pour the candy pecans into a blender and coarsely chop, then place into a large bowl.
- Slowly pour butter into the pecans, mixing until the pecans become "moldable."
- Place mixture into a pre-greased 9″ pie pan and shape into a pie crust. Refrigerate.
- Melt the chocolate and remove from heat.
- Add the coffee and stir until smooth.
- Allow the chocolate mixture to cool then beat in the egg yolks, one egg at a time.
- Whip 1 cup of the cream until stiff, then fold into the chocolate mixture.
- Beat the egg whites until stiff and fold into the chocolate mixture.
- Pour into the pie crust and chill until set.
- Whip the remaining cup of cream with the powdered sugar and spread over the pie.
- Serves 6-8.

Texas Pecan Pralines

3 cups sugar
1 cup "Milk-E-Whey"
Goat's Milk
½ stick Gandy's Butter
2-3 cups Pecan Valley
Pecan Halves

- Measure 1 cup sugar in black iron or heavy aluminum pot and caramelize.
- At the same time, bring goat's milk and remaining 2 cups of sugar to boil in saucepan.
- Add goat's milk mixture to caramelize sugar and cook together about 2 minutes. (Be careful when adding goat's milk to caramel as mixture bubbles up.)
- Remove from fire, add butter and beat until melted. Add pecans, continue beating until thick and ready to drop.
- Drop by spoonfuls onto waxed paper. Cool.
- Makes about 2 dozen.

ran out of gunpowder. And some said the dish had been run out of Italy by a government that was afraid its pizzaheads were becoming chili addicts.

Every steaming bowl of big red was different.

As Del McLane, the Supreme Allied Chili Commander of the Cow Creek Cookoff, pointed out, "Most of the recipes are carefully guarded secrets that have been handed down for generations. Well, they weren't exactly handed down. Most were thrown away. But a cook keeps his personal recipe such a secret that he won't even watch himself while he adds all the ingredients."

On a street corner in Eastland, an old man sits quietly, slowly shaking his head. He pays no attention to any of the concoctions. He doesn't have to. He says softly, "There ain't but two people in the whole world who can make good chili. And I'm both of 'em."

Trader's Village in Grand Prairie throws its cockeyed spotlight on the Cuzin Homer Page Invitational Eat-And-Run Stewed Prune Pit Spittin' Contest and a World Championship Pickled Quail Egg Eating Contest. Mike Sweet gobbled down thirty four of them in thirty seconds as he made one wild and probably last stab at lasting immortality.

Amongst the piny woods of East Texas, life drifts past at a slower pace. It almost crawls. And it is there, in the downtown streets of Gilmer, where God-fearing men and women all get together to praise the sweet potato and pay tribute to the oppossum at their annual Yamboree.

The proud, puritanical, professor of possumology would always say in his self-styled sermons, "The possum tastes a little like caviar. Very little." He even carried a cut chart along with him, helping people get the best possible P-bone, strip possaloin, posbelly, posham, and possabaloney at their favorite butcher store. The professor always referred to himself, with a certain amount of ham and humility, as one of the last great gourmet chefs of possums and yams.

He had been cooking one for four years. He told me, "It tastes better if you eat only the white meat."

"How do you get the white meat?"

"I usually soak it for a week in Clorox."

Dessert Tacos

2 cups semi-sweet
chocolate chips
1 oz paraffin
1 box Old El Paso® Mini
Taco Shells

- In a double boiler, melt chocolate chips and paraffin.
- Meanwhile, place taco shells on baking sheet and heat at 350 degrees for 5-7 minutes.
- Dip each shell in the melted chocolate mixture, coating all sides. Let excess chocolate drip off.
- Place open end down on a baking sheet lined with wax paper. Let stand until chocolate hardens.
- Fill each taco with your favorite fruits, ice cream or pudding.
- Makes 24 servings.

Mariano's Margarita Pie

Crust:
18 graham crackers
½ lb Vandervoort's Butter
⅓ cup sugar

Filling:
1 pkg clear gelatin
10 oz water
4 oz Mariano's Margarita Mix
¼ cup tequila
2 tbsp sugar
1 (12 oz) ctn whipped topping
lime rinds, shaved

- Put graham crackers in blender or food processor and chop to a very fine consistency.
- Melt butter and mix into graham crackers.
- Add sugar, stir well and then press into pie pan.
- Place crust in freezer for 2 hours to set.
- Dissolve gelatin in ¼ cup warm water.
- Place in a blender along with remainig water, margarita mix, tequilla, sugar and whipped topping. Blend thoroughly.
- Pour into chilled graham cracker crust.
- Garnish with a layer of whipped topping.
- Sprinkle with lime rind shavings.
- Serves 6-8.

Texas has many faces. And all of them are visible at San Antonio's Folklife Festival, sixteen acres of do-it-yourself history, wrapping around the grounds of the Institute of Texas Cultures, taking time to remember all of those ethnic groups that tamed a prairie and gave it statehood. There, children drive spikes into railroad cross ties or chop logs for a cabin that is being built. And you find sweat-and-callous demonstrations of the old-styled techniques for making lye soap, quilting, whittling, shingle splitting, water witching, corn shucking, rope making, and cooking with coon oil.

O. T. Baker, who founded the festival for the institute, spread the gospel of survival. He told folks, "Most who live today don't know that food comes from anyplace but the store. But the frontiersman survived, and you could, too, if you were out hunting or tramping around the mountains and got lost without any food. Of course, you have to be as smart as the old frontiersman was.

"He knew there was a lot of food value in a dried buffalo or cow or deer jawbone. Beat it up into a powder, boil it in water, and it could feed you for several days. We're just not in the habit of eating a lot of jawbones anymore.

"You would know to eat hickory nuts and berries. But mesquite beans have a lot of nutrition as well. And you're standing on a pretty good meal right now if you have leather sole shoes. Boil 'em for a couple of hours. They may not taste too good, but they'll flat keep you alive."

Weekends in Texas are alive with the sounds of music.

And tall tales.

Good times.

And good food.

They mark the distinct, unforgettable face of Texas that is forever laughing, always finding something new or something old to laugh about. But that's the way it is when Texans get together. And Texans can always find a reason to get together, even if it's just for hankerin' or hunkerin', swappin' lies or coon dogs, dippin' chili or snuff, spittin' tobacco or prune pits. That's the way it used to be. That's the way it is from border to border, river to river, in the midst of a whole other country.

Buyer's Guide

Baked Goods

Brazos Blue Ribbon Products (Brazos Blue Ribbon), Bryan
Cavazos' Sons, Inc. (Cavazos), Weslaco
Chef's Shadow, Inc. (Chef's Shadow, Inc.), Dallas
Collin Street Bakery (Original Deluxe, Collin Street, Navarro Farms), Corsicana
Custom Fortune Cookie Company (Custom), Houston
Dutch Regale Bakery, Inc. (Dutch Regale), Austin
Eilenberger's Butter Nut Baking Co. (Eilenberger's), Palestine
Frontier Meat & Supply (Frontier), San Antonio
Gladys' Cookie Shop (Gladys'), Flatonia
Glen-Mary Farms (Glen-Mary Farms), Hughes Springs
Hawkeye Hunting Club (Hawkeye Holiday Cake), Center
Heart Bakery (Heart Bakery), Austin
Heavenly Loaves Bakery (Heavenly Loaves), San Antonio
Kilkenny Cakes (Kilkenny), Austin
Kitchen Ltd., Inc. (St. Hedwig)
Kook-ie Man Corporation, The (The Kook-ie Man), Pearland
La Parisienne, Inc. (Armadillo Kiss), Corpus Christi
Lady Walton's Cookies, Inc. (Lady Walton's), Dallas
Larchmont House (Daddy Ray's Gingerbread), Houston
Laura's Cheesecake, Inc. (Laura's Cheesecake), Daingerfield
Lawler Foods, Inc. (Lawler's Cheesecake), Humble
Limon Bakery & Cafe (Limon Bakery), Austin
Lone Star Bakery, Inc. (Lone Star), San Antonio
Lone Star Cakes-In-A-Jar, Inc. (Lone Star Cakes-In-A-Jar), Dallas
Love Creek Orchards & Nursery (Adams Apples), Medina
Mac Crumbles of Texas (Mac Crumbles of Texas), San Antonio
Manske Baking Company (Manske Rolls), Hewitt
Miss King's Kitchen (Miss King's, Texas Ya-Hoo!), Sherman
Munch-A-Million (Munch-A-Million), Fort Worth
New York, Texas, Cheesecake, Inc. (New York, Texas), LaRue/New York
Pengelly's Famous Fried Pies (Pengelly's Famous Fried Pies), Burleson
Sonja's International Confections (Sonja's), Corpus Christi
Stone Meadow Bakeries (Stone Meadow Bakeries), Garland
Texas American Cookie Company (American Cowboy), Houston
Texas Duet (Texas Duet), Austin

Beverages

Aerobic Life Products, Inc. (Aerobic Aloe Hi-C), Dallas
Alamo Farms Winery & Vineyard (San Antonio, Fiesta, Alamo), Adkins
Artesia Waters, Inc. (Artesia), San Antonio
Bell Mountain/Oberhellmann (Bell Mountain, Oberhellman Vineyards, Oberhof), Fredericksburg
Brazos Beef Emporium, Inc. (Brazos Beef Emporium), Bryan
Buck Springs, Inc., Jasper
Dr. Pepper Bottling Co., of North Texas (Dr. Pepper), Dallas
El Paso Chile Co., Inc. (The El Paso Chile Company), El Paso
Everest Water Co. (Everest), Corpus Christi
Fall Creek Vineyards (Fall Creek Vineyards), Austin
G. Heileman Brewing Company, Inc. (Lone Star Beer), San Antonio
Good Flow Honey & Juice Company (Good Flow), Austin
Guadalupe Valley Winery (Guadalupe Valley), New Braunfels
Hilltop Herb Farm (Hilltop Herb Farm), Romayor
it'za NATURAL, Inc. (it'za SPRITZA, Hill Country Cellars), Austin
La Buena Vida Vineyards (La Buena Vida Vineyards, Springtown, Walnut Creek Cellars), Springtown
La Escarbeda XIT Vineyard & Winery, Inc. (La Escarbeda XIT), Amarillo
Lily of the Desert (Lily of the Desert), Dallas

Llano Estacado Winery, Inc. (Llano Estacado), Lubbock
Love Creek Orchards & Nursery (Adams Apples), Medina
Margarita Man, The (The Margarita Man), San Antonio
Mariano's Specialty Products (Mariano's), Richardson
Messina-Hof Wine Cellars (Messina-Hof), Bryan
Mixer Marketeers ("Fabuloso" Margarita Mix), Austin
Moyer Champagne Company (Moyer), Austin
Old City Brewing Company (Pecan Street Lager), Austin
Pearl Brewing Company (Pearl, Pearl Light, Texas Pride, Country Club Malt Liquor), San Antonio
Pedernales Vineyards (Pedernales Vineyards), Fredericksburg
Pheasant Ridge Winery (Pheasant Ridge), Lubbock
Piney Woods Country Wines, (Piney Woods Country), Orange
Preston Trail Winery (Preston Trail Winery), Roanoke
Ranger Foods of Texas, Inc. (Jump-Back Jack's, Shotgun Willie's, Ranger Luke), Austin
Reinheitsgebot Brewing Co. (Collin County Pure Gold, Collin County Black Gold), Plano
Richland Beverage Corporation (Texas Select), Dallas
Rife Vineyards (Rife Vineyards), Plano
Sanchez Creek Vineyards (Sanchez Creek Vineyards), Dallas
Skweezins Corporation (Skweezins), Dallas
Spoetzl Brewery, Inc. (Shiner Premium, Shiner Bock), San Antonio
Ste. Genevieve Wines (Ste. Genevieve, Domaine), San Antonio
Sundor Brands, Inc. (Texsun), Mt. Dora
Texas Beverage Packers, Inc. (Texas Soft Drinks), San Antonio
Utopia Spring Water, Inc. (Utopia), San Antonio
Val Verde Winery (Val Verde), Del Rio
Wimberley Valley Wines, Inc. (Wimberley Valley), Conroe

Candy

Acme Candy Company, Inc. (Acme Candies), Dallas
Ada's Candy Creations, Inc. (Ada's Candy Creations), Florence
Annie's Peanut Brittle, Mrs. (Mrs. Annie's), Floresville
Atkinson Candy Company (Atkinson Candy Company), Lufkin
Atwood Candy Company (Atwood's Old Fashioned), Forney
Aunt Lucy's Peanut Brittle (Aunt Lucy's Peanut Brittle), Jayton
Bluebonnet Candy Kitchen, Grapevine
Candyland & Nut Depot (George's Candyland), Colorado City
Clear River Pecan Company (Clear River Pecans), Schertz
Conchita's Fine Candies (Conchita's), Uvalde
Concho Candies (Concho Creamy Praline), San Angelo
Crawford Pecans, R.H. (Texas River Pecans), Arthur City
Delightfully Delicious Sweets (D.D.S.), San Antonio
Fredericksburg Fudge Company (Fredericksburg Fudge, Snapperr), Fredericksburg
Golden Confection, Inc. (Toros), Laredo
Golden Gal's Pralines (Golden Gal's Pralines), Clarksville
Jack's Batch Peanut Brittle (Jack's Batch), Roby
Kennedy Candy Company (Sir George Select Confections), Longview
La India Packing Company (La India), Laredo
La King's Confectionery (La King's), Galveston
Lammes Candies Since 1885, Inc. (Lammes), Austin
Madden Pecan & Fruit Farm (Pecans of Texas), Fort Worth
Madeline's Gourmet Foods (Madeline's), New Braunfels
Monterrey Products Company, Inc. (Monterrey Products), San Antonio
My Mama's Candy (My Mama's Candy), Amarillo
Nancy's Candies (Nancy's Candies), Rosenberg
Naomi's Kitchen (Naomi's Kitchen), Dallas
Old Fashioned Candy Company, Lufkin
Old Peanut Butter Warehouse (Peanut Pantry), Galveston
Oliver Pecan Company (Oliver Pecan Company · The Pecan Shoppe), San Saba

Pangburn Candy Company (Millionaires), Fort Worth
Pipecreek Texas Bullcorn (Pipecreek Texas Bullcorn), Austin
Ramage Farms, Hooks
Spirit of Texas (Spirit of Texas), Plano
Sweet Sensations (Sweet Sensations), San Antonio
Sweet Surrender (Sweet Surrender Chocolates), Katy
Texas Bess (Texas Bess), Fort Worth
Tyler Candy Company, Inc. (Dickies), Tyler
Webb's Candy Company (Webb's Candy Company), Boerne

Canned Goods

Allen Canning Company (East Texas State Fair), Siloam
  Springs, AR
Amigos Canning Company, Inc. (Amigos), San Antonio
B.B. Berzette's Foods (Lone Star Caviar), San Antonio
Country Woodcraft (Down Home Cookin'), Stonewall
El Arroyo (El Arroyo), Austin
Fiesta Foods, Inc. (La Cocina, La Fiesta), Dallas
Goldin Pickle Company, Inc. (Goldin's Silver Star,
  Pik-L-Giant), Dallas
Just the Best of Texas (Texas Windowpane Pickles),
  Duncanville
Lone Star Specialty Foods (Lone Star Butter Crunch, Lone
  Star Flavors), San Antonio
Millie's Kountry Kitchen (Kountry Kitchen), LaGrange
Old Orange Cafe/From Susan's Kitchen, Orange
Old River Trading Company (Jim's Fire, Ice Pickles), Freeport
Pet Inc. (Old El Paso Foods), St. Louis, MO
Pickleworks A.D., Inc. (Pickleworks A.D.), Midland
Special-T's (Texas Krispy Sweets/Dills), Richardson
Talk O' Texas Brands, Inc. (Talk O' Texas), Grand Prairie
Taormina Company (Gold Tip, Deer, Buffalo and Taormina),
  Donna

Cooking Woods

D & M Products, Inc. (Big Tex Brand), Dallas
Flippen Industries (Taste of Texas), Dallas
Flying W Wood Products (Flying W), Brady
G. A. T., Inc. (G & T), La Villa
Heart of Texas Mesquite (Mesquite Country Chips, Mesquite
  Country Blend, MC Bundlewood), Abilene
Hill Country Products (Hill Country Smoke), San Antonio
Indian Creek Mesquite, Inc. (Texas Smoke), Brownwood
J. P. Mesquite Co. (J.P.), Pearsall
Lil' Duke Sac-Of-Smoke (Larry's Bag-Of-Smoke), Houston
Lone Oak Vineyard (Grape Bar-B-Q Wood), Chico
Longhorn Mesquite & Produce (Longhorn Mesquite), Luling
Menard Manufacturing & Distributing Co. (Hill Country),
  Menard
Quality Texas Products, Inc. (Miss Keet), Bryson
Tree House Enterprises (Down Home Mesquite), Tyler
Wineta, Inc. (Sweet Smoke), Dallas
Wood Pile, The Woodsboro
WW Wood, Inc. (Western), Pleasanton

Dairy Products/Cheeses/Eggs

Alpine Specialty Foods, Inc. (Anne Ashburn's, Ashburn's,
  Arthur's), Dallas
Amy's Ice Creams (Amy's), Austin
Borden/Superior (Eagle Brand, Old Fashioned Borden, Lite
  Line, Lady Borden), Austin
Crystal Dairy Products (Chef Maurice), Gainesville
Fenton Egg Farm (Fenton's), Lake Brownwood
Gandy's Dairies, Inc. (Gandy's), San Angelo
Garland Beverage Company (Big K, Rocky Top, Golden
  Crown), Garland
Hygeia Dairy Company (Hygeia), Harlingen
Jake's Egg Company (Jake's Finer Eggs), Houston
La Parisienne, Inc. (Armadillo Kiss), Corpus Christi
Land O' Pines (Land O' Pines), Lufkin
Lane's Dairy, Inc. (Lane's), El Paso

Larsen Farms, Inc. (Larsen Farm's Texas Chevre), Dripping
  Springs
M-G, Inc. Egg Division (M-G, Morning Pride), Weimar
Maxim Production Company, Inc. (Maxim's), Boling
Milk-E-Whey Dairy (Milk-E-Whey), Hockley
Mozzarella Company (Mozzarella Company), Dallas
Pilgrim's Pride Corporation (Pilgrim's Pride), Dallas
Poncho's Range Chickens and Quail (Poncho's Range
  Chickens and Quail), Carrizo Springs
Purity Ice Cream Company (Purity), Galveston
Ricos Products (Ricos), San Antonio
Vandervoort Dairy Foods Company (Sealtest, Kroger, Texas
  Gold), Fort Worth

Flour/Corn Meal/Mixes/Sugar

Amber Waves Baking Products (Amber Wave Pancake Mix),
  Hereford
Brick Kitchens (Texas Chili Sauce), College Station
C & C Bakery, Inc. (C&C), Kingsville
Feelin' Your Oats Products (Power Pancakes, Mighty Muffins),
  Buda
Heart Bakery (Heart Bakery), Austin
Imperial Holly Corporation (Imperial), Sugar Land
Lamb's Grist Mill (Lamb's Stone Ground Mill), Hillsboro
Martha White Foods (Light Crust), Hurst
Morrison Milling Company (Morrison), Denton
Old Mexico Bakery, Inc. (Old Mexico Bakery), Austin
Panhandle Milling (Bakers Patent, H & R Flour), Canyon
Pioneer Flour Mills/San Antonio River Mill (Pioneer, White
  Wings, Angel Food, San Antonio River Mill), San Antonio
Shadowfox Farms (Shadowfox Farms), Elgin
Texas Sauce Products Company (Ole Ranch Hand, Brazos),
  Houston
Zebbies, Inc. (Zebbie's), Memphis

Fresh Produce

3-D Farms, Hillsboro
A & R Foods, Fort Worth
Ambrosia Orchards (Ambrosia Orchards), Arthur City
Agri-Tree, Inc. (Nueces Valley, Crystal Sweet), Crystal City
Amistad Orchard, San Antonio
Anchor Food Products, Inc. (Anchor), Appleton
Anders Greenhouses (Anders Tomatoes), Weimar
Anderson Produce (Tood's Best), Dilley
B & M Orchard, Wichita Falls
Bagley & Koetting (Bagley & Koetting), Amarillo
Bagley Produce Company, Inc. (Alita), Edinburg
Barrett Produce Company (Stan's Best, Muleshoe, Plainsman),
  Muleshoe
Barrett-Fisher Company (Tex Star, Barrett's Blue Chip,
  Springlake), Hereford
Barron's Blueberries, Lindale
Brazos Valley Orchards (Brazos Valley Orchards), Waco
Berry Country Farms, Brownsboro
Berryman's Fresh Fruits & Vegetables, Houston
Big State Produce Company, Inc. (Big State), San Antonio
Biz-zz Bee Farms (Biz-zz Bee, Naturally Texas), San Antonio
Blueberry Basket, LaRue
Blueberry Patch, Silsbee
Blueberry Valley Farms (Blueberry Valley Farms),
  Nacogdoches
Brick Kitchens (Texas Chili Sauce), College Station
Buckaroo Blueberry Ranch, Scottsville
Burges Orchards (Burges Orchards), Castroville
Burke Farms (Burke Farms), Roscoe
C & A Sales, Inc., (Curtis & Ashlie), Kingsville
Carlton Peach Farm, Wichita Falls
Caroland, Wichita Falls
Cee Dee Farms, Waco
Chaparral Fruit Sales, Inc. (Chaparral), San Antonio
Cokendolpher Orchard, Wichita Falls

Coker Farms (Coker Farms Brand), Yantis
Colville & Wilson, Inc. (Mission, Cimarron, Frio Town, Pride of Hereford), Hereford
Country Fresh Products (Country Fresh), Houston
Country Store & Orchard, Wichita Falls
Cowan Farms, Tulia
Cumings Enterprises, Rosenberg
Dallas Calco (Calco Sprouts), Dallas
Das Peach Haus, Inc. (Fischer & Wieser, Texas Wine Collection), Fredericksburg
De Bruyn Produce Company (Gulf, Deblo, Citation, Gold Rim), Hereford
Diamond Farm (Jewel), Grand Saline
Dome, The, Mexia
E & B Peach Orchard (Tru-Tex), Hempstead
Eastex Farms (Eastex), Rusk
El Kay Farms (El Kay), Montgomery
Engery Sprouts, Inc. (Fresh from Texas), San Antonio
Experimental Organic Agriculture, Whitney
Fincastle Nursery & Farms (Fincastle), LaRue
Fredericksburg Orchards, Inc. (Fredericksburg Orchards), Fredericksburg
Fredericksburg Peach Co., The (Fredericksburg Peaches), Austin
Fresh Farm Produce, Inc., San Antonio
Frio Foods, Inc. (Frio), Uvalde
G. D. Produce (G. D. Produce), Waco
Goldberg Horticulture, Rick (Lettuce Be Good), Austin
Good Earth Farm, Celeste
Grape Creek Vineyard (Grape Creek Vineyard & Garden), Stonewall
Griffin Organic Farm, Lockhart
Gro Tech Gardens (Gro Tech Gardens), Buda
H & S Produce Company (Hart), Hart
Hamilton Blueberry Farm (Hamilton), Livingston
Harvey, Jr., Robert E., Nixon
Herff Falls Vineyard (Herff Falls), Boerne
Hester, W.A. (Hester), Amarillo
High Plains Products of Texas (High Plains of Texas), Perryton
Hoelscher Farms (Hoelscher), Midland
Home Grown Sprout Co., The, Tulia
Huff, W. L., Call
Hutcheson, Sammy, Itasca
Hutton's Fruit Farm (Parker County Peaches and Pecans), Weatherford
Johnson Melon, Corporation, Knox City
King Tom Tomato Farms (King Tom, Gourmet), Guadalupe County
Kitchen Pride Mushroom Farms (Kitchen Pride), Gonzales
Klement's Grove, McAllen
Knapp-Sherrill Company (Ro-Tel, Gold Tip), Donna
Koetting, Mike, Amarillo
Kriegel, Laurance, Bovina
LC Food Products Company (Georgette's Western Brand), Austin
Lamar Farm (Lamar Farm), Kosse
Lazy D Berry Farm, Inc. (Lazy D), Winnie
Lee's Blueberry Haven, Silsbee
Lenz Apiary (Lenz Apiary), San Antonio
Little Seed Orchard (Little Seed Orchard), Amarillo
Longhorn Mesquite & Produce (Longhorn Mesquite), Luling
Love Creek Orchards & Nursery (Adams Apples), Medina
Lyles Produce Farm, Alba
M-M Orchard & Farm, Whitt
Madden Pecan & Fruit Farm (Pecans of Texas), Fort Worth
Madeline's Gourmet Foods (Madeline's), New Braunfels
Malamen, Sue, Hereford
Masson University Ranch (Athena Brand), Montague
Maxwell Orchards (Maxwell), Dimmitt
McKemie Home Grown (McKemie HomeGrown), Dale
Monterey Mushrooms (Monterey, First Harvest), Madisonville

Morath Orchard, Wichita Falls
Morrison, Glen (Morrison), Stanton
Mott Blueberry Hill Farms, Spurger
Navarro Mills Farms (Navarro Mills Farm), Purdon
New, John V. & Thelma, Hawley
O.L. Rozell Peach Farms, Tyler
P/2 Organic (P/2 Organic), Coupland
Pape Pecan House (Pape), Sequin
Peaceable Kingdom School (Peaceable Kingdom), Washington
Peach Basket (Hallford Orchards), Fredericksburg
Peach Springs Nursery, Winnsboro
Pedernales Valley Orchard & Farms, Fredericksburg
Penick Farms - P & L Canning (Penick Farms), Johnson City
Plainview Produce, Inc. (Red Rage, Julie Blond, Second Helping, Dueces Wild), Plainview
Plantation Pines Berry Farm, Tyler
Poor Farm, The, Wichita Falls
Poston Produce, Hillsboro
Proctor Brothers Vineyard, Lingleville
R Blueberry Farm, Gilmer
Ramage Farms, Hooks
Reinauer & Sons, Inc. (ECR, 3R), Hereford
Rhew Peach Orchard, Floresville
Richards Horticulture, Midland
Richardson Fresh Produce, Hawley
Riddick Farms, Jasper
Russell Vineyards (Texas Seedless, BesTex Seedless), Gardendale
Roberts Farm, Waco
Royal International, Ltd. (Regal Texas Pecans, Sugar Sweet, Royal International), San Juan
San Pit Enterprises, Inc. (De Zavala Vineyard), New Baden
Sandy Foot Farm (Sandy Foot), Livingston
Sandy Hill Farm (Noonday), Tyler
Schneider Hydro-Farms, Rockdale
Sem-Tex Produce (Sun-West Tex, Circle 7), Seminole
Shepherd Produce, Hutto
Shilo Vegetable Farms, Itasca
Smith's Peach Farm (Smith's Peaches), Pittsburg
Southern Blues Farm (Southern Blues), Vidor
Spear Orchard, Fischer
Spring River Farm (Spring River Farm), San Marcos
Stephenville Vineyard & Supply, Inc., Stephenville
Sterling Orchards (Panole Peaches, Panola Preserves, Panola Produce), Clayton
Storey Orchards, Avery
Sunbelt America, Littlefield
Sunray Corp (Sunray Corn), Sunray
Sunset Vineyard & Nursery, Sunset
Supreme Products, Inc. (Supreme), McAllen
T Bar C, Hedley
Tangram Nursery, Maxwell
Texana Fruit Company (Texana), McAllen
Texas Blueberry Marketing Association (Big Blues of Texas), LaRue
Texas Blueberry Plantation, Beaumont
Texas Citrus Exchange (Big Tex), Mission
Texas Fresh Products (Texas Fresh), Cedar Park
Texas Gunpowder, Inc. (Texas Gunpowder), Mesquite
Texas Orchard, Kerrville
Texas Ruby-Red Grapefruit (Texas Ruby Red Grapefruit), Mission
The Farm Country Club (Fresh Produce), Bandera
Thurber Garden, Pat, Whitney
TIE Demonstration Farm (TIE), Laredo
Top of Bosque Vineyard, Stephenville
Triple JD Ranch (Triple JD Ranch), Bandera
Tucker's Farm & Craft, Wichita Falls
Two Quail Crafts, Decatur
Valley Farmers Co-op, San Juan
Warehouse Farms, Inc. (Rio Queen), Mission

Webb Farms, Luling
Weber Ranch (Weber Ranch), Medina
Weidenfeller Trading Company, Fredericksburg
Westside Orchard, Wichita Falls
White Star Farm (White Star Farm), Fredericksburg
Whitmire, J.L., Tulia
Wieck, Willie, Dumas
Willmott Farms (Willmott Farms), Palestine
Woodrum Produce, Fruitvale
Young's Greenhouses, Wichita Falls
Young's Home Orchard (Young's Home Orchard),
    Wichita Falls

Gift Baskets

Accents, Conroe
Basket Works, The (The Basket Works), Duncanville
Das Peach Haus, Inc. (Fischer & Wieser, Texas Wine
    Collection), Fredericksburg
Gift Baskets & More (Gift Baskets & More), Hamilton
Giving Basket, The, Pasadena
Hubbell & Sons Foods Products, Inc. (Hubbell Quality,
    County Fair, 4-H, Old Bavaria), Houston
J&K Texas Distributors (J&K's Texas), Rockdale
Texart (Texart), Corpus Christi
Texas Fruit Baskets (TX Care Package, TX Special, TX
    Combo, TX Fruit Basket), Austin
Trinity Partners, Inc. (Texas Eats), Dallas
Tru-Tex Products (Tru-Tex), Hempstead
Westside Orchard, Wichita Falls
Zeys of Texas (Zeys of Texas), Mission

Honey/Syrup

B & Mc Enterprises (Chateau Cherie's), Fort Worth
Baker Apiaries (Baker Apiaries), Elgin
Bass Grocery, Chico
Biz-zz Bee Farms (Biz-zz Bee, Natually Texas), San Antonio
Blackland Apiaries Honey (Blackland Apiaries, Cajun),
    Prosper
Bluebonnet Apiaries, Inc. (Mama Kay's), McAllen
Best Apiary (Fancy Honey), Georgetown
Buckaroo Blueberry Ranch, Scottsville
Burleson's Honey, Inc. (Burleson's Honey), Waxahachie
Caldwell's Texas Honey, San Antonio
Cedar Grove, Sealy
Country Woodcraft (Down Home Cookin'), Stonewall
D & P Honey (D & P), San Antonio
Dabney Apiaries (Dabney Apiaries), Amarillo
Eastex Farms (Eastex), Rusk
Farley's New Era Sorghum (Farley's New Era Sorghum),
    Iowa Park
Gott's Buzzzy Acres (Gott's Buzzzy Acres), Round Mountain
Grape Creek Vineyard (Grape Creek Vineyard & Garden),
    Stonewall
Green Apiaries, (Russell Green), Ector
Gro Tech Gardens (Gro Tech Gardens), Buda
H. C. Honey House (H. C. Honey House), Schertz
Happy Honey Company (Happy Honey), Beaumont
Hoyts Honey Farm (Hoyts), Baytown
Hutchins, R.T. (East Texas Honey), Lindale
J & M Honey Company (J & M Honey Company, Texas Gold),
    Kempner
J & R Texas Honey (J&R), Fort Worth
J.J.'s Honey Bees (J.J.'s Honey Bees), McAllen
Johnny Boy's (Johnny Boy's), Rowlett
Killer "B" Honey Farms (Killer "B" Honey Farms), Houston
Lenz Apiary (Lenz Apiary), San Antonio
Little Mac Enterprises (Little Mac's Texas Tea Syrup), Nevada
Lone Star Honey Company (Lone Star Honey, Honey Affair),
    Leander
Madden Pecan & Fruit Farm (Pecans of Texas), Fort Worth
Mattson's Apiary, Austin

Niedecken Apiaries (Niedecken Honey), Coupland
Oliver's Honey (Oliver's), Waco
Orr's Apiaries, Bobby (Bobby Orr), Hurst
Pat Westmoreland (Ft. Bend County Wildflower Honey),
    Fulshear
Penick Farms - P&L Canning (Penick Frams) Johnson City
Rambo Bee Farms (Rambo Bee Farms, Pure East Texas
    Honey), Gilmer
Serendipity Of The Valley (Serendipity of the Valley), Lake
    Jackson
Shadowfox Farms (Shadowfox Farms), Elgin
Southern Gold Honey Company (Southern Gold), Vidor
Texas Duet (Texas Duet), Austin
Texas Fresh Products (Texas Fresh), Cedar Park
Texas Honey (Texas Honey), Vernon
Texas Honey Co-Op, Inc. San Antonio
Texas Natural Gifts Honey Co., (Texas' Natural Gifts), Dayton
Tule Creek Apiary (Tule Creek Apiary), Tulia
Uncle Red's Honey (Uncle Red's), Farmers Branch
Utopia Honey House, Utopia
Varsel Apiaries, Spring
Weaver Apiaries, Inc. (Weaver's Country Fresh, Weaver's Pure
    Country), Navasota
Weaver & Sons, Inc., Howard, Navasota
Winkler Pecan & Honey Farm (Winkler Farm), Moody
Yeager's Caddo Creek Crawfish (Caddo Creek Crawfish, Paul
    Yeager's Bees), Frankston
Youngblood Honey, Inc. (Youngblood), Pearsall
Z's and Key's Bees (Bottled Honey), Point

Jams and Jellies

Alamo Farms Winery & Vineyard (San Antonio, Fiesta,
    Alamo), Adkins
Angel Craft, Inc. (Angel Crafts, Pepper Palate), Chillicothe
B & M Orchard, Wichita Falls
Bass Grocery, Chico
Berry Country Farms, Brownsboro
Carole's Food Specialties (Carole's), Pearland
Country Canner (Country Canner), Seguin
Country Store & Orchard, Wichita Falls
Das Peach Haus, Inc. (Fischer & Wieser, Texas Wine
    Collection), Fredericksburg
Early Texas Tastes (Early Texas Tastes), Rody
Eastex Farms (Eastex), Rusk
Grandmother's House (Grandmother's House), Dryden
Green, Jeanne, Burkburnett
Hermitage Farm (Hermitage Farm, Organically Grown),
    Scroggins
Hill Country Foods, Inc. (Hill Country Farms, Across the
    Border), Dallas
Hilltop Herb Farm (Hilltop Herb Farm), Romayor
Jellies, Etc. by Jackie, Benavides
Kitchens of Serendip (Tejas), Bandera
Klement's Grove, McAllen
Lazy Susan, Inc. (Old San Antonio Style, Texas Gold), San
    Antonio
Little Red Hen Pantry, Inc. (The Little Red Hen Pantry),
    Neches
Londa's Gourmet Classics (Londa's), Wylie
Lone Star Specialty Foods (Lone Star Butter Crunch, Lone
    Star Flavors), San Antonio
Love Creek Orchards & Nursery (Adams Apples), Medina
Lowake Ranch Jelly's (Lowake Ranch), Lowake
Monterrey Products Company, Inc. (Monterrey Products),
    San Antonio
Nature's Song, Houston
New Canaan Farms (New Canaan Farms), Dripping Springs
Niedecken Apiaries (Niedecken Honey), Coupland
Old Orange Cafe/From Susan's Kitchen, Orange
Plum Creek Berry Farm (Plum Creek Berry Farm), Dale

R. G. Mexican Food Products, Inc. (Senor Pepe), San Antonio
Ramage Farms, Hooks
Reba's Country Cupboard (Reba's Country Cupboard), Washington
Rife Vineyards (Rife Vineyards), Plano
Sam Lewis & Associates, Inc. (Jalapeno Sam), San Angelo
Sandye's Country (Sandye's Country), Idalou
Serendipity Of The Valley (Serendipity of the Valley), Lake Jackson
Silva Swan, Inc. (Texas Fun Feed, Visions of Gourmet), Industry
Sterling Orchards (Panola Peaches, Panola Preserves, Panola Produce), Clayton
Tejas Pines (Tejas Pines "Southern Fixin's of East Texas"), Garrison
Tejas Specialties (Tejas), Fredericksburg
Texafrance, Inc. (Texafrance), Austin
Texas Jellies (Texas Jellies), Austin
Texas Original Mesquite Jelly (Texas Original), Port Lavaca
Texas Specialties (Texas Prickly Pear Cactus Jelly), Meridian
Texas Tamale Company, Houston
Two Quail Crafts, Decatur

Meats/Meat Products
3T Buffalo Ranch (3TR), Ben Wheeler
All That's Deer Ltd. (All That's Deer Ltd., Meier's Fulshear Farms, Red Deer Farms), Fulshear
Associated Rabbit Producers, Inc. (Associated Rabbit Producers), Hawkins
B3R Country Meats, Inc. (B3R Beef), Childress
Bear Creek Smokehouse Inc. (Bear Creek Smokehouse), Marshall
Ben's Longbranch Bar-B-Que, Austin
Bernhard's Quality Meats (Bernhard's), Ingram
Big Texan Steak Ranch, Amarillo
Brazos River Rattlesnake Ranch (Brazos River Rattlesnake Ranch, Texas Nature Exchange), Santo
Brenham Sausage Company, Inc. (Texas Star, Brenham), Brenham
Broadway Fish Market (Broadway), Port Lavaca
Buddy's Natural Chickens, Inc. (Buddy's Natural Chicken), Seguin
Cap Ranch Meat Market & Smokehouse (Cap Ranch), Mineola
Carlton Food Products, Inc. (Carlton's), New Braunfels
Cedar Mountain Buffalo Co. (Cedar Mountain), Odessa
Clamon Foods (Clamon), Palestine
Consolidated Smokehouse (Consolidated Smokehouse), LaGrange
Decker Food Company (Decker Beef Franks), Garland
Diamond "C" Productions, Henrietta
Dimmitt Meat Co. (Hopson's), Dimmitt
Double L Ranch, The (Lockhart's Double L), Waelder
Eddy Packing Company, Inc. (Imperial, Tasty), Yoakum
Edes Custom Meats, Inc. (Edes), Amarillo
Fischer's Meat Market (Fischer's), Muenster
Fisherman's Harvest, Inc. (Fisherman's Harvest), Anahuac
Fredericksburg Lockers, Inc. (Opa's), Fredericksburg
Frontier Meat & Supply (Frontier), San Antonio
Full Season Farms (Full Season Farms), Umbarger
Genesis Seafood, Inc. (Genesis Seafood), Stanton
Geronimo Sausage Co. (Geronimo), Laredo
Gonzalez Packing Company, Eagle Pass
Gordon Fowler Foods, Inc. (Gordo's Chili), Austin
Guadalupe Smoked Meat Company (Hickory Groves, Guadalupe Pit Smoked Meat), New Braunfels
H & H Foods (H & H), Mercedes
Halal International Trading Co., (Halal for Better Health), Arlington
Handy Packing Co. (Triple A, Plateau), San Angelo
Hans Mueller Sausage (Hans Mueller), Dallas

Harmony Packing Company, Inc., Palestine
Harrington Packing Company (Harrington Smoke Sausage), Winnie
Henneke Humpback Bluecat Fish, Hallettsville
Hickory House Bar B-Que (Hickory House), Denison
Highland Foods Company (Hudson's, Southwest), Austin
Hillman Shrimp & Oyster Company (Hillman Shrimp & Oyster Company), Dickinson
Hubbell & Sons Food Products, Inc. (Hubbell Quality, County Fair, 4-H, Old Bavaria), Houston
Inland Industries, Inc., McAllen
J-B Foods (J-B, Singletree Farms, Texas Smokehouse), Waelder
Jim's Meat Market, Seguin
Kitchens Hardware and Deli (Cap Ranch Meats), Mineola
La Grange Meat Market, Inc. (Country Style), La Grange
Lad-Pak, Inc. (Ladd's), Needville
Laguana Madre Shrimp Farms, Inc. (Laguana Madre Plantation, Plantation), Harlingen
Laxson Provision Co., (Laxson), San Antonio
Longhorn Meat Company, Austin
Majica (Majica "Naturally"), Houston
McCauley Export Marketing (EX'M Beef), Austin
Meat Link (Frazier's Natural Beef), Waelder
Meat Shop (Texas Jerky), Austin
Mesquite Bros. Barbeque & Catering, Greenville
Midway Fish Farm (Midway Fish Farm), Iowa Park
Miller's Seafood (Miller's), Seadrift
Naiad Corporation (Sysco Classic, Naiad), Liverpool
Nicholson's Meat Company (Hickory House, Mertzon Locker Plant), Mertzon
Ocean Venturess, Inc., Port Lavaca
Palo Duro Meat, Inc. (Farmer Dale Kitchens), Amarillo
Pedro's Tamales, Inc. (Pedro's), Lubbock
Plantation Foods, Inc. (Plantation), Waco
Poncho's Range Chickens Quail (Poncho's Range Chickens and Quail), Carrizo Springs
Prasek's Hillje Smokehouse (Prasek's Hillje Smokehouse), El Campo
Producer Perfect Beef, Valley Mills
Ranch House Meat Company (Ranch House), Menard
Rayner Foods, Inc. (Rayner, Old Plantation, Country Smokehouse), Houston
Riker Farm (Riker), Anton
Royal International, Ltd. (Regal Texas Pecans, Sugar Sweet, Royal International), San Juan
S&D Holmes Smokehouse, Inc. (Holmes Pecan Smoked), Rosenberg
Sadler's Bar-B-Que Sales, Inc. (Sadler's Smokehouse), Henderson
Sager's Seafood Plus, David (David Sager's Seafood Plus), Sugarland
Sam Kane Beef Processors, Inc. (Sam Kane Beef), Corpus Christi
Shadowfox Farms (Shadowfox Farms), Elgin
Sirloin Shops of Stephenville (Red Chain Farms), Stephenville
Signature Foods of Texas, Inc. (Signature Foods of Texas), Pittsburg
Sklar's Frozen Food Center, Inc., Wharton
Slaton Packing Plant & Lockers (Slaton Pack Meats), Slaton
Smokey Denmark Sausage Company (Smokey Denmark), Austin
Southwest Texas Quail Farms (Southwest Texas Quail), Houston
Square's Bar-B-Que Express (Square's), Abilene
Sun City Ocean Products (Sun City Ocean Products), El Paso
Sunday House Foods, Inc. (Sunday House), Fredericksburg
Sunrise Ranch (Sunrise Ranch Longhorn Lean), Liberty Hill
Sysco Food Services (Sysco), Houston
Texas Chili Company (Our Famous Texas Chili, Tex-O-Gold Chili, Tex-O-Gold Sauce), Fort Worth

Texas Crawfish Farmers Association, Frankston
Texas Hill Country Smoked Meats (Texas Hill Country),
    Kerrville
Texas Rabbit Processing Co., San Angelo
Texas Smokehouse Foods (Bar-B Foods), Lufkin
Texas Tender (Texas Tender), Houston
Texas Western Foods (Texas Western), Houston
Texas Wild Game Cooperative (Broken Arrow Ranch), Ingram
Triple C Meats (Triple C), Devine
Union Slaughter, Inc. (Que Rico), Del Rio
Uvalde Meat Processing, Uvalde
Valley Wholesale Meat Co., Inc. (La Rancherita/Country Girl),
    Alamo
Wilson's Rolling W Barbecue, Mesquite
Wolf Brand Products (Wolf), Dallas
Yaquinto Enterprises (Paisano Brand Italian Sausage), Dallas
Yeager's Caddo Creek Crawfish (Caddo Creek Crawfish, Paul
    Yeager's Bees), Frankston
Younger, Kay (Younger's Bros.), Amarillo
Yoakum Packing Company (Farm Pac), Yoakum

Nuts/Seeds/Peanuts

Agri-Tree, Inc. (Nueces Valley, Crystal Sweet), Crystal City
American Nut Corporation (Private Label, American, Nature's
    Farm), Lewisville
Anderson Pecans (Anderson Pecans), Seguin
Bar D River Ranch (Bar D River Ranch Pecans), Corpus
    Christi
Berdoll Pecan Farm (Berdoll Pecan Farm), Cedar Creek
Bessie Creek Groves (Bessie Creek Groves), Fulshear
Bluebonnet Apiaries, Inc. (Mama Kay's), McAllen
Caroland, Wichita Falls
Clear River Pecan Company (Clear River Pecans), Schertz
Cokendolpher Orchard, Wichita Falls
Cooking with Amber, Inc. (Cooking with Amber), Dallas
Country Store & Orchard, Wichita Falls
Crabtree Pecan Shoppe, Denison
Crawford Pecans, R.H. (Texas Red River Pecans), Arthur City
Dee & C Pecans (Dee & C Pecans), Lamesa
Dos Rios Ranch (Dos Rios), Gonzales
Durham Pecan Company, Inc. (Comanche Golden), Comanche
Early Texas Tastes (Early Texas Tastes), Roby
Flyover Farms, Houston
Friandise Desserts, Inc. (Friandise Desserts, Inc.), Houston
Frio Pecan Farm (Frio Pecan Farms), Leakey
Frog House, The (The Frog House), Wichita Falls
Grape Creek Vineyard (Grape Creek Vineyard & Garden),
    Stonewall
Great San Saba River Pecan Co., (The Great San Saba River
    Pecan Company), San Saba
Gro Tech Gardens (Gro Tech Gardens), Buda
Harmon Food Co., Allen
Hutton's Fruit Farm (Parker County Peaches and Pecans),
    Weatherford
Karen's Kracked Pecans (Karen's Kracked), Dallas
Klement's Grove, McAllen
Ledbetter Pecan Company, The, O'Donnell
Lee County Peanut Company, The (Lee County Peanut
    Company, Inc.), Giddings
Link Company, The (Jalapecanos), Allen
Lone Star Honey Company (Lone Star Honey, Honey Affair),
    Leander
Lone Star Specialty Foods (Lone Star Butter Crunch, Lone
    Star Flavors), San Antonio
M & W Pecans (M & W Pecans), Austin
Madeline's Gourmet Foods (Madeline's), New Braunfels
Martin, James G. (Martin's), Wharton
McKinley Pecans, Wichita Falls
Navarro Mills Farm (Navarro Mills Farms), Purdon
Nuts To You, Inc. (Vintage Wine Roasted Nuts), Dallas
Oliver Pecan Company (Oliver Pecan Company, The Pecan
    Shoppe), San Saba

Pape Pecan House (Pape), Seguin
Peach Basket (Hallford Orchards), Fredericksburg
Pecan Grove Plantation (Pecan Grove Plantation), Bastrop
Pecan Producers International (Texas Best, PPI), Corsicana
Pecan Valley Nut Company, Inc. (Pecan Valley), Stephenville
Penick Farms - P&L Canning (Penick Farms), Johnson City
Picosos Peanut Company, Inc. (Picosos), Helotes
Poor Farm, The, Wichita Falls
Premier Nut Company of Texas (Sandy Valley Farms of
    Texas), Cleburne
Ramage Farms, Hooks
Royal International, Ltd. (Regal Texas Pecans, Sugar Sweet,
    Royal International), San Juan
San Saba Pecan, Inc. (San Saba), San Saba
Serendipity Of The Valley (Serendipity of the Valley),
    Lake Jackson
Shepherd Produce, Hutto
Spirit of Texas (Spirit of Texas), Plano
Storey Orchards, Avery
Sundance Valley Fine Foods, Inc. (Richwood Farms), Dallas
Sunshine Nut Company, Inc. (Sunshine Country, Texas Pride,
    New Ace), San Antonio
Tobias Pecans (Texas River Bottom), Ellinger
Traylor Farms, Inc. (Tex-Goober), Maples
Tucker's Farm & Craft, Wichita Falls
Valentine Company, Inc. (Texas Roasted Peanuts), Woodville
Vanco Products Co., Inc. (Vanco), Houston
Westside Orchard, Wichita Falls
White Star Farm (White Star Farm), Leander
Wilson's Pecan Company, Sherman
Winkler Pecan & Honey Farm (Winkler Farm), Moody
Zinsmeyer Pecan Orchard, Castroville

Rice

Doguet Rice Milling Company (Doguets, Budget), Beaumont
Doguet-Dishman Rice Company, Inc. (Jasmine), Beaumont
El Campo Rice Milling Company (Fiesta, Elco, Island Girl),
    Louise
Early Food Group (Adolphus, Wonder, Blue Ribbon, Comet
    Rice), Houston
Lindsey Rice Mill, Inc. (Little Country Mill), Waller
RiceTec, Inc. (Texmati Rice), Alvin

Sauces/Relishes/Dips

Alamo Picante Sauce (Alamo Picante Sauce), Alamo
Amigos Canning Company, Inc. (Amigos), San Antonio
Angel Craft, Inc. (Angel Crafts, Pepper Palate), Chillicothe
Aunt Betty's (Aunt Betty's), Burleson
Bandito Foods (The One Armed Bandit), Fort Worth
Bass Grocery, Chico
Bennatte (La Pinata), Hempstead
Beto's Original Hot Sauce (Beto's Original Hot Sauce), Sonora
Big Mama's Bar-B-Que Company (Big Mama's), Hutchins
Blanca's Picante Sauce, Inc. (Blanca's Picante Sauce),
    Rosenberg
Blazin' Berry Company (Blazin' Berry), Wichita Falls
Bobby Free Farms, Inc. (Galante), Muleshoe
Brazos Beef Emporium, Inc. (Brazos Beef Emporium), Bryan
Brick Kitchens (Texas Chili Sauce), College Station
Cafe Maria, Inc. (Cafe Maria), Garland
Carmie's Kitchen (Manana Mexican Dip, Dallas Dill Dip, JR's
    Ranch Dip, TX Topper), Richardson
Carole's Food Specialties (Carole's), Pearland
Cattlebaron Foods, Inc. (Cattlebaron), Dallas
Circle D Farms (Circle D Farms), Millsap
Claude's Sauces, Inc. (Claude's), El Paso
Cotton Picken Productions (Manuels Sauces), Dallas
Country Classic Foods (Country Classic), Devine
Country Woodcraft (Down Home Cookin'), Stonewall
Dickie Davis' Sweet & Hot (Dickie Davis' Original), Menard
DiFranco Foods, Inc. (DiFranco's, Gourmet Bubbaque Sauce,
    Tex-Mex Bubbaque Sauce), Austin

Early Texas Tastes (Early Texas Tastes), Roby
East Texas Best Sauces, Inc. (Texas Best Sauce), Nacogdoches
El Paso Chile Co., Inc. (The El Paso Chile Company), El Paso
Fiesta Fresh (Fiesta Fresh), El Paso
Figaro Company, Inc., The (Figaro), Dallas
Goldin Pickle Company, Inc. (Goldin's Silver Star and Pik-L-Giant), Dallas
Gourmet Garnishes, Inc. (Gourmet Garnishes), San Antonio
Guadalupe Smoked Meat Company (Hickory Groves, Guadalupe Pit Smoked Meat), New Braunfels
Guiltless Gourmet (Guiltless Gourmet), Austin
Hall & Company Texas Barbecue, Ken (The Sauce), Fredericksburg
Hast Foods Company (Hast), Dallas
Hell On The Red, Inc. (Hell on the Red), Telephone
Hill Country Foods, Inc. (Hill Country Farms, Across the Border), Dallas
Honey Creek Farms (Ticklin Picklin Squash Relish), Dallas
James Fine Food (Geneva's Specialties), Houston
Janet's Own Home Sweet Home (Janet's Own Home Sweet Home), Austin
Jardine's Texas Foods (D.L. Jardine's, Shotgun Willie's), Austin
Jellies, Etc. by Jackie, Benavides
Jumping J Jalapeño Ranch (Jumping J Jalapeño Ranch), Arlington
Knapp-Sherrill Company (Ro-Tel, Gold Tip), Donna
L-C Food Products Company (Georgette's Western Brand), Austin
Lazy Susan, Inc. (Old San Antonio Style, Texas Gold), San Antonio
Londa's Gourmet Classics (Londa's), Wylie
Madeline's Gourmet Foods (Madeline's), New Braunfels
Miguel's, Inc. (Miguel's Gourmet Mexican Sauce), Humble
Millie's Kountry Kitchen (Kountry Kitchen), LaGrange
Monterrey Products Company, Inc. (Monterrey Products), San Antonio
National Convenience Store (Stop & Go) (DL Jardins, Pace, Carlton Sausage), San Antonio
Nelson's Kitchen, Inc. (Goose Creek), Baytown
New Canaan Farms (New Canaan Farms), Dripping Springs
Novella's Picante Sauce (Novella's Texas Style Picante Sauce), Bandera
Old Orange Cafe/From Susan's Kitchen, Orange
Pace Foods, Inc. (Pace), San Antonio
Pet, Inc. (Old El Paso Foods), St. Louis, MO
Pedro Gatos' Salsa, Inc. (Pedro Gatos' Salsa), Austin
Penick Farms - P&L Canning (Penick Farms), Johnson City
Pizzo Enterprises, Inc. (Daddy's Hot Stuff), Smyrna, GA
R. G. Mexican Food Products, Inc. (Senor Pepe), San Antonio
Ranger Foods of Texas, Inc. (Jump-Back Jack's, Shotgun Willie's, Ranger Luke), Austin
Renfro Foods, Inc., (Dixieland, Mrs. Renfro's and Private Labels), Fort Worth
Ricos Products (Ricos), San Antonio
Rudy's Food Products, Inc. (Rudy's Tortillas), Dallas
Sam Lewis & Associates, Inc. (Jalapeno Sam), San Angelo
Satay, Ltd. (Satay's Original), Austin
Silva Swan, Inc. (Texas Fun Feed, Visions of Gourmet), Industry
Square's Bar-B-Que Express (Square's), Abilene
Texafrance, Inc. (Texafrance), Austin
Texas Chili Company (Our Famous Texas Chili, Tex-O-Gold Chili, Tex-O-Gold Sauce), Fort Worth
Texas Duet (Texas Duet), Austin
Texas Heat, Inc. (Texas Heat), San Antonio
Texas Prairie, Inc. (Texas Prairie), Plano
Texas Sauce Products Company (Ole Ranch Hand, Brazos), Houston
Texas Sisters Food Products, Inc. (Texas Sisters Chow-Chow), Odessa
Texas Sting, Ltd. (Texas Sting), Austin
Texas Tamale Company, Houston

Tornberg Foods (Jefe), Houston
Tres Chic of Texas, Inc., Lago Vista
Tru-Tex Products (Tru-Tex), Hempstead
Two Women Cooking Inc. (Take Stock), Richardson
Van De Walle Farms, Inc. (Van De Walle), San Antonio
Vivacé, Inc. (Vivacé), Houston
Wolf Brand Products (Wolf), Dallas

Seasonings/Chili Mixes

Adams Extract Company (Adams), Austin
Adkins Seasoning Company, Inc. (Adkins, Texas Pride, Texas Style), Dallas
Aunt Betty's (Aunt Betty's), Burleson
Baldy's Seasoning (Baldy's), Houston
Big Daddy Finchums Texas Cajun ("Big Daddy" Finchum's Seasonings), Orange
Bobby Free Farms, Inc. (Galante), Muleshoe
Bolner's Fiesta Products, Inc. (Fiesta), San Antonio
Boone's Texas Shake (Boone's Texas Shake), Valley Cuero
Brooke's Seasoning, Inc. (Brooke's), Irving
Bubba's Spice Company (Bubba's Red Dust), Riverside
Caliente Chili, Inc. (Two Alarm), Austin
Dallas International Marketing (Authentic Texas Seasonings), Irving
El Paso Chile Co., Inc. (The El Paso Chile Company), El Paso
Fajita Fiesta (Fajita Fiesta), Houston
Fredericksburg Herb Farm, Fredericksburg
Fuzzy Hicks Seasoning (Fuzzy Hicks Seasonings), Houston
Gilroy Foods, Inc., Fabens
Goerlitz, Harley (Harley's Texas Style Barbeque Seasoning), Giddings
Ham I Am! (Hog Wash), Plano
Hell On The Red, Inc. (Hell on the Red), Telephone
Herbal Gems (Herbal Gems), Frankston
Hermitage Farm (Hermitage Farm, Organically Grown), Scroggins
Hill Country Foods, Inc. (Hill Country Farms, Across the Border), Dallas
Hoyt's Texas Chili (Hoyt's Texas Chili), Dallas
J.P.'s Enterprises (Texas Seasons), Brazoria
Janet's Own Home Sweet Home (Janet's Own Home Sweet Home), Austin
La India Packing Company (La India), Laredo
Lantana Seasoning (Lantana), New Caney
Londa's Gourmet Classics (Londa's), Wylie
Lone Star Cafe, Inc. (Lone Star Cafe, Chez Fred), Austin
Lone Star Specialty Foods (Lone Star Butter Crunch, Lone Star Flavors), San Antonio
Longneck Seasonings, Inc. (Longneck), Dallas
McCarty Greenhouses (McCarty Greenhouses Certified Texas Organic Herbs), Dripping Springs
Muzzy's Products, Inc. (Cajun Seafood Seasoning), Austin
Navarro Mills Farm (Navarro Mills Farm), Purdon
Old Orange Cafe/From Susan's Kitchen, Orange
Opryshek's (Opryshek's Seasoned Salt), Arlington
Patchwork Herb Farm (Patchwork Herbs), Denison
Patty's Herb's, Inc. (Patty's), Pearsall
Peaceable Kingdom School (Peaceable Kingdom), Washington
Peach Basket, Fredericksburg
Pendery's Inc. (Pendery's), Fort Worth
Ranger Foods of Texas, Inc. (Jump-Back Jack's, Shotgun Willie's, Ranger Luke), Austin
Red Eye Company (Red Eye), Florence
River Manufacturing Company (Jimmies Chuckwagon), Mount Enterprise
Rosehill Herbs (Rosehill Culinary Herbs), Tomball
Shadowfox Farms (Shadowfox Farms), Elgin
South Texas Spice Company, Inc. (Menchaca, Yellow Rose, South Texas Spice), San Antonio
Sunset Vineyard & Nursery, Sunset

Tejas Pines (Tejas Pines "Southern Fixin's of East Texas"), Garrison
Texafrance, Inc. (Texafrance), Austin
Texas Duet (Texas Duet), Austin
Texas Heat, Inc. (Texas Heat), San Antonio
Texas Spice Company (Texas Spice), Austin
Tru-Tex Products (Tru-Tex), Hempstead
Van De Walle Farms, Inc. (Van De Walle), San Antonio
West Brand, Inc. (West Brand Texas Chili), Dallas
White Oak Farms (White Oak Farms), Fredericksburg

Tortillas/Taco Shells/Chips
Bernard's Tortilla Factory (Bernard's), Midland
C & C Bakery, Inc. (C&C), Kingsville
Cavazos' Sons, Inc. (Cavazos), Weslaco
El Azteca Tortilleria (El Azteca), Laredo
El Galindo, Inc. (El Galindo, Inc.), Austin
El Lago Tortillas (El Lago), Austin
El Tepeyac (El Tepeyac), Laredo
Guiltless Gourmet (Guiltless Gourmet), Austin
Jasso's Tortillas & Bakery, Inc. (Jasso's, Del Tule), Austin
La Malinche Tortilla/Tamale Factory (La Malinche), Corpus Christi
La Supreme Tortilleria (La Suprema Tortilleria), Dallas
Mayan Tortillas (Mayan, Raul's), Laredo
Mexico Bakery, Inc. (Mexico Bakery, PoPo, Mortena), Kingsville
R.G. Mexican Food Products, Inc. (Senor Pepe), San Antonio
Rudy's Food Products, Inc. (Rudy's Tortillas), Dallas
Ruiz Tamale & Tortilla Factory (Ruiz), Corpus Christi
Tornberg Foods (Jefe), Houston

Miscellaneous
Amy's Food Company (Amy's), Austin
Carter Processing (Tejas Gold, Texas Gold, Moore Pop), Sunray
Confection Technology, Inc. (Texas Treats), Roaring Springs
Del Sol Food Company (Briannas), Brenham
Fitzwater, Eugene, New Ulm

Foodmaker, Inc. (Jack-In-The-Box), Dallas
Gourmet Garnishes, Inc. (Gourmet Garnishes), San Antonio
Hart of Texas, Inc., Fort Worth
Houston Calco (Calco), Houston
Jesse's Honey Crunch (Jesse's Honey Crunch), Pipe Creek
Joseph Products, A. (Chef A. Joseph), Dallas
Lee's Organic Foods (Lee's Organic Fruit Jerky), Wellington
Little Red Hen Pantry, Inc. (The Little Red Hen Pantry), Neches
Los Tios Mexican Restaurants, Inc. (Los Tios), Houston
Microw Pop, Inc. (Texas Microwave Popcorn On The Cob), Hereford
Miller's Seafood (Miller's), Seadrift
Minh Foods Corporation (Minh Egg Rolls), Pasadena
Nena's Gourmet Foods (Nena's Gourmet), Houston
O.B. Macaroni Company (QQ Fideo Vermicelli), Fort Worth
Orchard Properties, Inc. (Aunt Muriel's), Humble
Penick Farms - P&L Canning (Penick Farms), Johnson City
Penrich Enterprises, Inc. (Penny's Oat Bran Granola Cereal), Houston
Perry Products (Old Fashion), Giddings
Pet, Inc., Old El Paso Foods (Old El Paso), St. Louis, MO
Ruiz Tamale & Tortilla Factory (Ruiz), Corpus Christi
Sealantic, Inc. (Clearwater Tilapia), Katy
Silva Swan, Inc. (Texas Fun Feed, Visions of Gourmet), Industry
Tekita House Foods, Inc. (Tekita House), El Paso
Texafrance, Inc. (Texafrance), Austin
Texas Deli Foods (Double D Deli Masters), Pasadena
Texas Duet (Texas Duet), Austin
Texas Popcorn, Inc. (Caraway's Original Texas Popcorn), Honey Grove
Texas Tamale Company, Houston
Threadgill's (Threadgill's Vegetable Entrees), Austin
Tres Chic of Texas, Inc., Lago Vista
Tropi-Cool Frozen Food Products, Inc.. (Tropi-Cool Paletas), San Antonio
Valley Wholesale Meat Co., Inc. (La Rancherita, Country Girl), Alamo

Index

Notes

Notes

Notes

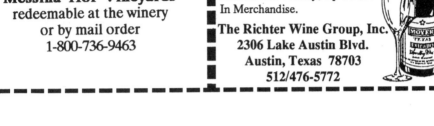

BUY TEXAS . . .
IT WILL PAY YOU BACK

• A $19.95 value offered at a suggested retail price of $16.95
• Texas manufacturers coupons inside the book are valued over $30

Please send ___ copy (copies) of **THE GENUINE OLD FASHIONED, DOWN-HOME, HOME GROWN OFFICIAL TEXAS COOKBOOK** @ $16.95/copy, plus $2.50 freight to:
(Make check or money order out to LeisureTime Publishing, 9029 Directors Row, Dallas, TX. 75247)

Name:_____

Address: _____

City/State/Zip:_____ Phone:_____

BUY TEXAS . . .
IT WILL PAY YOU BACK

• A $19.95 value offered at a suggested retail price of $16.95
• Texas manufacturers coupons inside the book are valued over $30

Please send ___ copy (copies) of **THE GENUINE OLD FASHIONED, DOWN-HOME, HOME GROWN OFFICIAL TEXAS COOKBOOK** @ $16.95/copy, plus $2.50 freight to:
(Make check or money order out to LeisureTime Publishing, 9029 Directors Row, Dallas, TX. 75247)

Name:_____

Address: _____

City/State/Zip:_____ Phone:_____